PRAISE FOR REME

M000169544

"Ryan Walters has exposed the real battle within the GOP, one that has been brewing for nearly thirty years. This isn't a "boys on the bus" book about a single election in Mississippi, but a deep discussion about the future direction of conservatism in America and the seedy tactics the establishment wing of the Republican Party will use to gain and maintain power. Before Trump vs. the establishment, there was Reagan vs. Ford and Buchanan vs. Bush and Chris McDaniel vs. Thad Cochran in Mississippi. That election foreshadowed the Trump revolution of 2016. Readers will be left wondering how they ever supported or voted for sellouts like Cochran and will wish for a do-over."

—**Dr. Brion McClanahan, author of** *The Politically Incorrect Guide to the Founding Fathers*, *The Founders' Guide to the Constitution*, **and** *How Alexander Hamilton Screwed Up America*

"Desperate to maintain power, the ruling establishment pulled out every dirty trick in the book in order to crush a popular pro-liberty insurgency—including smearing the insurgent candidate and his followers as racists. Did this happen in a foreign country that the US Government has targeted for regime change? No, it happened in the United States, specifically in the 2014 Mississippi GOP primary battle between pro-liberty insurgent Chris McDaniel and long-term establishment Senator Thad Cochran. Every member of the liberty movement who still labors under the delusion that the political class will abide by the Marques of Queensbury rules or can ever be 'won over' to the side of individual liberty and constitutional government needs to read this book."

—**Ron Paul, former US Congressman and Presidential Candidate**

"Chris McDaniel successfully fought the political class of both parties' establishments in Washington, D.C. That's why the swamp sewer in Washington fears him so much. In many ways, the open warfare between the grassroots and establishment that led to President Trump's victory started in the Mississippi summer in 2014 when the establishment engaged in dirty tricks against Chris. He's a warrior. This book is a must read."

—**Matthew Boyle, Washington Political Editor, Breitbart News**

"As someone who got to know Chris McDaniel in and away from politics it was appalling to see to what depth the establishment of the Republican Party would sink to protect Thad Cochran. That tactic was to link Chris to the KKK, where no such link exists. As Conservatives we expect that from the Democrats but this treatment came from the GOP. As Republican voters move closer to the Constitution and libertarians are seen as the future, the establishment is doing whatever it takes to hang onto control. This book chronicles that struggle between the big government insider class versus the new wave of limited government Conservatives."

—**Andrew Wilkow, host of *The Wilkow Majority* on SiriusXM Patriot**

"Chris McDaniel's bold conservative leadership breaks the mold. His unapologetic fight for conservatism, limited government, strong national defense, and traditional family values is a clarion call for our time, and exactly what the United States needs. *Remember Mississippi*, the official history of Mississippi's 2014 Republican primary, shatters the notion that establishment Republicans will include conservatives in their 'big tent.'"

—**Ken Cuccinelli, former Virginia Attorney General and President of the Senate Conservatives Fund**

"The story of what happened to Chris McDaniel and Mississippi conservatives in 2014 is one of the most important modern political tales to be told. For it was really the first time the lies, frauds, and schemes hatched by the GOP—to go after conservatives harder and dirtier than they ever do Democrats—first came to light with the general public. May this book let even more of the light pierce the darkness, because we know cockroaches can't handle the light."

—Steve Deace, host of the Steve Deace Show on CRTV and contributor to *Conservative Review*

"This just threw gasoline onto the flames of the civil war. What happened in Mississippi will resonate for years to come. It will become the battle cry, just like the Alamo. We will remember Mississippi."

—Richard Viguerie

REMEMBER MISSISSIPPI

REMEMBER MISSISSIPPI

How Chris McDaniel Exposed the GOP Establishment and Inspired a Revolution

by

RYAN S. WALTERS

Foreword by Erick Erickson

REMEMBER MISSISSIPPI

Copyright © 2017 by Ryan S. Walters

World Ahead Press is a division of WND Books. The views and opinions expressed in this book are those of the author and do not necessarily reflect the official policy or position or WND Books.

Paperback ISBN: 978-1-944212-98-8
eBook ISBN: 978-1-944212-99-5

Printed in the United States of America
16 17 18 19 20 21 LSI 9 8 7 6 5 4 3 2 1

*To all the men and women across Mississippi
and the nation who volunteered, contributed money,
invested time, and cast a ballot to elect Chris McDaniel
to the United States Senate in 2014.
Though we had the rug snatched from beneath us,
your hard work was not in vain.*

CONTENTS

"'Men don't follow titles,' said Republican McDaniel. 'They follow courage.' He was quoting from the movie *Braveheart*, he said, citing William Wallace – an ancestor of the largely Scots-Irish crowd of 50 or so – as played in blueface by Mel Gibson. Wallace was McDaniel's model. He fought against the English elites, just as McDaniel was fighting against the old, pork-loving Bourbon Republican establishment, people like former Governor Haley Barbour and Senator Thad Cochran, who would compromise their principles in order to get public-works projects for the state."

—Joe Kline, *Time Magazine*

ACKNOWLEDGMENTS

During the presidential campaign of 2012, President Obama made an extraordinary statement, one that rightfully upset a lot of people. While speaking about opportunity and the economy, he told those who had created small businesses that "you didn't build that." Any success in life, the president said, was due to help from someone else.

Although I disagree with most of what Mr. Obama said that day, at least as far as writing a book is concerned, I must begrudgingly agree with him. Although I did no outsourcing with the writing, in the creation of this book I had the help and assistance of a great many people—those I interviewed, those who sent me material, and certainly those who gave me advice on the book's structure and content.

First and foremost, this book would not exist without Chris McDaniel. I consider Chris one of my very best friends, the type of friendship where we both have each other's back. He can depend on me for anything and I know that is true with him. So when I got the idea to do this book in the summer of 2015, I approached him with it. He enthusiastically agreed and I began the research. Before long I was banging out a manuscript. By the summer of 2016 I had a very rough draft in place. I then sat down with Chris for two lengthy interviews. Although I was very much involved in the race, and obviously know Chris very well, I wanted to conduct formal interviews and get his side of the story since quite a bit of time had passed. His words and his assistance throughout this long process were invaluable. In reality, it's as much his book as it is mine.

I also specifically want to thank Melanie Sojourner, Jack Fairchilds, Tiffany Parrish, Keith Plunkett, Cindy Wilkerson, Richard Sager,

Talib Bey, and Glynn Branch for their time and input. They all kindly answered questions, made phone calls, and sent material when I needed help with certain aspects of this book.

But, unfortunately, a number of the people I wanted to interview and get their take on the events in 2014 kindly refused. As you will see within these pages, there are many reasons why such fear pervades the political climate in Mississippi.

My publishers at World Ahead Press, a division of WND Books, have been exemplary. Daniel Horowitz, the editor of *Conservative Review*, made the initial contact, so I must credit him for his assistance. Mike Klassen, as the Director of Author Acquisitions at WND, was invaluable throughout the process. He was always patient with me, even as it took some time to get the project off the ground, and he was always there when I needed him.

As any writer will tell you, or should tell you, a good editor will make a book much better, if you listen to the advice. My editor at WND, Geoffrey Stone, was a Godsend. His input, corrections, and organizational ideas made this book much better than my original manuscript.

Finally, like all human beings, I am prone to errors and mistakes. These great friends who graciously helped me on this project are not responsible for any blunders within these pages. So as for any mistakes and faults herein, they are entirely my own.

— Ryan S. Walters
Arlington, TX

FOREWORD

Prior to the adoption of the seventeenth amendment in 1913, senators were most often appointed, often confirmed by state legislative bodies after nominations from governors. The result was that states truly had federal representation. The appointment system also made state legislative elections much more influential and diffuse.

Once senators were elected, the rapid march toward expansionist federal government policies proceeded unabated. And with that came new powers through party machines seeking to preserve power in Washington and grow power in states. Concurrently, states abandoned party conventions to choose nominees. Over time, under pressure from progressive activists, state political parties began using primaries to nominate candidates. The tenure of politicians in office in Washington directly corresponds to the shift from conventions to primaries. No longer did politicians have to be faithful to principle and party. They could just raise a bunch of money and destroy any opponent through negative ads.

Southern states were some of the last to abandon conventions for primaries, but even they ultimately succumbed. After the Civil War and Reconstruction, southern states began growing and, led by people like Huey Long in Louisiana, built elaborate welfare statements dependent on federal cash flow to subsidize state expenditures. Bringing home the bacon and getting kickbacks kept politicians in office and created a new welfare class where voters were dependent not just on Uncle Sam, but on individual politicians too. Mississippi was no different and, with the welfare state, expert political dynasties rose up to protect the cash flow and reward friends. Oftentimes political parties could shift in control of power, but the same people kept getting rewarded. Meanwhile, the taxpayers saw their taxes go up, spending go up, the national debt go up, and the future bills of their children and grandchildren go up.

With Barack Obama's election in 2008 and an expansionist federal government growing even more rapidly, aided and abetted by supposedly conservative Republicans, tea party groups sprouted up across the country. Before taking the fight to Democrats, they took the fight to a Republican Party that preached fiscal restraint and practiced reckless spending. In 2010, a Republican wave spread across the country from coast to coast. The destruction the Democratic Party saw at the local, county, state, and federal level was the worst since the 1890s. Whole towns in the South overnight saw all Democrat city councils become all Republican. The media mantra that Republicans could not win in New England saw Republicans winning across New England.

But the work was not done.

Undeterred, in 2014, the tea party proceeded. By now, though, the establishment Republicans had learned a few lessons. In some cases, they would actually seed a field with multiple conservatives who would fight each other while a moderate candidate consolidated support to win. In other cases, they would rally Democrats to their side to cling to power. In other cases, they would spend massive amounts of money destroying conservative primary challengers.

It had nothing to do with principle and everything to do with keeping the gravy train moving. Principle had given way to the acquisition of power. Ideas did not matter. Money did and, more precisely, control of that money did.

Into this entered a Mississippi State Senator, Chris McDaniel, who had a well-established track record of defying his own political party. In Mississippi, McDaniel had a reputation for putting principle first, including fighting his own side in support of fiscal restraint and limited government. He had ruffled many a feather and attracted conservative attention. Mississippi's king of pork, U.S. Senator Thad Cochran, was up for re-election. Conservatives encouraged McDaniel to oppose Cochran in a primary.

Thus began one of the nastiest, dirtiest senate campaigns in modern American politics. Faced with the loss of power and a potential

Senator who might stop the gravy train, the Republican Establishment, Mississippi political dynasties, and Democrats rallied together to fight against conservatives and fiscal integrity. They never expected to get such a run for their money. McDaniel's hard fought campaign remains, years latter, a rallying cry for conservatives who saw supposed friends and allies so easily bought off and so quickly abandoning principle.

Chris McDaniel's story is a real testament to those who put principle over power and fight for the cause out of conviction, not as mercenaries. The good guys might not always win, but their fights often find unknown good guys willing to make a stand. McDaniel's campaign ushered in a new era of conservative grassroots politics and helped cement an anti-establishment wave that continues to bludgeon the Republican Establishment.

— Erick Erickson

INTRODUCTION

CHRIS MCDANIEL
AND THE CONSERVATIVE INSURGENCY

In what can be described only as a stunning political upset, Donald J. Trump, a billionaire real estate tycoon with no political or military experience, captured the Republican nomination by defeating sixteen leading GOP candidates. Then on November 8, 2016, he won the presidency of the United States in a campaign for the ages. Yet political pundits and experts are still at a loss as to why Trump defied the odds, and their predictions, to reach the unreachable. How could a man who seemed to be just another fringe candidate win a major party nomination? In any other presidential election year he probably would not have survived Iowa and New Hampshire.

The answer lies in the mass conservative insurgency that rose up among the grass roots to take down the ruling Republican Establishment, and the catalyst of the uprising was the GOP primary for a US Senate seat in Mississippi in 2014. In that campaign the Establishment reached a new low by shamelessly trashing a rising conservative star, Chris McDaniel, and by doing so, unwittingly ignited a full-blown political rebellion.

The Republican Party has been in the throes of "civil war" for years. The conflict rages between two opposing forces: the Establishment, the old party elites beholden to their big donors seeking to maintain the status quo at all costs, and conservatives, the ideological purists who seek to reform the government from top to bottom and to return to America's founding principles. Both sides equal to the task; both sides determined to win. It is an epic struggle that has only worsened over time. But even with Trump's victory, it's far from over.

The nastiest skirmish in this internal struggle, and the one that led directly to Trump's triumph, was the 2014 Republican race for a US Senate seat in Mississippi, an all-out political brawl that became the most hotly contested race in the nation during that year's mid-term election cycle, and through several contentious weeks from May until the end of June, Mississippi became the center of the American political world.

The 2014 Mississippi Senate contest pitted two candidates: one young and rising, the other an elder statesman at the twilight of his career. The incumbent senator, Thad Cochran, who had served Mississippi in both houses of Congress for over forty years, was well known in Washington Establishment circles and hoped to stay in DC for a seventh term in the US Senate. Chris McDaniel, a state senator near the end of in his second term in Jackson, represented the true conservative movement in what was the latest and most effective effort to oust a longtime member of the Establishment.

The result of the clash of these two political titans was one of the most raucous, topsy-turvy, rough-and-tumble Senate campaigns in recent memory, if not ever. Throughout Mississippi history, US Senate races have never been tough on newsroom ink supplies and almost never generated much national press, if they ever did. Yet this one was the most talked about in state history and by far the most written about in the 2014 national cycle, encompassing thousands of stories from small, local papers to the biggest national periodicals and magazines. Geoff Pender, writing for the state's major paper, the *Clarion Ledger*, called it "one of the most bitter, mudslinging-est, bizarre political hootenannies in state history." Sean Sullivan of the *Washington Post* labeled it the "nastiest primary in the country."[1] One writer for Buzzfeed thought it was worthy of a good John Grisham novel.[2] Others simply called it "weird" and "ugly," and in many ways it was both.[3]

Regardless of the names pinned on it by political journalists, it's without a doubt a great story that surpasses most presidential campaigns in sheer excitement, an epic tale that included vicious mudslinging and personal attacks, suspected affairs, deplorable race baiting, big-name appearances, a crashed press conference, two alleged "break-ins," five arrests, a legal challenge that reached the state supreme court, and the tragic suicide of a well-respected attorney and political activist. All in one Senate primary in Mississippi.

First things first, however. In the spirit of full disclosure, this book is not an unbiased look at the 2014 US Senate race in Mississippi, nor does it pretend to be. I am a dedicated conservative who loathes the Establishment. To be brutally honest, I downright hate it. And like all writers, whether they divulge it or not, I am unashamedly biased, but at least I will admit it. So don't expect a pity party for Thad Cochran, the Barbour Boys, the National Republican Senatorial Committee (NRSC), or anyone else in the Republican Establishment in Washington or Mississippi. This is a critique of the Establishment's stranglehold on Mississippi (and to some degree the nation) and an unapologetic defense of Chris McDaniel and his campaign against Thad Cochran in my own words, the words of many of those closest to the campaign, and those of Chris McDaniel himself. I also drew heavily from the hundreds of articles and journalistic pieces written about this race in newsrooms across America.

I've known Chris McDaniel since our days in grade school together in our hometown of Ellisville, Mississippi, in Jones County—the "Free State of Jones." He graduated from high school a year ahead of me and our paths briefly diverted. I bumbled around for several years in a never-ending quest to see just how long it would take me to earn a college degree after high school. He plunged straight through college and law school and then worked as a federal law clerk for two years before settling down in Jones County to practice law.

We rediscovered each other around 1999 when I was working to help Pat Buchanan in his third race for the White House. We ate lunch often at one of our favorite hangouts, Pasquale's in Laurel, and talked politics. I was a frequent listener to his radio show and was proud to serve on his campaign committee when he first ran for the State Senate in 2007, a race he won easily.

It was obvious to me, as it was to many, that Chris McDaniel was destined for more than a career in the Mississippi Senate. Congress, governor, or an even higher office was not out of the realm of possibility to those of us who knew him best. He had the combination of intelligence, oratorical skill, charisma, and "the look" to go far in politics. Even one of the state's leading Republican Establishment websites, Y'all Politics, listed him as *the* top rising star in state politics, a designation also awarded him by the news site *Jackson Jambalaya* and reported by the *Clarion Ledger.*[4]

Chris and I began discussing the possibility of a challenge to Thad Cochran in the early months of 2012. With the election more than two years away, the prospect of knocking off Cochran was well worth exploring even though we both knew it would be a David versus Goliath battle. We talked about it often and after a quick review of all the Senate seats that would be up in 2014, we both concluded that a challenge to Cochran could very well end up being the definitive race that season.

As a historian, I knew that since the advent of the Seventeenth Amendment, which gave the people the power to elect senators, Mississippians usually didn't run off their US Senators, at least not those who had been elected to full terms or had served as long as Thad Cochran. Yet in the past century, two full-term Senators had been "primaried" and beaten: James K. Vardaman in 1918, because he opposed World War I, and Hubert D. Stephens, who fell victim to the popular former governor Theodore G. Bilbo. Although those incidents came at a time when the Democratic Party was the only game in town, so primaries, in essence, were general elections, therefore it could be done in Mississippi, depending on how you viewed it.

The possibility of taking on such a strong incumbent frightened a great many potential supporters who would not commit to such a race either publicly or privately, but the challenge did not scare me in the least. I was not only a conservative and very accustomed to being an underdog, but also a former Buchanan supporter who was then drifting the halls of academia in pursuit of graduate degrees in American history. I was very familiar with being the least popular team in town, and I'd take to any cause that I believed in, no matter the opinion of the so-called experts. And I believed in Chris. I was on-board right from the start. And judging from other successful primaries in recent cycles, the political climate was perfect to defeat a longtime Establishment

Republican with a record that fell far short of the conservative beliefs held by most Mississippians.

Once the effort did kickoff, I was a campaign insider throughout, though not a paid staffer, which surprised many who knew of my closeness with Chris. But the decision was the result of many developments, not the least of which were the baseless media attacks on me, as well as those of the Cochran camp, which would only serve to distract from the real issues in the campaign. To be on the official staff, though, did not mean as much to me as it might have to others. I was more interested in seeing my friend elected to the US Senate to represent our great state than any self-aggrandizement on my part.

In politics, as I well knew, there are show horses and workhorses, and I was quite comfortable in the behind-the-scenes, workhorse mode. So I put my knowledge to good use as an unofficial advisor, speaking with Chris as often as possible, texting my thoughts, appearing at many functions, and harnessing my writing and research skills in the creation of a new political website, *Mississippi Conservative Daily*, a title I came up with using the first three letters of McDaniel—MCD.

And because the Cochran camp was desperate to use anything and anyone to smear Chris, I felt it best to serve in my blogging capacity as an anonymous editor. There was simply no good reason to make myself an issue. But I did have fun watching Cochran's Establishment minions try to figure out who was behind *MCD*, many of whom openly criticized my decision to remain secret all while they themselves were also anonymous on social media. I authored many of the nameless articles on *MCD*, but there were other writers who also wanted to remain anonymous. Such was the atmosphere in Mississippi during the McDaniel-Cochran race in 2013–14.

This book deals with a number of intertwining issues—obviously politics, but also the state of American democracy, corruption, and the modern-day political machine, which is, despite the opinions of some, still very much alive, though in a much different form than it was in bygone eras. It is about what really happened in this very important Senate race, the real story told from the perspective of those involved in the race on the side of Senator Chris McDaniel, including many words from McDaniel himself. It's got all the whats, hows, and ultimately the whys that went into the campaign's major decisions. But it's also an indictment of Mississippi's politics, and by extension, the nation's as well, especially for those who reside in states that are caught in the same trap of corruption and machine politics. And, of course, it provides our answer as to why Trump won the Republican nomination in 2016, and ultimately the White House.

But why, you might ask, should the focus be on this particular race? Why would anyone want to read a book about a US Senate primary in the Deep South in 2014? Why is it important for conservatives and the national ideological movement to fight for limited government? The 2014 race for the US Senate in Mississippi was historic for a number of reasons. For one, it was more than a statewide race. It had for all practical purposes become a national campaign. It revealed to the entire nation the great division within the Republican Party, and it exposed just how far the Establishment is willing to go to destroy serious conservative challengers, which can, if we learn from them, help point the way forward for those of us who consider ourselves movement conservatives. Finally, it is the main reason why Republicans across the country in 2016 threw the Establishment overboard in favor of an anti-Establishment presidential candidate in Donald J. Trump, something no one thought remotely possible.

The ideological divide within the party is the most crucial element that led directly to the insurgency in 2016, and the McDaniel-Cochran race, like no other, shined an enormous spotlight on the great disagreement within the GOP, a split between the moderate/liberal Establishment wing, many of whom continue to masquerade as conservatives, and those who are the true bearers of conservatism and the true representatives of the people at the grass roots. It's a race that pitted the Machine versus the People, the main protagonists in the "civil war" within the Republican Party for the soul of the conservative movement, a battle in which the Establishment has enjoyed the upper hand in recent years.

Simply put, the US Senate race in Mississippi in 2014 was the height of the Establishment war on conservatives, a war they and their wealthy interests had no intention of quitting. They were very much Goliath, with all the money and heavy machinery, able to raise millions of dollars in a single night; we were David, with nothing more than a few small donations we scraped together from working families who cared about the future of their country. But sometimes that's all you need—a few rocks and a slingshot.

Thad Cochran and Chris McDaniel are the personifications of this Republican divide, representing two distinct versions of conservatism—one false, one true. Thad Cochran can be called a conservative but only in the textbook sense of the word, which is the maintenance of the status quo, meaning to conserve, preserve, and maintain the current system. *Time* magazine once dubbed him the "Quiet Persuader," meaning he works behind the scenes, but to conservatives in Mississippi it means he never raises his voice in defense of true conservatism, an issue Chris brought up repeatedly on the campaign trail.[5] And it's behind the scenes where all the deals are struck and the compromises hashed out. Cochran has no problem compromising with Democrats, as he has shown throughout his more than forty years in Washington. Keep things as they are, that's the Establishment way.

By contrast, Chris McDaniel is a true conservative reformer in the historical and traditional sense, meaning an adherence to the Jeffersonian conservative philosophy that came out of the American Revolution. He supports principles such as limited government, federalism, low taxes, no debt, a prudent foreign policy, and a strict adherence to the Constitution, principles advocated by conservative icons like Calvin Coolidge, Robert Taft, Barry Goldwater, and Ronald Reagan. These tenets are pillars of the conservative philosophy, and they do not include compromising with the destructive ideas of liberalism. As a state senator, Chris has never cut deals with Democrats that would be damaging to the founding ideals of the republic and would also advance liberalism in any way, shape, form, or fashion. Roundly criticized in some Republican circles because he won't compromise, Chris McDaniel is a warrior for conservatism who believes we must fight liberalism and roll it back. Thad Cochran, on the other hand, believes in détente with Democrats, that we must get along with them in the spirit of bi-partisanship and compromise to strike deals. But as Chris stated throughout the race, it's that very attitude that has led the nation into the trouble it's in today. And that, in a nutshell, is why he ran.

What transpired during the course of the race is something no one anticipated. It was obvious the Establishment would go to great lengths to maintain the status quo by destroying any conservative they viewed to be dangerous. This race should be a wake-up call to true conservatives that our presence in the GOP, beyond simply acting as voters for the Republican ballot line, is unwanted. And the proof of that statement is the subject of this book—the 2014 Mississippi US Senate race.

As Patrick Howley wrote on the conservative site *Breitbart,* "Establishment Republicans treat the GOP much the way checked-out old sports owners like Jerry Jones treat their teams. They get to go sit up in the owner's box with their families or their dates, they get to control the season ticket packages, they can drive up prices for the fans, and they don't really care if the team wins or not. And there's nothing the fans can do. But now the fans are taking over the team. And the owners are trying to wreck the team in order to save their ownership of it."[6] And attempt to wreck the party they did. In 2014, the GOP Establishment's all-out effort to lie, cheat, and race-bait their way to "defeat" Chris McDaniel had great consequences throughout the party. It was the turning point in the conservative movement and is a major reason why the "fans" took over in 2016 and rebelled against the Establishment by electing Donald Trump as the GOP candidate.

More than just a "boys on the bus" anthology, this book also takes a hard look at the state of American Democracy. It has become a very messy, corrupt affair across the country, as reflected in Mississippi in June 2014. It may be hard to say but our beloved republic is a sham in many ways. We may boast of the finest government crafted by the hand of imperfect man in the history of the world, but it's a shadow of what it once was. Today, as a nation, we no longer follow the Constitution, routinely break laws, often ignore rules, no longer live by any standards, and most disturbingly, we openly steal elections. We promote electoral democracy around the globe but don't practice it at home because our elections are full of fraud and corruption, and that's certainly not a strong signal to send around the world.

Mississippi's US Senate race in 2014 exposed the deficiencies and corruption of the national party and solidified these facts to those of us who are natural skeptics of men and their motives. It should have clearly enlightened those who are naïve idealists and believe people always act on their best impulses and on behalf of the lasting interests of the people, yet despite the multitude of issues and problems this race brought to light, there are those in Mississippi and elsewhere who will say, as they've been saying since June 2014, that we should just "get over it," let sleeping dogs lie, and look to the future. I'm sure the Establishment would love for us to do that, to leave them free to continue with their reign of terror against conservatives. And if we do shut up, if we do back down, if we do walk away, then they win. And that is something we can never let happen. Even though the Establishment was dealt a crippling blow in November 2016, we conservatives must continue to fight to restore the Founder's Republic. Our future generations deserve no less of us. And soldier on we must until victory is ours.

THE COURTHOUSE
ELLISVILLE, MISSISSIPPI
THURSDAY, OCTOBER 17, 2013

The day arrived overcast and rainy with a bit of a fall nip in the air. But the gathering crowd would not let the cruddy weather put a damper on what was truly an historic and exciting day in Chris McDaniel's hometown of Ellisville, Mississippi. The throng of supporters believed they were witnessing history, the start of something big. And the many who gathered there on that day brought their children and grandchildren to witness the event firsthand.

The famous county of Jones in south Mississippi, where Ellisville sits, is no stranger to being in the spotlight and producing notable residents. Ralph Boston, the 1960 Olympic gold medalist; Tom Lester, the actor from *Green Acres*; and Ray Walston, of *My Favorite Martian*, were all born in Laurel, just seven miles up the highway, as was NFL quarterback Jason Campbell, actresses Parker Posey and Mary Elizabeth Ellis, and opera singer and Presidential Medal of Freedom winner Leontyne Price.

The small, yet far from sleepy, southern town of Ellisville, the county's other seat, which would be the host of the day's anticipated event, has also seen its fair share of excitement in two centuries of existence. The local junior college—Jones County Junior College—has produced national championships in football, basketball, and baseball, and a two-time national runner-up in women's softball. Actor and

Elvis bodyguard Red West played football for the JCJC Bobcats in the '50s and Billy Cannon, the 1959 Heisman Trophy winner from LSU, attended in the mid-1960s, though it was in the classroom and not in the backfield.

Tiny Ellisville also has a few famous alums of its own. Mary Alma Hughes Carson, the mother of Redd Foxx, the legendary stand-up comedian of *Sanford and Son* fame, was from Ellisville, and more recently Lance Bass of the pop band N'Sync. Lorenzo Johnson, a star on the court for South Jones High School, played eight professional seasons in Europe, and also played with the Houston Rockets and the Harlem Globetrotters. Two of the most renowned residents were major leaguers: Buddy Myer of the Boston Red Sox and Washington Senators had more than 2,100 hits in seventeen seasons, including the 1935 American League batting title. Harry Craft played a few seasons for the Cincinnati Reds but made his name as a manager for several major and minor league clubs in a lengthy career, including the first manager of the Houston Colt .45s. He was later given credit by both Mickey Mantle and Roger Maris for making them the great players they later became.

Famous residents were not Ellisville's only excitement. It has had its share of notable historical events, most of them political. One evening more than two hundred years ago, Vice President Aaron Burr slipped into town and spent what must have been a sleepless night at Parker's Inn on his flight to the Southwest to escape pursuing federal authorities. In 1863 a group of concerned yet valiant citizens met in the midst of a bloody civil conflict to consider a withdrawal from the Confederacy and the formation a Free State.

On a cold morning in 1909, President William Howard Taft made a brief speech from the back of his train as it stopped on the tracks running through the middle of town. In more recent times, Ellisville's citizens received visits by Vice President Gerald Ford, former House Speaker Newt Gingrich, Supreme Court Justice Antonin Scalia, and in 2008 by former President Bill Clinton, who stopped by in the midst of a tumultuous national campaign to gather support for the possibility of another President Clinton in the White House.

Those days were certainly newsworthy events that sparked much discussion, though most of us have no memories of the earliest ones, having only the accounts in the local newspapers and history books. But October 17, 2013 was a day for all of us true conservatives, our day, which we hoped would be long remembered and one that would prove to be the most exciting yet.

I jumped out of bed extra early that morning with a euphoric feeling that many planning to join the festivities at the courthouse likely felt. Despite the premature hour, I felt as refreshed as I had been in a long time. As a true, dyed-in-the-wool conservative, this was a day I had long awaited, a day with a big announcement, one that could change everything for those of us who were Jones Countians and lifelong Ellisvillians.

Even though Ellisville was named for a US Senator from Mississippi, Powhatan Ellis, and as storied as the history of Jones County, Mississippi has been, a saga rich enough to spark a new Hollywood film about our days as a Free State, Jones County had never sent anyone to the United States Senate, nor have we had a candidate strong enough to take on the challenge of defeating a sitting United States Senator.

In the preceding weeks, the excitement and anticipation only grew because of rumors our favorite son might throw his hat into the ring. If he did, conservatives would finally have a solid candidate from among us who had a great chance to win. He was a man who would speak for those of us who believed we no longer had a voice in Washington, someone with the courage to step up to the plate to challenge Mississippi's six-term US Senator, Mr. Establishment himself, Thad Cochran, who had not faced a seriously contested race in decades, if he really ever had.

In Chris McDaniel we had a native son at center stage, doing something we all believed to be good and decent, something that we could all be proud of, something that needed to be done. We all believed that soon conservatives across Mississippi would see our candidate the same way Jones County saw him, as a serious conservative in the mold of Senators Ted Cruz, Mike Lee, and Rand Paul, who would soon join them in the US Senate to fight for a better Mississippi and a stronger America. Hopefully, with a good effort and God's blessing, we could add his name to the list of notable local citizens.

Most everyone in Jones County thought highly of Chris McDaniel. "I don't have anything bad to say about Thad Cochran, but Chris is just as fine a fella as you'd want to meet," said Vern Getty, an eighty-four-year-old Ellisvillian and owner of Western Auto. "You just always knew he was going places."[1] Tea Party activist Tiffany Parrish was ready for new leadership. "I believe our country needs change and term limits," she told me in an interview. "It has been past time for Thad Cochran to retire. I do not have a passion to run for office but I do have a passion to get the good ones in office and Chris is one of the good ones! The thing I like best is he didn't wait his turn to run or sit back and be told from the Establishment what to do, how to do it and when to do it. Unlike some of the others, he can actually think for himself. This is the type of leadership we deserve."[2]

Chris's longtime friend and radio sidekick, Jack Fairchilds, summed up why many were throwing their support behind the challenger to take down a Goliath like Thad Cochran. "Chris as a public servant is very rare because he's always honest with you, and you don't find that this day and age in politics. He's very accessible to people and even if the answer he gives you is not the popular answer but it's the true answer, then he's going to give you that answer. He fights the hard fights even if that is not the popular fight. We need more like that."[3]

As for me, this challenger, this new, emerging national leader was a good friend of mine as well. I was honored that he asked me to attend a prayer session before his announcement speech and then to stand on the steps of the courthouse in our hometown to watch as he delivered his long-awaited announcement that he was launching a campaign to take down the aged Senator Cochran.

Waiting for the event to begin, the clock seemed to move ever more slowly. The assembling crowd seemed unusually small and a few of Chris's out of town guests, fellow state senators and other dignitaries, lingering with the rest of us, began to worry. "Don't be alarmed," I told them. "Ellisvillians always arrive just at the right moment, usually right at kickoff."

As the event finally commenced, the drizzle miraculously stopped, the skies cleared, and the sun began to peak through. Was this a sign from heaven that we are on the right track? We believed it was.

Finally, the moment came. State Senator Chris McDaniel stepped up to the podium on the steps of the 110-year-old courthouse to announce that he was throwing his hat into the ring against Cochran. The crowd had swelled to several hundred, filling Ellisville's courthouse lawn, which was quite a scene for a Thursday at lunchtime. My parents were there, along with my two nephews. I recognized, and knew, many in the crowd, but there were quite a few who had come from afar to hear from a great young leader.

Thanking the throng of supporters who came out on their lunch break, Senator McDaniel likened this new crusade to the struggle the United States faced as it fought for its independence from England:

I am reminded of that first revolution, and how important it was, because it didn't just change the leading cast of characters, it changed everything. For the first time in man's relationship to man and his government, we didn't just remove a king and replace him with another king, we removed the king and replaced him with the will of the people. That revolution brought us the consent of the governed.

We are the people now. They must listen to us. That is truly revolutionary. And it's that idea, that concept we stand to defend today. Because all across this country when that revolution took place lamps were lit in the hearts of men and women, in the hearts of free men and women, and the whole world witnessed liberty. They looked from afar and they traveled to these shores with new dreams. My Irish ancestors, my Scottish ancestors, they came here with an idea that was bigger than self, it was about liberty, it was about freedom and we fight for that today. But ladies and gentlemen the lamps of liberty are going out across this republic. The republic is in trouble. You sense it. You recognize this dire need we have to turn things around. Millions of people feel like strangers in their land. You don't recognize your country. An old America has faded away, a new America rises to take its place, the traditions and the morals that we find important, they don't find important. And so we recoil.

I do not mean to overstate this but I want to be perfectly clear: We are engaged in a battle between two opposing visions of America's future. Someone will win. And so we stand here today to make a very public choice and to ask you to join me in choosing to become more. To be better. To be what this country was always intended to be—a beacon of liberty. Now is the time.[4]

Ending his speech, he spoke of the vast struggle he and those of us who supported him were about to enter. The fight was going to be a tough one but we would endure to the end. "With apologies to one of my early heroes, Winston Churchill: we shall go on to the end," he said. "We shall fight in academia. We'll fight in the classrooms and in the newspapers. We'll fight with growing confidence in the natural rights of mankind. We will fight in the marbled halls of Congress. We'll fight in the state capitols. We'll fight in the cities. We'll fight in the streets. We'll fight in the countryside. And, if for a moment, which I do not believe, this country and its liberty were somehow subjugated, I will expect a new generation of Americans to stand, with the Constitution as their guide, and reclaim what's rightfully theirs. This is our fight, if necessary for years, if necessary alone."

He didn't yet know it but this Churchillian statement, before the race was over, would come frighteningly close to prophecy.

CHAPTER 1

CHRIS MCDANIEL:
A SON OF MISSISSIPPI

He was a native son who embodied the traditions and values that most Mississippians held dear. Though long rumored to have a familial connection to the Kennedys of Massachusetts, he was a true son of Mississippi: hardworking, responsible, self-reliant, honest, independent, loyal, charitable, hospitable, dependable, a family man with a servant's heart who was capable of self-sacrifice. He was also a true conservative who could fire up the Republican base like no one else in the entire state. And, what's more, he cut quite the contrast to the ancient Senator Thad Cochran, in looks but also youth, energy, ideas, and their legislative records and life stories. In short, he was the Establishment's worst nightmare.

Chris McDaniel grew up in the small town of Ellisville, Mississippi, as did I, not a rock's throw from each other. Though it has changed somewhat over the decades, the quaint little hometown of our formative years featured just one red light, only a couple of fast-food joints, no modern hotels, and certainly nothing outstanding on the entertainment scale. It was a community where everyone knew each other, supported one another, and there was no rancor or division to speak of. It was the kind of place where you didn't have to lock your doors at night but if any of us youngsters decided to do something against the rules, you could bet your parents knew about it before you got home. And as teenagers we knew that all too well.

Chris and I attended the same elementary school. In high school Chris got good grades and played varsity basketball. After graduation, he attended our local junior college to play basketball at the same place his father, Coach Carlos McDaniel, taught a full load of courses. From there Chris went to William Carey College in nearby Hattiesburg, barely twenty miles down the road from Ellisville, before heading north to law school at Ole Miss in Oxford.

Chris McDaniel's political views, though, were formed not in these influential high school and college days, as they are for so many of today's youth, but years earlier while just a young teenager under the tutelage of his father. His dad called him into the living room one evening in 1984 to watch a nationally televised political speech by Ronald Reagan. "My father said, 'Listen, you've got to watch this,'" Chris would tell audiences on the campaign trail. "'You've got to see what this man is saying.' And there on the TV was this former actor from California. And he looked right at me. He looked right at my father. But he was really speaking to the entire nation. And he said things to us that intuitively made sense. He talked about liberty and freedom. He talked about balanced budgets. He talked about traditional values and personal responsibility. And my father looked at me and said, 'Well, son, we must be Republicans.' And, indeed, we were, and are. That's the party I joined."

And he's been with that party ever since. "I was a Republican because Reagan was a Republican," he often said, breathing a sigh of relief that it wasn't Nixon who had been speaking that night. Reagan changed his life. Because of Reagan, Chris developed an interest in history, literature, philosophy, public policy, the law, and even theology. But it was the law, not politics, which first spurred his intellectual interests. "As far as politics, I have always been fascinated by it, but I wasn't that guy planning my career path like some of these kids are nowadays," he told me. "I was a Young Republican in college, of course, but I wasn't out there thinking, 'I'm gonna run for Office A this year and Office B next year.' It never dawned on me. My whole thought process was to go to law school, and be a good, hardworking successful lawyer."

His focus was to go into private practice and perhaps possibly run for a legal office, not a political one. His lifelong dream was always to be a federal judge, to make critical constitutional arguments he'd talked about so many times on the campaign trail. "A federal judge is what I've always wanted to be," he told me in an interview. "I thought my talents were better in that setting and that's one of the reasons that I was so fortunate to be a federal law clerk for two years. That was an incredible amount of experience and I thought it was going to put me on the fast track to perhaps one day be a federal judge."[1]

Being raised by a professor, the great game of politics, as it's known, was simply not a part of the McDaniel household. His family was not political and certainly not out networking, shaking hands, and making backroom deals, like some other families. "I thought everything in the world was nice, generous, and wholesome," he told me. "I never heard my dad say a curse word. I never saw him take a drink of alcohol. I never heard him say a negative word about anybody, so I thought that's how the whole world was. Of course, then I went to law school and started practicing law and I realized quickly that my father was just a very special human being. So I was a little naïve growing up because I was in that type of household."

After law school, Chris obtained a two-year federal law clerkship under Judge Charles Pickering at the United States District Court in Hattiesburg, a post that was a rare and distinguished honor. As he began work at the court, he still had to pass the bar exam. Preparing for the rigorous test, his new boss gave him some last-minute words of encouragement, "I wish you the best, but if you fail, you're fired." Whether joking or not, Judge Pickering's advice worked, for Chris did not fail. He passed with flying colors.

While at the federal court, Chris received valuable experience that could never be purchased. Like the medical profession, the law has its own version of a residency where the best young lawyers out of law school can serve as a clerk to federal judges, giving them a unique insight into the inner workings of the bench. "When you come out of law school, you don't know what's going on behind the judge's bench," Chris told me. "What's really going on back there? What are they talking about? It can be quite scary. But when you live behind the bench for two years and help them write opinions, it's an eye-opening experience and made me a much better lawyer because it was on the trial level and in my opinion the most important level for a federal court because that is where you see the best lawyers in the world doing the work that really matters from a criminal standpoint and a civil standpoint. There you are, able to sit and watch these guys, the best lawyers in the country, making these arguments. And that was really influential to me because I was able to see what good lawyers do and how they behave and what bad lawyers do and how they behave. It made me a better lawyer today, and it made me more respectful of the entire process, even the whole jury process."

After finishing his two-year clerkship with Judge Pickering in Hattiesburg, Chris moved back home to Ellisville in the summer of 1999 to begin private practice at a firm in Laurel. He was also soon to be married to his long-time girlfriend, Jill Tullos, and his father was to be his best man. Life was certainly good, and he looked forward to a long, fruitful life practicing law in Jones County.

Late one evening, though, at the age of twenty-seven, just days away from his wedding, Chris's life took a dramatic turn and he entered a true trial by fire. Such a horrific tragedy, though, can only be told by him in his own words:

It's been years, and yet I seldom discuss that night.

The date was July 13, 1999. It was the most horrifying and impactful day of my life. Perhaps it is best described as the evening the old Chris passed away, and a new one took his place.

My dad asked me to help him with a new SUV purchase in Jackson, MS, which is roughly 90 miles away from our home in Ellisville. I agreed and drove him up to the dealership, with the idea of following him back later that evening. After negotiating with the salesperson all afternoon and acquiring the new vehicle, we begin our trip home that night. He was excited about his new SUV and was absolutely thrilled about the idea of showing it to my mom -- he loved her dearly and always sought her approval. He was happily out in front; I was dutifully following. The drive was beautiful.

As fate would have it, the way home from Jackson led through Collins, his boyhood home.

We stopped there for a moment as we were passing through the city. Like many Southern towns, Collins has a small downtown area -- bustling during the day, but quiet at night. We pulled over there for a few seconds, stretched our legs, and talked about the day.

He was always so proud of Collins. As folks around here will tell you, he was Mr. Collins High School in 1960 and was a basketball standout for the Tigers. The stories from his childhood permeated my youth -- it seemed as though I knew the town and its inhabitants, his teachers, his friends. The streets, buildings and the names were all familiar. I spent much of my childhood there. Even the smells were comforting.

Looking back on that night, it was the last time he would visit his hometown. Maybe, perhaps stopping there was the Lord's way of reminding me of our roots, but also for him to have a final visit with the community that raised him from a boy to a man.

In any event, it was time to head home. We talked for a while, he hugged me and said, "I love you, son."

I'll never forget that moment, his blue eyes, his glasses, his wristwatch, his smile, his laugh. Little did I know, it would be the last time.

From Collins, two highways lead home to Ellisville – Highway 588 and Highway 84. Each road can take roughly 25 minutes to make the trip.

He chose Highway 588, and I followed closely.

We weren't strangers to that old two-lane highway. To the contrary, it was a road my family knew very well. When I was a little boy, it's how we traveled to my grandmother's home. It was our trail to the family on Thanksgivings and Christmases; it was our path to Sunday lunches and long naps during football games. And on the way back in the evenings, my dad would sing Amazing Grace and other hymns as I would stare out into a limitless night sky while imagining myself an astronaut or superhero.

My mom and I loved to hear him sing. And when he wasn't singing, he was telling stories -- funny ones. He loved to laugh, and we enjoyed his tall tales, even when she had to correct him from time to time. And how we laughed! I can still hear them both talking and chuckling about some big fish that managed to escape or an exciting basketball game in the late 1950s. Those conversations are among my favorite memories. Highway 588 is where he taught me how to drive. All of those good thoughts, it was a comfortable, familiar and happy place. But that was about to change.

I remember it being late. It was dark.

A few miles outside of Collins, still in Covington County, the highway curves slightly leftward with a long but subtle downhill decline. He made the turn and began down the hill.

Shortly after that, I saw his brake lights flash for a brief second, as his headlights quickly reflected on a huge truck blocking both lanes of traffic. He never had time to stop, and he crashed at almost full speed into the side of the tractor-trailer.

Unthinkable. Unimaginable.

Because of the suddenness of the impact, I had no choice but to swerve into a ditch to avoid the collision.

The next few minutes changed my life forever.

I exited my car, rushed over to him, but he was trapped inside, with much of his new SUV twisted and destroyed under the trailer.

I called for him. I begged for him. I cried out for him to answer. But the most I heard was strange metallic sounds, the creaking of materials and God forbid, what sounded like groans. Then an eerie silence.

My heart was racing. I convinced myself it was a dream -- just another nightmare. I would awaken soon; I kept telling myself. I was in shock. I did my best to reject reality, to convince myself it wasn't real. Wake up, Chris. Just wake up. Seconds turned to minutes. Minutes into eternity. Despite my best efforts, I could not get him to respond.

So I broke the glass. Pulled apart metal and plastic. Ripped the flesh on my hands, arms, and torso. But I gained entry.

And that's when I found him.

He was still buckled, seat belt intact. Sitting in the driver's side seat. Horrible injuries. A terrible scene. Stuff I still can't forget although it's been eighteen years.

I tried to perform CPR, but there as no room. No place to move. Not that it would have mattered.

I prayed for a miracle. I prayed to wake up. I prayed for God to give me some type of sign, however small.

But I was met with silence.

And that's when I knew.

This is real. This is not a nightmare; I'm not waking up from this one. Ever.

I placed my head on his shoulder and cried. I hugged him. Through the smell of smoke, airbag dust, and bent metal, I kissed him on the cheek. I thanked him for being my daddy, and I told him how much I loved him.

Then I said goodbye.

I held him, whimpered, closed my eyes and waited.

Time stood still. I specifically remember a man, perhaps the driver of the rig, telling me the SUV was on fire. I recall someone using a fire extinguisher. I remember others screaming at me to get out of the vehicle, telling me "don't do that to yourself." But I also remember thinking I had died, too. Smoke was in the air. It was hard to breathe. But there was no way I was leaving my daddy's side. If he was going to burn, then so was I. Loyal to the very end.

Sometimes at night, even now, when things get still, and I let my mind wander, I still relive the scene, wishing I could have done something different. Wishing I could have saved him. Begging for one more second. Hoping it was all still a dream. Perhaps I could have led; he could have followed me. Maybe I should have been driving his new SUV. Why couldn't I have chosen another way? Another day? Another direction? Another moment?

I guess I'll always have doubts. Life has a way of being difficult, doesn't it?

My father died on Tuesday, July 13. It was dark. He was 57. His name was Carlos McDaniel. And there's not a day that goes by when I don't miss him.

As midnight struck, on July 14, 1999, I was a different person. The old me was gone; a new one had emerged. I was shattered, all innocence lost. My faith splintered.

And the next two years were the most painful of my life.

I had to overcome. I had to be stronger. I had to develop a backbone. Then I had to rediscover my faith.

All in good time, Chris. All in good time.

It was truly a life-altering experience, as it would be for anyone. Carlos was not just Chris' father; he was his best friend on earth and soon to be best man. Life was now in turmoil. The wedding was cancelled and Chris fell into a period of deep refection. "My life has changed dramatically since that day when I lost my dad and the manner in which I lost him. It couldn't have happened in a more inopportune or uneasy time in my life, considering I was transitioning between being a law clerk and to a law firm setting." His father, Carlos, was a big part of why he became a lawyer. He pushed Chris to be the very best he could be, to read, think, and question everything. So the loss became a very transformative experience, causing him to fall into a two-year period to doubt some of the biggest pillars of his life, things he would never have questioned before, like God and his faith. "I was angry for a long time," he said, "but not at people, just at my circumstance."

Such tragedy would have destroyed a lesser man, as it has countless numbers of people over the years. But great men rise above those nearly irresistible opportunities to wallow in grief and self-pity. It is the true measure of a man in how he responds to tragedies. And Chris McDaniel certainly lived up to the standards of a godly, Christ-centered life. He decided to move forward, not to simply exist under a dark, oppressive cloud of grief, but live his life as his father would have wanted.

Many eminent people have lost at least one parent early in life, either in childhood or early adulthood. Throughout history, a total of sixty-seven percent of British Prime Ministers lost at least one parent by age sixteen. In fact, twelve out of the first forty-three men who have held the US presidency had lost their fathers while they were young.[2] Chris's personal tragedy has the same impact. It made him a better human, it taught him perspective, and exposed him to so much pain at such a relatively young age, and this taught him something important: "I could stand firm for the things in which I believe, and even if I were criticized or attacked, or even if I lost a race because of it, I knew that there was nothing my political enemies could do to really hurt me."

Unlike some who tend to hurl responsibility for personal calamity at God, Chris never blamed the Lord for the tragedy. He couldn't have known it in 1999 but such a personal tragedy did prepare him for what was to come. During the 2014 campaign people marveled at how he handled all the negative attacks thrown at him, without once compromising his views. He remained steady in the face of the onslaught. "When you go through that kind of shock and pain," he told me once when reflecting on his father, "there's nothing that my political enemies can do to me that can even compare with what I've been through. The worst pain imaginable." And that puts him in a unique position as a politician because he can stick to his core set of principles. After surviving the initial shock of the tragedy, everything became much clearer. He now understood what was most important in his life.

In the long run, the tragedy also made Chris much stronger. Even though in the immediate aftermath of the accident, his life was seemingly turned upside down. After putting his wedding on hold, he did the honorable thing by moving back home to care for his widowed mother, who had just lost the only husband she had ever known, in a family that was extraordinarily close. His family was never apart. His mother never had a driver's license. His father drove her everywhere, usually with young Chris in tow. They went everywhere together. So he had to spend the next two years helping her transition to a whole new phase of life.

Tragedies happen in life. We make mistakes, experience failure, heartache, and defeat. Those things are not the true measure of a person. It's how we deal with such mistakes, failures, and defeat. It's what we do when those storms of life arrive. Do we wallow in self-pity or rise up, overcome the sorrows, and move forward with our lives?

Chris McDaniel chose the latter, but he also questioned his faith along the way. He had walked through the fire. He had been in the valley of the shadow of death. And as the Holy Scriptures teaches us, emerged as gold. In the end, his faith became stronger because of the accident, not weaker.

In August 1999, just three weeks after the accident, Chris began his law practice at the Hortman & Harlow offices in Laurel. It was a very sad time, a very scary time. But God blessed him with a wonderful law firm with some of the most incredible Christian lawyers and amazing human beings who supported him through such a trying time. Over the next few years he put his head down and worked hard practicing corporate law, which earned him the honor of being named one of the top fifty lawyers in Mississippi. Ninety-five percent of his practice is corporate law and defending businesses from civil lawsuits. The remaining aspect of his practice mainly concerns constitutional issues.

Chris McDaniel's life up to that point had been nothing short of exemplary, and he owed this to his upbringing, the lessons he learned at the feet of his father. His conservative bona fides were stellar. So in 2003 he took his strong conservative convictions to the world of talk radio, launching a second career of sorts as host of a new, local show he dubbed *The Right Side*, with co-host Jack Fairchilds. The show had great ratings, broadcasting across much of south Mississippi's Pine Belt region, and it eventually went national, being produced out of Chicago and streamed live on the Internet.

The show's phenomenal success helped launch Chris's political career when Jones County's State Senate seat came open in 2007. After deciding to run for the seat, he asked me to join his campaign committee, which I was honored to do. But moving into politics was not something he ever imagined, especially before his father's tragic death. Had his father not tragically lost his life, it is quite likely that he would have never gone into politics. Being as dedicated as he was to his family, he had already made plans to remain in Ellisville with them, making sure they could grow old together, while he continued to practice law and possibly teach some classes at the junior college.

But sometimes our lives turn on a major decision, for better or worse. Looking back on our past, we can usually pick out an event or decision where things changed. For Chris McDaniel it was the day his father passed away. "That was the turning point in my life in so many ways," Chris said. He didn't decide to become a politician right way, but the things Chris considered important prior to July 13, 1999 were not the same things he considered important after July 13, 1999. He had an entirely different perspective on life at that point. "It's kind of weird to have two lives in one, but I do," he said.

Whether it's fate, fortune, or the hand of God, whatever you want to call it, Chris did go into politics, and the people of Jones County are certainly thankful for it. After easily dispatching his Republican opponent in the primary in the summer of 2007, then winning 60 percent of the vote in November against a well-known Democrat, he was now Senator Chris McDaniel and began what has turned out to be a stellar legislative career thus far.

Unlike Thad Cochran, whose career is based on promoting an activist government and the interests of the donor class, Chris McDaniel's has been an exemplary advocate of true conservatism and the lasting interests of the people. And much of these core beliefs came from his upbringing and his church, where much of his social conservatism originated. His dad was a deacon in the Southern Baptist church, but he started out as a Missionary Baptist, which are even more ultra-conservative than the Southern Baptists. "We've been at West Ellisville Baptist Church my entire life," said Chris. "Every time the doors were open, and that is where my social conservatism came from."

It was this upbringing, and an attachment to the teachings of Christ, that shaped his worldview. Chris has his dad's Bible today. The verses that really mattered to him are underlined and there are notes in the margin. Carlos stayed in the Bible, and Chris was always taught that nobody was perfect, which is why we needed God. "Frankly that's why we need conservatism because we are all sinners," Chris told me. It is a philosophy that fit perfectly within this Scotch-Irish, strong individualist, anti-centralized kind of guy. Since we are all sinners, Chris has always wondered why, as a nation and a people, we would want to consolidate authority and power in the hands of another sinner. "We need more freedom, not less, and we need less power in the hands of another man."

The philosophy of conservatism, rooted in the values of Christianity, the Declaration of Independence, and the Constitution, cut quite the contrast with liberalism and its roots in another value system. Liberalism is not a mind-set, Chris would often say, but an old impulse to control others. Modern liberals do it under the guise of freedom and tolerance, but they are the most intolerant of people. They want more of your money to throw at problems to assuage their guilty conscience. "It's not Christ-like," he said of the liberal philosophy. "Christ was not a liberal or a socialist. He recognized free will and recognized the ability of people to make decisions and he expected us to make wise decisions, the most wise of which was to follow Him. But He would have never passed a law forcing people to follow Him. And He would have never taken money by force from His fellow neighbors to make sure His ministry was intact and successful. Free will is a big part of who He is. And there's no free will in liberalism. When someone says, 'I'm a liberal,' that just means they are for force and coercion."

That, in a nutshell, is Chris's political philosophy of the world. And he recognizes that having free will means that everyone is not going to be in agreement. True conservatives respect those that have liberal viewpoints, even if we disagree with them. It is the liberals who don't show respect when they try to force their viewpoints on others, whether it's through economic policies or whether it's through social policies. And, making matters worse, liberals don't respect the balance of powers in government or the limitations imposed by the Constitution, using those tactics to empower the collective over the individual.

For Chris McDaniel, social conservatism, what he sometimes called "traditional values," is just as important but also requires free will. And in 2014 he was often attacked for advocating traditional values, which his political enemies twisted into a supposed belief in segregation and racism. Yet traditional values are those rooted in Christianity, like free will, individual responsibility, self-reliance, respect for all human life, freedom of religion, and defense of the most vulnerable in society.

As a member of the Mississippi State Senate, Chris has fought to advance the principles of conservatism and safeguard the freedoms, liberties, and traditional values that most Mississippians hold dear. To help perpetuate this effort, he founded the State Senate's Conservative

Coalition, an idea based on the historical group that fought FDR's New Deal in the 1930s. From the start, Chris took up his pen and began writing laws that work. He is the author of the Mississippi Student Religious Liberties Act, a law that protects prayer in public schools, and has been used several times to protect the rights of students to freely exercise their religious liberty. He authored the Unborn Child Protection Act of 2011 and Karen's Law, a law that protects child victims by instituting harsher punishments for criminals who prey on society's most vulnerable.

In 2010, Nathan Key, a five-year-old boy in Laurel, Mississippi was struck and killed instantly by an impatient punk who swerved around the stopped bus as Nathan was exiting at home after a day at school. In response to the tragedy, Chris introduced Nathan's Law that strengthened the penalties for passing a stopped school bus, which included stiffer fines, lengthier jail time, and suspension of driver's licenses.

Another traditional value that many Americans hold dear is the right to keep and bear arms. In the Mississippi Senate Chris has fought as hard as anyone to safeguard the Second Amendment and protect the gun rights of Mississippians. He authored the Federal Firearm Ban Cooperation Act to prohibit firearm bans in the state of Mississippi and the Concealed Carry Protection Act to protect the rights of concealed permit holders. He also sponsored legislation to require Mississippi to honor any valid concealed carry permit issued by another state and to confer enhanced carry benefits to members of the military. This bill, which became law in 2014, also granted the Department of Public Safety continued authority to enter into written reciprocity agreements with other states if those states require such an agreement before recognizing Mississippi carry permits.

And to keep the iron hand of the federal government from crushing gun rights in Mississippi, Chris sponsored a bill that outlined the constitutional principles that protected gun rights and demanded that the federal government "cease and desist" in actions that are beyond the scope of its constitutional delegated authority. If Washington oversteps its bounds, then the bill directs that "all compulsory federal legislation which directs states to comply under threat of civil or criminal penalties or sanctions or requires states to pass legislation or lose federal funding be prohibited or repealed."

In 2013, Chris authored the Second Amendment Preservation Act, which would prevent federal infringement on gun rights and nullify all federal acts that violate the Second Amendment. He has also sought to protect Mississippians from acts of terror, authoring a bill that made terrorism a crime punishable by death, thereby making it easier to impose the death penalty in state courts in cases of terrorism.

Although Chris is supportive of law enforcement and tough-on-crime legislation, he also sought to protect the liberties of the people against government overreach by writing the Educational Data Freedom Act to allow parents to opt out of student mandatory tracking systems in public schools and the Fourth Amendment Protection Act to prohibit Mississippi government agencies from implementing and cooperating with NSA spying programs. Furthermore, he introduced a Senate resolution to express opposition to the National Defense Authorization Act of 2012, a federal law that would allow the government to forever detain terror suspects, including American citizens, without trial and also allowed the US military to conduct anti-terror operations on US soil in clear violation of the Bill of Rights and the federal Posse Comitatus Act.

As our borders remain wide open and our immigration system broken, Chris fought for jobs and protection against illegal immigration. He authored the Immigration Reform Act to prevent Mississippi from becoming a "sanctuary" state and introduced a number of other pieces of legislation relating to immigration, including bills to prohibit undocumented workers from receiving federal and state benefits and to require illegal aliens to pay out-of-state tuition at state schools. He also authored the Employment Protection Act in 2008, also known as the E-Verify law, which requires all Mississippi companies to use an Internet-based system to check the legal status of potential employees. The enactment of this law would also prohibit Mississippi companies from employing illegal immigrants.

Fiscal conservatism is also a major part of the McDaniel platform, unlike the spendthrift ways that has come to define the modern Republican Party, especially Thad Cochran. I dubbed Chris "Mr.

Fiscal Conservative" in Mississippi and his record proves his fiscal bona fides. He's been very supportive of small business, sponsoring legislation designed to give owners of small businesses more say about state regulations that could affect their livelihoods. His bill established the twelve-member Small Business Regulatory Review Committee that examines state rules and laws that could impact businesses with fewer than one hundred full-time employees and less than $10 million in gross annual sales or revenues. He has also fought to cut taxes, authoring the Mississippi Income Reduction Act of 2014, the End the Corporate Franchise Tax Act of 2013, the School Fundraiser Sales Tax Exemption Act of 2013, and the Hunting Supplies Sales Tax Holiday Act of 2012. He also fought tooth and nail against every proposal to raise taxes. His mantra: "No more taxes! Not one cent!"

Of conservatism's cornerstone, freedom and liberty, there can be no greater aspect than that of private property rights. In Mississippi it was Senator Chris McDaniel who led the successful fight to protect private property from the prying hands of encroaching government. As Mississippi governor, Haley Barbour, in partnership with private corporations, believed businesses should have the power to take private property for their own use, in clear violation of the Constitution. Chris disagreed and authored a bill to safeguard property rights. After Governor Barbour vetoed his bill, Chris led the fight to override it, which came up just two votes short. Far from being deterred, Chris led the grassroots campaign that resulted in a new constitutional amendment that guaranteed that private property rights in Mississippi would be protected from the clutches of private corporations.

But in his most audacious stand, Chris led the fight in Mississippi against the disastrous Obamacare bill, filing his own federal lawsuit in 2010 when Mississippi's attorney general, Democrat Jim Hood, would not stand up to Washington in defense of average Mississippians. I agreed to be one of the original three plaintiffs, along with fellow Jones Countians Michael Shotwell and Richard Conrad. In fact, I was the lead plaintiff. I'd never sued anyone in my entire life, but I was now filing a suit against Attorney General Eric Holder and three other cabinet secretaries, including HHS Secretary Kathleen Sebelius, to try to block the implementation of Obamacare. The suit was filed as Ryan

S. Walters, et al v. Eric Holder, et al. and was eventually joined by Mississippi Governor Phil Bryant.[3]

As the case moved through the system, it was increasingly likely that we would have our day in court, which would include plaintiff testimony administered by Obama Justice Department lawyers. One day I got a phone call from Chris. "I need one of you to testify in a court hearing to face off against Holder's lawyers," he said. "And congratulations you're the one." It was one of those gut-punch moments in life, but without stopping to consider just exactly what I was agreeing to, I said, "Let's do it."

As I began brushing up on my arguments, familiarizing myself with all possible constitutional and legal curveballs that Holder's lawyers might throw at me, I recognized that the argument Chris put together was simply brilliant. Of course the case would center on the usual argument about the government forcing citizens to purchase health insurance, but there was another major component. Chris was going to argue that the way Obamacare was set up would require the government to gain access to our private health records. It was a necessary component or the law simply could not function. But the problem is that health records are considered privileged information, part of the doctor-patient dynamic.

Chris's argument broke down like this: The federal courts had found a right to privacy in the Bill of Rights, which they used in *Roe v. Wade* to safeguard a woman's right to choose to have an abortion. In essence, the courts concluded that an abortion was a medical right to privacy. So why did the same right to privacy not exist with Obamacare? With this argument, the government would find itself backed into a legal corner. They would have to either grant us the same right to medical privacy as *Roe* had, which would ultimately gut Obamacare, or they would have to throw the arguments made in *Roe* overboard. I was anxious to see their response to this one.

Unfortunately, that day never came. US District Judge Keith Starrett in Hattiesburg, where we filed our suit, threw out the case for a lack of legal standing. The court's reasoning was simple. Since the law had yet to go into effect, there was no injury to adjudicate. Therefore, we had no standing to sue. It was a case of having to wait until the government injured us before we could defend ourselves. I guess preemptive strikes are only legal if the federal government undertakes them.

Although Chris's case was not successful, through no fault of his own, it was bold stands like this one that has earned him numerous awards and recognition from influential groups and organizations. He was named legislator of the year by MADD (Mother's Against Drunk Driving), Mississippi State Troopers Association, and the Oil & Gas Association. *Mississippi Business Journal* named him one of the state's top fifty attorneys, while Mississippi's Business and Industry Political Education Committee (BIPEC) named him a business champion. He also proudly serves as an attorney for Mississippi Right to Life.

Boldness and taking decisive stands is something Chris is known for, even as a freshman member of the Mississippi Senate. Soon after the 2007 state elections, Republicans controlled the Senate but Democrats maintained their lock on the House, where they have exercised dominance since 1875. But that hold was slipping and they knew it. So state Democrats came up with a new redistricting plan designed to maintain their grip on the House for years to come. It was sleazy and probably illegal. Unsurprisingly it passed the House and faced stiff opposition in the GOP-controlled Senate. The worry, though, was that it might slip through. Lt. Governor Phil Bryant had one man in mind to speak in opposition to the bill and persuade the chamber to vote it down, and that man was freshman senator Chris McDaniel. Bryant's words to him that day were simple: "Take the podium and stop this thing." Chris delivered an impassioned plea to the Senate that was so persuasive that not only did every Republican vote to kill the redistricting plan, but several Democrats crossed over to vote against their own party's bill. That's real leadership.

"Chris is one of the brightest legal minds I've ever met and he's as genuine a conservative as I've ever met," said Keith Plunkett, who would serve as his policy advisor during the campaign against Cochran. "He has a concern and vision for the future that sets his own personal and political self-interest aside. It's a refreshing thing to see such leadership in today's politics."

But the sheer gravity of the situation could unnerve even the most seasoned political veteran, particularly if Cochran jumped into the race. "This is Thad Cochran we are talking about, the Godfather of Mississippi politics!" Chris said to me during one of our interviews after the campaign. "Thad Cochran! Even his name has a certain level of distinction. It isn't Fred. It isn't Sam. It is Thad!" Growing up that's all we ever knew. The name 'Thad' was synonymous with "Senator." He was Mr. Republican in Mississippi.

In November 2013, with Chris already committed to the race, Cochran announced his intention to run for a seventh term. So this would be a McDaniel-Cochran race, which begged an obvious question: Why in the world would anyone want to run against Thad Cochran, a man considered untouchable by any political expert who weighed in? Because Mississippi needed a philosophical conflict, the party needed a philosophical conflict. As Chris put it, we were called "the most conservative state in the republic yet I kept seeing us beg for federal dollars." People claimed Mississippi wanted state sovereignty, "but I kept seeing us surrender that sovereignty to the central authority. I kept reading that we were this great social state but saw nobody take a stand in defense of social values." Chris kept hearing how conservative Thad was, but he was *not doing anything in defense of conservatism.*

There is certainly a big difference between being a Republican and being a conservative, and Thad Cochran was very much the former. He wasn't conservative at all, didn't have a conservative bone in his body. He grew up in the '60s as a moderate and openly talked about being a moderate as a Democrat. And even today he defends his moderate positions on every viewpoint. Chris saw that as a sin against the party. "We're $20 trillion in debt and the biggest spender is our Senator. Yet he and his supporters claim he is a conservative. He's in one of the most powerful positions in DC to effectuate change yet does absolutely nothing to effectuate change. He has got over forty years' experience and if he'd only raise his voice occasionally in defense of conservative values, you can rest assured we'd be a much better country today because of it. But I can't think of any issue that he has raised his voice on unless it's pork."

Because of Cochran's reluctance to confront the real issues and problems facing the nation, Chris made that all-important decision to run against Thad Cochran for the United States Senate. In a teasing press release just days before his official announcement speech in Ellisville he wrote: "We are in difficult times. Our state and country are suffering from a lack of confidence in our current leaders. Our Republican Party is in the process of reinvesting in the principles that made us who we are, and that has not been an easy time. I hope my decision will aid in bringing us back to agreement on the values we all support and hold dear, and give Mississippians the ability to move forward into the future with a purpose of reclaiming those values for our children."

But although he brimmed with confidence, the thought was a bit unnerving at times. "Look, it was a scary thing because you are not running against Thad Cochran; you are running against a powerful political machine. It's the most incredible machine I've ever seen. Not built on loyalty or principle, just on pure fear and force. Not a bit of loyalty or principle in the whole bunch of them. They don't care about Thad Cochran; they care about Thad Cochran paying them. And not a one of them can defend his record."

In order to expose Cochran's liberal record and defeat him in the election, Chris needed an effective organization comprised of many skilled people, and those would be hard to come by. Why? Because no campaign managers would touch it. No one wanted to represent Chris McDaniel in the state of Mississippi. Not one. "I talked to people," he told me. "I went around the state. And I heard the same refrain everywhere I went: 'Hey man we are with you but we can't touch this.'" Chris wasn't even able to have an in-state fundraiser. People seemed to support him, but nobody wanted to take on the job of running a campaign against Thad Cochran.

To head up the effort he chose a fellow Senator, Melanie Sojourner, the first Republican ever elected to serve District 37 in the State Senate. In her first run she had the full support of the state party and during her term became the first freshman to be tapped for a chairmanship in the history of the state. Like Chris McDaniel, she was named a rising star in the party and some were already putting her on the watch list for higher office.

Chris has always thought very highly of Sojourner. "I think Melanie was the best choice for a campaign manager," he said. "Melanie is one of the most capable communicators I've ever met and one of the most principled conservatives I've ever met. She was the perfect complement to the campaign because of her ability to fundraise, her ability to communicate, and because of her connections to the agricultural community, which is an important part of Mississippi's politics." This was very significant because Thad Cochran's claim to fame is the most recent federal "Farm Bill," so the campaign had to have a more important structural tie to that community. And Melanie was it.

The pick, like Trump's choice of Kellyanne Conway, was historic. Of all the US Senate campaigns across the country in 2014, Melanie Sojourner was the only woman to serve as a campaign manager. "Committing to work with McDaniel was one of the easiest professional decisions I ever made," she told me. "McDaniel is easily the smartest and most politically intuitive person I've ever worked with. He has an absolutely brilliant constitutional and legal mind coupled with being a gifted orator." But that didn't mean everyone liked it. Melanie received warnings and threats from establishment insiders more than once.

"Following adjournment one afternoon," Melanie told me. "I was one of the last people to leave and I had a member of Lt. Governor Tate Reeves' staff come up to me on my way out of the Senate chamber. He said, 'I know you and several others here are good friends with Senator McDaniel. We know he is considering a run against Cochran. Don't make that mistake.' When I ask him what he meant by that he pointed his finger very firmly and closely toward my face and said, 'Don't get involved.' Before he concluded he tapped his finger right at my chest close to my collarbone and continued, 'It's going to cost you if you do. Don't do it.'"

And of course the ensuing campaign was full of political attacks against Melanie. The Cochran machine ended up spreading rumors of infidelity and attacked her character and appearance. They stopped at nothing. There were even calls for Chris to fire her during the campaign. But as Chris knew, "loyalty in this life is the one thing, in politics especially, that we can't find anymore, so when you find people that really want to fight for principles, you better surround yourself with them. And that's what we did."

Loyalty was a value that Chris prized above most others and he stacked his campaign with those kinds of people, many of whom were volunteers. "That's the way I wanted it. Loyal, principled people that were fighting for principles and not just for personal advancement or even for me but for the set of things we believe in. So we found people who were strong, like-minded, and were thick-skinned enough to do it. And we surrounded ourselves with them."

But all the attacks aside, Chris knew he was doing the right thing, not for himself but for all of Mississippi. It was time for the people of the state of Mississippi to decide what kind of Senator they wanted representing them and their values in Washington. Chris believed that right was on his side, that Mississippi Republicans would vote to make a new change, and he would take his conservative values to Washington in January 2015. "Ladies and gentlemen," he announced to those assembled in Ellisville, "the next time Ted Cruz stands on that floor, the next time Mike Lee stands on that floor, the next time Rand Paul stands on that floor to fight for you, a son of Mississippi will stand next to them."

CHAPTER 2

THAD COCHRAN: A LIBERAL WOLF IN CONSERVATIVE SHEEPSKIN

If there was ever a politician that could rightfully be called the "Creature from Washington," Thad Cochran was it. He was loathed and even hated by true conservatives, who pegged him as their number one target for the 2014 mid-term elections as soon as Chris McDaniel jumped into the ring. Unlike Chris, though, Senator Cochran had no right to call himself a "son of Mississippi," if he ever could. He had left those values behind a long time ago, if he ever possessed them at all. He was nothing like Goldwater or Reagan, shared no passion for principles or for the Constitution, and what's more, he could spend taxpayer money like no one else in the entire country.

Despite his decades of service to the state, personal appearances were a rarity. Like many Mississippians my age, especially those of us who live in south Mississippi, I had never laid eyes on Thad Cochran and, even with the long Senate campaign that lasted from October 2013 until June 2014, to this day I still haven't. Elected to the US Senate in 1978, when I was five years old, Cochran almost never visited the state, choosing to remain in DC for a majority of his years of service. If he came at all, it was usually to north Mississippi, his home base. It was certainly no stretch for any of us to consider Senator Cochran as a "man from Washington" who had lost touch with many people back home, particularly the most conservative element of the voting public.

Cochran is known mainly as a big spender, the "King of Pork." Looking over his long career, it's certainly no stretch of the facts to suggest that Cochran has outspent many Senate Democrats on the Hill and that seemed to be just fine with homegrown Democrats in Mississippi. Had McDaniel defeated Cochran, a major spendaholic would have disappeared from Washington, and the economy, at least in the eyes of the Democratic Keynesians, would suffer.

Conservatives should not have been surprised to hear such news, for Cochran's own voting record, not just in recent years but as far back as the early '70s, is reflective of his friendship with liberal Democrats and his opposition to staunch conservatives. And how could we think he would do anything differently? Aside from more than forty years collecting a paycheck from the taxpayers, Thad Cochran has little accomplishments in the real world. No business success, no legal achievements to speak of, and certainly no recognition of any kind outside government.

But as all Establishment Republicans try to do, especially in a tight race with a conservative challenger, Cochran sought to convince the conservative base of the party that he had long service as a foot soldier in Reagan's army. The McDaniel campaign well knew that he could not be allowed to define the race and himself as a defender of Reagan. A slight scratch in the surface of his record in the last few years was not going to cut it. We had to dig as deeply as we could to expose Cochran for what he was and what he has always been—a liberal hiding in the clothing of a conservative.

For those who have been around long enough, or know enough conservative political history, the battle test for a claim of service in Reagan's army can be definitively proven by one's actions in 1976. And that came down to the Republican National Convention in July in Kansas City, Missouri. Throughout the presidential primaries that year, Ronald Reagan, the former two-term governor of California, had challenged the unpopular President Gerald Ford, who had angered a good many citizens by pardoning Richard Nixon before any charges were ever brought against him in the Watergate scandal. The economy was in shambles, with high inflation, and Ford's foreign policy, allowing South Vietnam to fall to the North without any response and signing the Helsinki Accords, an agreement that essentially handed the Soviets control of Eastern Europe, was a disaster.

Reagan, seeking to give Republicans a conservative choice of "bold colors, not pale pastels," stumbled out of the blocks during the early primary season, losing the first six contests, but roared back in North Carolina and Texas, as well as other more conservative Southern and Western states. When it was all said and done, Reagan had captured twenty-three states. Arriving at the convention, though, neither candidate had a majority of delegates, so the nomination would come down to the slate of uncommitted delegates. And both camps lobbied them heavily.

National attention soon focused on Mississippi, as its delegation, led by Clarke Reed, adopted a unit rule, whereby the entire voting bloc would swing to one candidate based on the majority vote of the delegation. So, in other words, if sixteen of the thirty delegates voted for Reagan, the whole thirty-vote bloc would go to Reagan. Mississippi became a major prize sought by both potential nominees.[1]

With its steadfast conservatism, it was widely believed Mississippi was solidly in Reagan's camp. However, Reagan did make a strategic mistake, although not a catastrophic one. Before the convention began, he picked a liberal Republican Senator from Pennsylvania, Richard Schweiker, to be his running mate, hoping to pick up that state's crucial delegates. This caused anger among many conservatives, particularly in Mississippi, and some began switching to Ford.

To be sure, the Schweiker pick was bad on Reagan's part but that did not mean the overall convention would have supported it. Furthermore, in exchange for the nomination, Reagan could have been pressured to drop him. Even the *Clarion Ledger* in Jackson mentioned the Schweiker pick as a "potential" choice for vice president.[2] Yet no one knew what the crucial state of Mississippi would do.

Perhaps the major blow came on the day a pair of Mississippi congressmen, and later US Senators, Trent Lott and Thad Cochran, publicly endorsed President Ford over Governor Reagan. Clarke Reed then switched his vote and the entire Mississippi delegation went for Ford, as did the convention. Most historians and political scientists of all partisan stripes have credited Mississippi with tipping the balance toward Ford. But apparently not satisfied with his work to simply nominate the moderate Ford, Congressman Cochran even flew with the president on board Air Force One back to Mississippi to parade in front of the cameras and gloat before the general public.

As a reward to conservatives, President Ford slapped the other cheek when he picked moderate Kansas Senator Bob Dole as his running mate. So instead of a strong conservative at the top of the ticket, no matter who his VP might be, the Republicans picked two moderates to lead them in the fall against Jimmy Carter. Even Haley Barbour knew the ticket did not stand much of a chance, though Reagan might have. "Gerald Ford is a safe 47 percent, but he can't win," he said. "Reagan may get forty, but he may get fifty."[3]

Haley Barbour was proved correct as President Ford lost to Carter in a close race with the former Georgia governor winning Mississippi, the last time a Democrat has won the Magnolia State. Of the whole sordid affair, one Reagan supporter in Mississippi said it best, "We would a whole lot rather have Reagan with Schweiker, than to have Jimmy Carter. And most of us perceived Reagan as the only person who could beat Jimmy Carter."[4] But thanks to Thad Cochran, the nation did not get a true choice in the November election. Instead he gave us four years of President James Earl Carter.

During the Carter years, Cochran won his Senate seat and in order to do so he had to defeat a fellow Republican, a state senator from Jones County who, interestingly enough, would later serve as a federal judge after appointment by President George H. W. Bush, one Charles Pickering.

A young Haley Barbour chaired Cochran's US Senate campaign in 1978 and throughout the campaign, though, Cochran portrayed himself as a "man of the people," who would always see to the needs of his fellow citizens. "I wouldn't think . . . that Senate seat belongs to Thad Cochran at any time during my service," he told *The Capitol Reporter*.[5] It was obvious that Thad Cochran felt very much entitled to the Senate seat from Mississippi. Just a year or so before Chris McDaniel entered the 2014 race, a prominent officeholder in Mississippi sat down with Cochran in his office in Washington. After their conversation on government matters, this particular elected official, knowing Cochran was nearing the end of his term and advanced in age, told him that he would be interested in the Senate seat should he retire after the term ended. To that Cochran got up out of his chair and loudly proclaimed, "This is *my* seat!" then stormed out of the room.

Nearly four decades prior to that outburst, Thad Cochran exhibited a much different character. He ran as a conservative who believed in limited government and balanced budgets and touted his six-year record in the House. "I've got a voting record that shows where I stand." Mississippians want "a Senator who has proven he can do what the other candidates are promising they will do."[6]

With Jimmy Carter in the White House and Democrats in control of Congress, the sagging economy and government spending were the big issues in 1978, so Cochran believed he better toe the conservative line if he wanted to serve in the prized upper chamber. "I think we have to consider very seriously a constitutional amendment to force a balanced budget except in times of national emergency," Cochran told the *Jackson Daily News*. "There is no excuse for a $50 billion deficit in peacetime," an amount that was a tidy sum in those days.[7]

At a speech at the Jackson Rotary Club in October 1978, as reported by the *Jackson Daily News*, Cochran stuck to his limited government message. "The primary theme [of the speech] was that the government should assume more responsibility for creating inflation through deficit spending. 'The time has come for the government to realize that it is the culprit,' Cochran said, 'not the working people and taxpayers.' He quoted Ronald Reagan as saying that 'high prices and costs are not the cause of inflation, that is inflation.' He said he supports the Carter Administration proposal for voluntary restraints in wages and prices but added he would like to see the plan tied to specific recommendations for reduced spending." And on at least two occasions in the campaign, Cochran voiced his opposition to excessive regulations: "Congress must move to control excessive regulations on businesses, which . . . are pushing up prices unnecessarily."[8]

Aside from his crafty campaign rhetoric, making him sound more like Ludwig von Mises than the Thad Cochran we have become accustomed to over the years, in 1979, his first year in the Senate, he appeared to follow a conservative script. He announced very early after taking his seat in January 1979 that he would be "co-sponsoring a constitutional amendment to demand a balanced federal budget." And to balance the federal budget, he said, Congress needed to cut back on government spending. "We need to take a careful look at all government programs. A 2 percent across-the-board cut could be digested," he said of a proposal then before Congress.[9]

Understanding that it might be tough with Jimmy Carter in the White House, Cochran warned that it was a "very cautious Congress" but that conservatives would target big spending programs anyway. He promised the people a "strong effort" to limit government spending to get the deficit under control. "I think that right now what Americans want most from their government is less government," he said.[10]

But the reality was very different. Despite his campaign rhetoric, Cochran soon felt right at home with the tax-and-spend liberals that dominated the times. He voted for Carter's Department of Education to pacify the teacher's unions, supported the Food Stamp program, backed a windfall profits tax, and voted against an income tax cut. He voted in favor of Carter's Energy Mobilization Board, a special panel with the power to overrule any local, state, or federal law that hindered the implementation of a prioritized energy project. He also backed the Council on Wage and Price Stability, a board authorized to monitor and combat inflation. This was contrary to the conservative approach of allowing the free market to work. He consistently voted against budget targets, or caps on federal spending, throughout his years of service in the 1970s.

Thankfully, President Reagan arrived in 1981 and ushered in an era of conservatism. Along with his supporters in Congress, Reagan worked tirelessly throughout his eight years in the White House to craft an administration centered on conservative values. He had two main goals: (1) gain control of spending and balance the budget, and (2) build up the nation's lagging defenses to push back the Soviet Union. To do this Reagan had to struggle against a recalcitrant Democratic Congress to rein in federal spending and needed help from every conservative Republican. That would not include Cochran, who did not support any of Reagan's efforts to cut spending and shrink the government. He remained a Big Government Republican, despite what he had told the people of Mississippi during his campaign in 1978.

During Reagan's administration, Cochran was hell on wheels with regard to spending and blocking the conservative fiscal policy agenda. In the fall of 1981, conservatives sought to implement small cuts to three Cabinet departments: a 5 percent cut at the Interior Department, 2.6 percent at Agriculture, and 4 percent for Transportation. Even though the cuts were relatively minor, Senator Cochran opposed all three bills. In 1982 he voted with liberal Democrats to increase the debt ceiling by $1.2 trillion to keep the pork flowing. The next year he voted for a $25 billion bailout for the Department of Housing and Urban Development.[11]

He also voted against a bi-partisan effort to give President Reagan the power to impound funds of up to 20 percent on various federal programs if Congress failed to meet previously agreed upon deficit targets. Cochran also supported the 1983 Social Security bailout bill that included $100 billion in new Social Security taxes. In 1984, as spending and deficits grew worse, he voted against an amendment to cut federal spending across the board by 10 percent.

In 1985, the moderate Bob Dole introduced a bill that would set budget targets, eliminate more than a dozen federal programs, and allow defense spending to be indexed to inflation. Senator Cochran voted to kill it. The next year Cochran supported an increase of over $1 billion for farm programs even though the appropriation would push federal spending over the budget limits set by the Gramm-Rudman-Hollings Deficit Reduction Act, which he had supported the previous year. Later in 1986 he supported a budget resolution that increased spending and created a budget deficit of $144 billion. The eventual deficit that year was over $200 billion, a time when the entire federal budget was less than $1 trillion.

In March 1987, Democrats, in control of both houses of Congress, passed an $88 billion highway bill filled with pork-barrel earmarks. President Reagan immediately vetoed it, angering the big spenders who vowed to override it, a group that included thirteen Republican Senators. To try to keep spending under some semblance of control, Reagan needed to persuade at least a few of those thirteen to stand with him, so he traveled up to Capitol Hill to personally lobby them to sustain his veto. Reagan wrote of the meeting in his diary, and specifically mentioned Senators Thad Cochran and Mitch McConnell. At the meeting in Bob Dole's office, the president said, "I beg you to vote with me on this."[12] But Cochran turned his back on Reagan yet again, joining the liberals in overriding the veto.

Reagan slammed those thirteen senators. "I have no respect left for that thirteen," he wrote. "They were voting on strictly the pressure they were getting from the construction industry and they were voting *against* trying to balance the budget."[13] So much for being a soldier in Reagan's army.

And the spending just kept on coming and Cochran supported it no matter what, including liberal anti-poverty programs. In 1987 he supported a $1 billion spending bill to assist the homeless, a big issue pushed by the media at that time. When Senator Phil Gramm, a major budget hawk, authored an amendment to remove tax increases from a budget bill and cap spending at 1987 levels, Cochran voted to kill it. And when Reagan asked for the line-item veto that year, Cochran was against that budget-cutting measure too.

Democrats still try to argue that it was President Reagan and conservatives who ran up the debt in the 1980s. In reality it was the Democrats, along with the help of liberal Republicans like Thad Cochran.

Despite supporting many spending increases for pet projects, and in typical liberal Democratic fashion, Cochran was never bashful about slashing funding for defense. In 1982 he voted against an amendment that would have frozen domestic spending and increased defense spending by 7.5 percent. That year he also voted to cut $80 million from the Titan missile program, voted against increases in the MX missile system, and opposed spending for the "Midgetman" missiles that President Reagan wanted as part of his defense buildup. And if these actions were not enough of a slap in the face, Cochran couldn't even bring himself to vote for a Jesse Helms amendment to sanction the Soviets after they shot down a Korean civilian airliner in 1983, the incident that caused President Reagan to label the Soviet Union "the face of evil in the modern world."

When George H. W. Bush ran on the message of a "kinder, gentler America," Cochran must have interpreted the slogan as "tax and spend more." He supported the disastrous October 1990 budget compromise that included the largest tax hike in American history up to that time. He also voted that year to increase spending for the Departments of Labor, Health and Human Services, and Education by $11.5 billion more than President Bush sought. In July 1991 he voted against a budget freeze but voted in favor of a congressional pay raise of nearly $24,000 per member. So within the span of just nine months, Cochran greatly hiked the taxes on working Mississippians and allocated himself a fat pay raise. Nice work if you can get it. Later that decade, when conservatives attempted to stop President Clinton's spending spree, Cochran voted against another attempt to freeze federal spending.

During the Bush I years, Cochran was not always supportive of efforts to maintain a strong national defense. He voted against aid to the Contras in Nicaragua in 1989 (even though he supported Central American assistance under Carter in 1980), voted against the operation to remove drug pusher Manuel Noriega from Panama, and opposed sanctioning trade with China after the Tiananmen Square massacre.

Although Cochran supported the withdrawal of support for freedom fighters in our own hemisphere, in a strange vote in 2000, Cochran supported President Clinton in sending American troops to Kosovo, where the US had no vital national security interests. He even refused to stand with conservatives to block the UN Law of the Sea Treaty, which critics charged would have eroded US sovereignty and effectively turned over the world's oceans, including the sea floor, to the United Nations.

Cochran has also supported amnesty for illegal immigrants. Two of his worst votes occurred in 1982, when he voted for an amendment that would allow amnesty for illegal immigrants, and in 2006 by opposing an amendment that would have stripped the amnesty provisions out of an immigration bill, the same W. Bush–backed bill that conservatives were working overtime to kill and eventually did, no thanks to Cochran.

On the all-important conservative issue of gun rights, Cochran voted for his buddy Joe Biden's massive gun control bill, which banned numerous firearms and imposed waiting periods. He supported federal background check law on private gun sales and transfers that overtook existing state law. And in 2004, he voted for a bill that prohibited the sale of all guns that did not have the federally approved safety device.

On the culture front, including the important issue of abortion, Cochran's record is less than stellar. National Right to Life gave him a score of only 75 and called his record on life issues "mixed," a distinction which they do not consider to be a pro-life voting record.[14] Most of the pork-filled appropriations bills Cochran has supported over the years have included funding for Planned Parenthood, the nation's leading abortion provider. Three times in the 1980s, as pro-life conservatives fought for the rights of the unborn, he voted against amendments that would have cut the use of federal funds for abortions in the District of Columbia. In 2007 he supported embryonic stem cell research, a process that destroys human embryos. During Clinton's presidency, he voted for both of his Supreme Court nominees—Ruth Bader Ginsberg and Stephen Breyer—both steadfast supporters of abortion rights.

In 1991 Cochran voted to kill a Jesse Helms amendment that would have denied funding to the National Endowment for the Arts for any programs that promote pornography or any explicit sexual activities. He also failed to support his fellow Mississippi Senator, Trent Lott, in 1992 when he attempted to freeze funds for the Corporation for Public Broadcasting, an outfit that runs the outrageously liberal PBS. In 1980, 1987, and 1991, Cochran voted against efforts to cut funding to the Legal Services Corporation, a congressionally created private, nonprofit organization that provides free legal representation to the poor that has been in the crosshairs of conservatives for decades.

Despite loud boasts during campaign season that he is a conservative, Senator Thad Cochran has been a kind friend to the cause of active and energetic government, the very thing Thomas Jefferson warned us was "always oppressive."[15] Aside from his support for the Energy Mobilization Board and wage and price controls, Cochran also voted for the Americans with Disabilities Act, a law intended to aid those with disabilities but instead has been a burden for business. In the long run, the bill has actually made it more difficult for the disabled to find jobs because the conditions placed upon employers made it more likely that they would not hire someone with a disability. This is a perfect example of a well-intentioned law producing the opposite of its intended effect.

Cochran also voted for the 1991 Civil Rights Bill that conservatives charged would establish minority quotas and set-asides. He supported John McCain's campaign finance efforts in 2001 and 2003, which critics called the "Incumbent Protection Act" because it limited the amount of money citizens could give to federal candidates and also prohibited participation in the political process within sixty days of an election, a clear violation of the First Amendment that the US Supreme Court later struck down as unconstitutional. In a related issue, he voted against an effort to cut the franking privilege, a program of tax dollar financed postage that all members of Congress use (and abuse) come election time. And in 2012 he voted against a constitutional amendment to institute congressional term limits.

Cochran has also been in line with the liberals on many of their environmental crusades in recent years. In 1985 and 1986 he voted billions of dollars into the Superfund, a federal fund to clean up toxic waste sites, which was so bad even Bill Clinton called it a "disaster."[16] In 1990 he voted for the industry-busting Clean Air Act. In 2012 he supported increased funding for the Land and Water Conservation Fund that allows the federal government to acquire more land, as if they don't have enough already.

So, as we dug up and brought to light Thad Cochran's record, it was obvious that he had supported every single liberal Democratic cause—increased domestic spending, enlarged entitlements, cuts in defense, open borders, gun control, opposition to restrictions on abortion, federal control of health care, racial quotas, environmentalism, restrictions on liberty and free speech, and pay raises for himself while raising taxes on the people. My first thought was, with a record this atrocious, how would he get any votes at all against Chris McDaniel? But more than that, how has this man been elected in Mississippi for six terms?

The people had to know the truth: Thad Cochran's legacy reflects a career politician who believes the Senate seat he holds actually belongs to him and not the people of Mississippi, despite what he said in his first campaign in 1978. He is not nor has he ever been a principled, limited government conservative, but a Democratic wolf in conservative Republican sheepskin. We believed very strongly that if we could just get this information into the hands of the voting public—the Republican voting public—Cochran would be in serious trouble, particularly when contrasted with the stellar record of Chris McDaniel.

When we began pointing these things out, showing the people that Cochran did not reflect the views of a majority of Republicans in the state, and once many Mississippians began to conclude that it was long past time for change, we believed his bid for an unprecedented seventh term would look bleak, to say the least. But the Cochran camp had a huge trick up their sleeve, a multi-million dollar strategy they hoped would send us reeling back to Jones County. And that secret weapon was the moneyed, unscrupulous political machine of Haley Barbour.

CHAPTER 3

THE SAGA OF UNCLE HALEY: THE BARBOUR MACHINE AND THE NATION'S MOST CORRUPT STATE

Within an hour of his announcement on October 17, State Senator Chris McDaniel boarded his campaign bus in Ellisville and headed north for his first big event, a stop in Oxford, deep in the heart of Cochran country, to work the Ole Miss-LSU football game.

The race against Thad Cochran was going to be an uphill battle for sure, but everyone backing Chris felt deeply that it was a cause worth fighting for, even though the political mountain did resemble Everest at times. Cochran had name recognition, sky-high poll numbers, a vast campaign war chest, a major network of donors, an enormous stack of unredeemed political IOUs, and, perhaps most importantly, his not-so-secret weapon: unyielding support from Haley Barbour's immense political machine.

In the world of Mississippi politics there was but one machine, and that's all there ever has been. In the old days longtime senator and powerhouse James O. Eastland, who knew as much about raw political power and how to use it as any man in the history of democratic government, led this perpetual organization. Stories of Eastland's power wielding abound in the state, as he led a political network reminiscent of the old Gilded Age machines, complete with patronage, get-out-of-jail-free cards, and full support for candidates who could keep the ball rolling in the right direction.

After Eastland's retirement in 1978, when Cochran succeeded him in the Senate, the machine fell to Trent Lott, being the more conservative member of Congress. Now the political network, and very lucrative lobbying operation, is headed up by former governor and RNC chair Haley Barbour.[1]

Over the years Haley Barbour had become so powerful, and so resented, that many Mississippians began privately referring to him as "Boss Hogg," both for his expanded midriff and his propensity to make racist remarks. His chief objective, along with nephews Henry and Austin, was to maintain control of the state and wipe out any and all opposition. In short, Haley Barbour dominates and controls the entire state. *The New Republic* dubbed him the "K Street evil genius who took over Mississippi."[2]

Haley Barbour's vast personal fortune came from lobbying, the act of influencing public officials on behalf of special interests. It's simply legalized corruption. As Ronald Reagan once remarked, "It has been said that politics is the second oldest profession. I have learned that it bears a close resemblance to the first." And that's not too far from the truth about lobbyists and their trade.

Barbour's lobbying career began decades ago, long before his years of public "service" as governor of Mississippi and chairman of the Republican National Committee, a high-profile stint he held from 1993 to 1997 and probably his most well known position. Prior to that, he'd served as a political director in the Reagan White House. But he'd always been involved in politics. Even as a young law student in 1973 he was selected as the executive director of the state Republican Party, at that time still in relative infancy in Mississippi. As a lawyer in Yazoo City, he chaired Thad Cochran's first Senate campaign in 1978 and made his own unsuccessful attempt to join him when he ran against the state's most powerful senator, Democrat John C. Stennis, in 1982.[3]

In 1991 Barbour's lobbying career took off when he co-founded with two former members of the first Bush administration, Lanny Griffith and Ed Rogers, the BGR Group, a firm that was named by *Fortune* magazine in 1998 as the second most powerful lobbying group in the country. With offices just a stone's throw from Capitol Hill, the BGR Group has easy access to the levers of power, lobbying on behalf of the defense industry, pharmaceuticals, alcohol interests, Big Oil, and Big Tobacco, to name but a few.[4]

In 2003 Barbour decided to try again for an elective office, throwing his hat in the ring for Mississippi governor. Nephew Henry Barbour managed his campaign, and it was conducted, in the words of *The New Republic*,

> exactly the way you'd expect a lobbyist to: by parading a contingent of suits through Mississippi to vouch for his bona fides. George W. Bush showed up, as did Dick Cheney, Elizabeth Dole, and cabinet secretaries Donald Evans and Rod Paige. Then-RNC chairman Ed Gillespie, another longtime lobbyist, gushed to *The New York Times Magazine* that the national GOP would "do everything that we're legally allowed to do" to elect Barbour. When it was all over and Barbour had won, even his celebration betrayed his K Street provenance. "One of the interesting things about his inaugural was how sparse the crowd was," notes former Mississippi governor Ray Mabus. "He just didn't know many Mississippians."[5]

With little competition in the GOP primary, Barbour easily gained the nomination and defeated the unpopular incumbent, Ronnie Musgrove, in the general election with a little more than 52 percent of the vote. Haley raised more money for that race than any other candidate had ever raised in Mississippi, and he spent more than any other candidate had ever spent. The real story was the fact that he barely defeated Musgrove, even with such a massive war chest. But, more importantly, the vast money binge sent a strong message to all the ambitious in Mississippi—the road to political success was aboard the Haley Barbour Express. So whatever Haley said began to rule the day.

Barbour took office in January 2004 and had to leave the lobbying behind for a time, or so he said. He told the press that he had "no ownership or stock in the [BGR Group]," and announced that he was putting all his wealth into a blind trust while he was serving the people. He told the *Clarion Ledger*, "I can't have anything that's a conflict of interest." After being in office just six weeks, however, "Barbour still had a stake worth $786,666 in the publicly traded parent company of Barbour Griffith & Rogers Inc., as well as pension and profit-sharing plan benefits from the lobby firm," Timothy J. Burger of *Bloomberg* reported. While serving as governor, "Barbour receives $25,000 per month, or $300,000 a year, from it. He lists the trust in his annual Mississippi ethics filing as his only source of income outside his $122,160 salary as governor." And when questions emerged, Barbour refused to discuss his personal finances, even though he was in public service, so who really knows what went on behind the scenes.[6]

But just because Barbour was not involved with the BGR Group while in the governorship, that doesn't mean the lobbying came to a screeching halt. As reported in *The New Republic*:

> In many ways, Barbour has replicated Tom DeLay's K Street Project in Jackson. After his election in 2003, Henry and Austin Barbour joined Capitol Resources, a lobbying firm just steps from the governor's mansion--much like Barbour Griffith & Rogers overlooks Capitol Hill. The firm shares a number of BG&R's clients, including Northrop Grumman and Lorillard Tobacco Company. Most lobbying shops in Jackson are small, single-person firms, which, while business friendly, have rarely dominated the legislature the way that Capitol Resources has, with its 15-strong battalion. "They made a habit of going after other lobbyists' clients, saying, 'If you want anything done in the Mississippi legislature, you better hire us,'" says one Democratic legislator.
>
> One of the advantages Henry and Austin had in this competition was their unusually close access to the governor. Austin, for example, has spent a considerable portion of his expense account on his uncle's employees, according to filings with the Mississippi secretary of state. One night in 2006, he plunked down over $800 at a restaurant called Tico's for a meal with twelve members of the governor's staff. "That is highly unusual," says Mabus, the former governor. "I don't think my staff ever went out with a lobbyist."[7]

Strong-arming potential clients with shakedown tactics, influence peddling, raking in huge sums of cash from whoever will provide it for whatever cause they seek is the Barbour Way.

When we think of lobbying today, we tend to think of it in terms of Washington, but it's just as bad in our state capitals and in some respects may be worse, not because of the amount of money that's brought to bear but the ease of influence. The lobbying class in Washington and Jackson are very much associated with one another. People may think there are these two distinct lobbying organizations: one in Washington and the other in our state capitols. But in reality it's "all part of the same big mass of lobbying power," Chris told me. The elite that can afford lobbyists reside in positions of power, whether that's in Jackson or Washington. They need laws to suit them, and special treatment from time to time.

Governor Barbour's personal lobbying might have subsided while he was in office, at least officially, but his mind was still on his clients, as were his actions. During his first term, the legislature proposed cutting the sales tax on groceries in half then making up the revenue by adding a dollar tax on a pack of cigarettes. It seemed a very reasonable proposal designed to help the poor and the elderly with their grocery bills, particularly since the state had one of the lowest tax rates on tobacco products. But the tobacco-lobbying governor, whose firm had received $3.8 million in fees from four big tobacco companies from 1998 to 2002 and another $2 million after Barbour became governor, would have none of it, vetoing the proposal when it hit his desk.[8]

"To this day," wrote *The New Republic*, "few in the GOP have dared to cross Barbour on the matter." One cowardly member of the legislature admitted that he was afraid Barbour would "dump more money into my opponent's campaign." The governor utilized the flow of money to purchase the loyalty of politicians who then abandoned the party platform in favor of their loyalty to the Barbour machine out of fear of losing their positions. The same timid legislature allowed the "Governor of Big Tobacco" to kill Mississippi's anti-smoking program, which was once billed as "the nation's most successful."[9] It is a rare thing for the state of Mississippi to be ranked first in a worthwhile endeavor, but since it conflicted with Barbour's lobbying clients, it had to go.

Bradford Plumer and Noam Scheiber wrote about Barbour's ties to the tobacco industry:

> In August 1997, as Congress was putting the finishing touches on a balanced-budget agreement with the Clinton White House, two sharp-eyed freshman senators spotted something odd. Someone had convinced Newt Gingrich and Trent Lott to slip a $50 billion tax credit for tobacco companies into the bill at the last minute. For a month, the mystery raged across Washington: Who could have engineered such an audacious giveaway? Finally, *Time* discovered the culprit: Haley Barbour, the former RNC chair cum millionaire tobacco lobbyist.[10]

In addition to keeping the skids greased for Big Tobacco, Barbour also used the power and influence of his office to get things done for other clients. While in the governor's chair, he worked hard for the construction of a new experimental coal power plant in Kemper County, a facility that is supposed to turn Mississippi's abundance of lignite coal into a type of natural gas called synthesis gas to power electricity-generating turbines. It's a process not everyone agreed could work, but that never matters when it's someone else's money.[11]

Mississippi Power, a subsidiary of the Southern Company, would construct the plant and operate it. Southern Company had been a client of Barbour's for four years before his election as governor in 2003. But once Barbour took office, his son, Haley Jr., served as a lobbyist for Southern Company and "pushed" the governor to approve the project, which began in June 2010. And it's been nothing short of disastrous for Mississippi. No matter, for once he was out of office, Barbour went right back on the Southern Company's payroll. In an op-ed in the fall of 2013, Barbour blamed the problems with the plant on the Sierra Club, but like so much of the Barbours dealings, he didn't bother to mention his ties to Southern Company. In the summer of 2017, the $7.5 billion plant was shut down because it did not work.[12]

The goals of the Barbours are simple: support big-spending Republicans so they can make loads of dough. To Chris McDaniel, this smacks of hypocrisy. "I'll give Haley all the credit in the world," he said, "because he's a capitalist and he's a good lobbyist but at the end of the day it's not about principle to him. He ran the RNC, which is beholden to a platform, and the Republican Party works every year for a platform, where they are supposed to uphold the provisions of that platform. But if the party simply exists to perpetuate their own power, not a core set of principles, then it seems to me that we are all just wasting our time at this point."

And if compromise with liberals is necessary to keep Big Government Republicans in office, they are quick to do it. Anything to stay in power. Case in point: Nephew Henry Barbour, a member of the Republican National Committee, helped craft a GOP-administered report, the *Growth and Opportunity Project*, that identified the problems with the presidential loss in 2012 and recommended changes to policy proposals. The report stated, "The perception, revealed in polling, that the GOP does not care about people is doing great harm to the Party and its candidates on the federal level, especially in presidential years. It is a major deficiency that must be addressed."[13]

To satisfy the deficiency, the report recommended moving the party to the center. Henry even went so far as to advocate liberal agenda items like raising the minimum wage. "As Republicans, in my opinion, we shouldn't just stiff arm that because there are legitimate needs of working people. You've got single moms who are trying to pay for two kids and make the rent and pay for groceries and medical bills. If she's working for $8.00 an hour and she's got two different jobs, we've got to be very sensitized to the worker in America and their needs."[14] Henry and the RNC, though, failed to address issues like global free trade and amnesty for illegal immigrants, which the Barbours consistently propagate, both of which hurt American workers and do far more to depress wages than any other policy, two issues Trump used to win the White House in 2016.

Back in the Clinton years when he was RNC chair, Barbour seemed to seek what all conservatives seek, the destruction of liberalism and the supremacy of conservatism, once saying, "Compromising with the Democrats is like paying the cannibals to eat you last."[15] But no more. Now there's money to be made. This is why they say they are only interested in Republicans that can win, meaning Republicans that will maintain the status quo. They detest conservatives like Chris McDaniel because he wants to reform the system, which will most assuredly hurt their livelihood. The word *reform* is akin to political blasphemy.

The Barbours, and those like them, are nothing more than influence peddlers, and they can easily ply their trade in the vast sewer of corruption that is Mississippi. Politics and corruption, at least on some level, has always existed, but Mississippi has never been known as a land of blatant dishonesty. The first thoughts that usually come to mind in regards to the political history of the Magnolia State are racism and white supremacy, not thievery and influence peddling. Not so now. Although once *the* main bastion of Jim Crow, supported by unadulterated violence to uphold it, Mississippi has exchanged its political past for a future based on monetary perversion. Several studies in recent years have determined that Mississippi is the "most corrupt state in the nation."[16] If you think about it through the prism of history, it's quite a transformative accomplishment, though not one Mississippians should brag about.

In just the last few years the state has seen major scandals in the state's prison system, ensnaring the commissioner, Chris Epps;[17] and the Department of Marine Resources (DMR), that also entangled the director. In the Department of Corrections scandal investigators believe the corruption might be as high as $800 million and perhaps more.[18] At the DMR, the executive director, Bill Walker, his son, and five others employees were convicted of defrauding the government to the tune of $1.2 million.[19] Making matters worse, the state auditor, Stacey Pickering, cousin to a former congressman and nephew to a former federal judge, was held in civil contempt of court for illegally withholding documents related to the case from the prying eyes of the media.[20] He has since been guilty of ethics violations and is presently under an FBI investigation. After all this mess, at the end of 2015, the Center for Public Integrity gave Mississippi a grade of D- for the state's campaign to deter corruption.[21]

When and how all this began in Mississippi is anyone's guess but most contend it began during the 1990s when Christian conservative Mississippi turned in a new direction, one that our leaders promised would keep us awash in vast new sources of tax money and solve many problems—the new grand panacea of dockside gambling. But, as we soon found out, immense amounts of new money, especially in the wrong hands, always begets corruption.

In 1990, the state legislature passed a law allowing the establishment of casinos along the Mississippi River and on the Gulf Coast. The powerful and influential Baptist groups worked hard to try to keep the gambling boats out but ultimately failed with the allure of the potential payoff for the state. The money will go to our schools and the kids, we were told, which was pretty much the same excuse used when they sought the legalization of alcohol years before. And when the casinos opened for business, the money rolled in throughout the 1990s and 2000s, providing well more than $100 million per year, not counting the vast local government take. But as more casinos were built, more problems soon mounted. Aside from crime and other moral tribulations, more public employees were convicted of corruption, four per every ten thousand employees, according to the Pew Research Center, a number that leads the nation.[22]

When gambling cash proved not enough, the state sought a new target: Big Tobacco. The eventual tobacco settlement would provide a nice financial windfall, but it soon became a debacle in a unique combination of corruption and stupidity. Mississippi led the attack on the major cigarette producers for causing health problems that taxpayers had to pay for. Although individuals had tried for years to successfully sue Big Tobacco, all to no avail, one Mississippi attorney named Michael Lewis came up with the idea that the state should go after these corporate behemoths in order to recoup Medicaid and other health related expenses that the state had paid out for smoking related problems. Of course, this was well before Tobacco Governor Haley Barbour gained complete control over the state.[23]

Lewis knew just who to contact to get the tobacco ball rolling, Mississippi's attorney general Mike Moore. Moore thought the idea great and readily agreed to this new legal strategy. The AG then sought assistance from another Ole Miss chum, Richard "Dickie" Scruggs, the brother-in-law of Senator Trent Lott. Scruggs had experience with such cases, having already made a large fortune suing companies over asbestos-related health problems. And he would continue his "good work" with Moore on behalf of the state. In 1988, Moore's first year in office, he named Scruggs a "special assistant attorney general" and sent him after these "evil" companies. For his work, Scruggs' firm kept twenty-five percent of any monies the state recovered, and those funds went well into the tens of millions.[24]

Although it seems like such an operation should be illegal, at the time it was never determined to be so. Again, because of more cronyism and corruption. When Scruggs began his quest to take down Big Tobacco, state auditor Steven Patterson, elected in 1991, began peering into the strange relationship, not so much to root out corruption, which is kinda his job, but to knock out a potential rival for the governorship, for which Patterson was seeking. In this case, AG Mike Moore seemed to be his chief obstacle. Patterson was convinced this partnership of government and private attorneys could not be legal, especially given the fact that the legislature had never approved it. If Patterson did strike a lethal blow at the tobacco effort, Scruggs' crusade would be over before it started.[25]

Enter Senator Trent Lott, who contacted a major player inside Eastland's old operation, Presley L. Blake. Blake was a big-time farmer in the Delta who had played football at Mississippi State in the 1950s, then three seasons in the Canadian Football League. He was still very much "in the know" and could still "fix" things that needed fixing. In fact, Blake was still very much part of Lott's own political machine. He met with both Patterson and Scruggs at his home in Greenwood, convincing Patterson in no time to stop his inquiry. What was decided, or promised, is not known but the state auditor agreed with Blake's assessment, eventually writing a letter to the district attorney in Jackson that he had found "no evidence of criminal conduct." The fight against Big Tobacco was back on.[26]

But to make sure they covered their backside, the endeavor would need some legal authorization from the state legislature. State Senator Roger Wicker, an Ole Miss alum from Tupelo, added a 73-

word amendment to a Medicaid appropriations bill that gave the Mississippi state government the authority to "employ legal counsel on a contingency basis." Soon, when it became apparent that Mississippi was about to hit the jackpot, 46 states joined the tobacco lawsuit.[27]

Scruggs soon went to battle, likening the lawsuit to a crusade, complete with wartime rhetoric—it was a "war" against the "devil" and the "merchants of death" said Scruggs—in the end the states agreed to a settlement with the tobacco companies, a case of the lawyers and Big Tobacco "simply cutting a deal," in the words of Timothy P. Carney. Mississippi's share was more than $4.4 billion, payable in annual installments over twenty-five years.[28]

For his part, the warrior Scruggs made off with what he said was approximately $300 million in fees but what others claim might be closer to $1 billion. One of the most powerful trial attorneys in the nation, he was prominently portrayed in a Hollywood film on Big Tobacco, which featured the Mississippi tobacco suit, *The Insider* with Al Pacino and Russell Crowe. But soon Scruggs went too far and met an ignoble end. After trying to bribe state judge Henry Lackey in a case involving Hurricane Katrina litigation, he found himself, along with his son, indicted, convicted, imprisoned, and disbarred. Enough is never enough for some people.

And Steve Patterson, the crusading state auditor who initially wanted to go after both Moore and Scruggs, eventually had to resign his office soon after beginning a second term for filing a false affidavit to keep from paying state car taxes. He later found himself in worse trouble when he was caught in the same snare as his new pal Scruggs. Patterson eventually pleaded guilty to a charge of conspiracy for the attempted bribery of Judge Lackey, for which he received twenty-four months in prison.

The tobacco money was supposed to go a trust fund to reimburse Medicaid and help with the state's healthcare costs, which would only rise over time. But various reports indicate that a very small percentage of the funds have actually been used for its intended purposes by many of the states that ended up involved in suing the tobacco companies. Within two years, Mississippi's legislature began diverting funds to other areas, which should have surprised no one.[29]

Under Governor Kirk Fordice, a Vicksburg businessman and the first Republican governor in Mississippi since Reconstruction, the brakes were applied quite forcefully against the spending schemes coming out of the legislature as the new funds came rolling in. But in 1999, with the fiscally tightfisted Fordice term-limited out of office after eight years, Democrats managed to re-capture the governor's mansion in a once-in-a-lifetime election by the legislature. Under the state constitution, if no candidate receives a majority, the election is thrown into the House. The presence of a fringe, third-party candidate did just that, and in the only instance in state history, the Democratically controlled House of Representatives chose Democratic lieutenant governor Ronnie Musgrove over Republican congressman Mike Parker, even though Parker had won more counties.

In Musgrove's one term in office, the fiscal damage was done. The freewheeling Democrats, perhaps seeing it as their last hurrah, engaged in spending that was a disservice to drunken sailors. In Governor Fordice's two terms, the state had a balanced budget, a surplus of revenue flowing into state coffers, and had built the second largest "rainy day" fund in the country, around $700 million. Times were definitely looking good for the state of Mississippi. But by 2004, at the end of Musgrove's term, the rainy day fund was dry, the surplus was gone, and the state was $700 million in the red. And the tobacco trust fund, which should have contained approximately $2.5 billion, was virtually empty.[30]

With such overflowing new tax revenue, the state should have been singing "Happy Days Are Here Again," but that has not been the case, at least not for everyone. The tobacco lawyers and advocates of the casinos sang a happy tune, as did the lobbyists and other well-connected big wigs, but the state as a whole did not gain very much. In fact, most of the problems have only gotten worse. But we do have wealthier lawyers and politicians, and an abundance of them too. Where all the money really went, what good it has done, or into whose pockets it wound up, is anyone's guess. It's a question that has been asked around the state for many years.

Sadly, these few examples constitute just the tip of the tip of the iceberg. Unbeknownst to most Americans, today Mississippi is the center of an intricately connected web of money and power, a deadly combination that drives the corruption and influence peddling racket. The bulk of the members of this vast network reside in Jackson and points north. As we saw with the tobacco cabal, most of them attended Ole Miss for both undergraduate work or law school, if not both. All know each other and have worked for one another at various times. The state's top offices, both US Senate seats, and three of the four US House seats are all tied together in this web of corruption, all while the machine works to keep the trains on the track and running on time.

The connections are deep and vast. Mississippi's other, lesser-known US Senator is Roger Wicker, the same Roger Wicker that secured authorization for Scruggs' tobacco war. He's from North Mississippi, attended Ole Miss, represented the district around Tupelo in the State Senate, and has been involved in state politics since he was a teenager. After law school at Ole Miss and four years active duty in the Air Force, Wicker worked in Washington for longtime Mississippi congressman Jamie Whitten and for then-congressman Trent Lott before winning his seat in the Mississippi State Senate in 1988. In 1994, when Whitten announced his retirement from the US House, Wicker ran for his old boss's seat and won. His State Senate seat went to Alan Nunnelee.

After nearly fourteen years in the US House, Barbour appointed Wicker to succeed Lott in the US Senate in 2008, after Lott's hasty retirement. Since before the Civil War it was always tradition that one US Senator would be from North Mississippi and the other from the southern half of the state, but Barbour's move placed both US Senate seats in the hands of North Mississippians, the center of the machine's vast network. In 2010, Nunnelee won Wicker's old seat in Congress. And who knows what path Nunnelee's career would have taken had he not tragically passed away in 2015 after a long fight with brain cancer.

Wicker is an Establishment man who backed Cochran and is very well entrenched within the web as "one of those who made up the new generation's core of the old Eastland network," writes Curtis Wilkie.[31] Beginning his climb up the political ladder over forty years ago, he's had his fingers in the Establishment pie as far back as 1973. While at Ole Miss, Wicker supported Karl Rove for national chairman of the

College Republicans, as did "his buddy Lanny Griffith,"[32] the same Lanny Griffith who is partnered with Barbour in the BGR Group.

Wicker's daughter, Caroline Wicker Sims, works as a "senior government relations advisor" at the Jackson office of the powerful Butler Snow law firm, a cushy, high-paying job that can have but one responsibility: when something is needed she calls Senator Daddy in Washington. Butler Snow is the same firm used by Thad Cochran, which played a pivotal role near the end of the McDaniel-Cochran race, and where Haley Barbour is also currently employed, at least in the use of his name. Caroline Wicker Sims is married to Kirk Sims, who served as Governor Phil Bryant's Chief of Staff before resigning in 2013 to manage Cochran's campaign against McDaniel.[33]

The Butler Snow law firm, a mainstay within the state, touches every part of state government. Filled with bureaucratic hacks, it's the firm used by the Establishment elites, as well as the state government. It is perhaps the most important cog in the machine's wheel. McDaniel advisor Keith Plunkett calls it "Mississippi's shadow government, from the municipalities and county government, all the way to the state government. They crack the whip and the politicians run like scared dogs. Butler Snow is the biggest source of the corruption in Mississippi."[34]

The connections there are nothing short of extraordinary. Butler Snow employees include: Paul Hurst, former chief of staff for Haley Barbour; Tray Hairston, a former policy advisor to Governor Phil Bryant; Rebekah Staples, who, even while working for Butler Snow, was also a policy advisor to Barbour and Lt. Governor Tate Reeves; Amanda Tollison, married to State Senator Gray Tollison of Oxford, who also advised Barbour; and Heather Ladner, a former legal counsel to Barbour.[35]

Other employees of Butler Snow have been appointed to various state boards and commissions: Tommie Cardin, appointed to the Charter Schools board by Lt. Governor Reeves; Mark Garriga and John Harral, both donors to Phil Bryant in his successful run for governor in 2011, were both appointed to the Judicial Appointments Advisory Board by Bryant once he took office; Ryan Beckett, appointed to the chairmanship of the Tort Claims Board by Governor Bryant; and Wilson

Montjoy, appointed to Bryant's transition team on energy policy. And for good measure, Barry Cannada, also a Bryant donor, serves on the board of directors of the Mississippi Energy Institute, who, according to one well-connected Mississippi blogger, is working to bring nuclear waste to the state with the full support of both Barbour and Bryant.[36]

Today Butler Snow is in the process of transitioning out of a law practice to more of a professional lobbying enterprise, which is evident with some of their employees and the work they do. For instance, Butler Snow hired lobbyist Sidney Allen, Jr., who previously worked in the same capacity for Comcast and was also a Phil Bryant donor, to lobby the state legislature on Butler Snow's behalf.[37]

But where there's lobbying, Haley Barbour is close by. "Haley Barbour recently opened a brand-new business development firm billed as a wholly owned subsidiary of Butler Snow, which will be using federal dollars to seed these companies," Chris told me. The name of the new firm is VisionFirst Advisors, with offices in Tallahassee and Orlando, Florida. "And of course there's a finder's fee, because anytime federal dollars come through Butler Snow or Haley's business, he evidently finds a way to keep a fraction of it through high hourly rates or otherwise."[38] Yet despite this flurry of economic development money, Mississippi remains dead last economically. If you follow the money trails of just about everybody in some position of authority in Mississippi, they all lead to Butler Snow, which represents a lot of supervisor boards in the counties and the campaign met a lot of resistance from these boards because Butler Snow had told them to back away from Chris McDaniel.

Like Haley Barbour, Butler Snow does not want true limited government but a government to work for their interests and their people, which includes Congressman Gregg Harper, who is from Jackson and attended Ole Miss Law. Congressman Harper is good friends with Governor Phil Bryant and will most likely get the nod to replace Cochran when the time comes. Harper proved his worth on the campaign trail by going all out for Ole Thad, essentially serving as a surrogate candidate on many occasions.

Preceding Harper in the Third District House seat was Charles "Chip" Pickering, Jr., another Ole Miss alum, cousin of State Auditor

Stacey Pickering, and the son of former Federal District and Appellate Court Judge Charles Pickering, who served in the same State Senate seat now held by McDaniel and who ran for the GOP Senate nomination against Thad Cochran in 1978. Charles, Jr. was seen as a young, rising star in Mississippi politics that everyone knew was destined for the US Senate, having also served, like Wicker, as a Washington aide to Trent Lott. He won his first race for the US House in 1996 to succeed the retiring Sonny Montgomery, with his campaign under the management of none other than Haley's nephew Henry Barbour. And if not for a personal scandal, Pickering quite likely would have been the pick to succeed Lott in 2008, rather than Roger Wicker. And the story behind his downfall is quite amusing.

In August 2007, in his sixth term in the House, Pickering abruptly announced he was uninterested in a Senate seat, as rumors of Lott's departure mounted, and would retire from Congress instead of moving up the ladder. The following July he filed for divorce from his wife Leisha. Then the sordid details emerged. It seems Pickering was spending an inordinate amount of time at 133 C Street SE in DC, a house registered as a "religious and commercial building" and affiliated with Christian groups such as the "Fellowship Foundation," which sponsors the National Prayer Breakfast attended annually by the President of the United States. But spending time at such a place might not seem so bad, given Pickering's Christian faith and advocacy of those causes, but it's what he was doing at this religious center that caught everyone's eye, as well as who he was doing it with.[39]

Pickering, who ran for Congress touting his moral "values," including two years of work as a missionary in Eastern Europe, was spending more than a little quality time at the C Street house with a lady named Elizabeth Creekmore Byrd, who also takes pride in her missionary work in Eastern Europe, as well as Christian studies at the University of Texas and at Vanderbilt, along with other various philanthropic endeavors. The time they spent together was, in fact, so close that Chip's wife, Leisha Pickering, sued Byrd for alienation of affection, a relationship she alleged ruined the Pickering marriage and destroyed Pickering's promising political career, although it seems Ole Chip was doing pretty well with that on his own.[40]

But with the Pickering-Byrd affair there was more than just love in the air. Just after leaving Congress, Pickering was hired as a high-priced telecommunications lobbyist on Capitol Hill for Cellular South, a Mississippi company founded by the parents of none other than Elizabeth Creekmore Byrd.[41]

And what about Pickering and Wicker's old boss Trent Lott? Also an Ole Miss grad, he's very much in the network because he was Senator Eastland's successor as head of the machine. And although Lott and Cochran were rival Senators from the same state, known to have a spat or two about appointments and other dealings inside Mississippi, as well as Lott's control over Eastland's old network, it now all seems like one big happy family, as Lott, like his cronies, jumped in to support his old Senate colleague, even going so far as to trash the Tea Party and conservatives in general. As Haley Barbour said himself during the campaign, "Thad Cochran, Trent Lott and I have been allies, working together for Mississippi for 40 years."[42] But, truth be known, they were working for themselves.

After his rather abrupt departure from the Senate at the very end of 2007, just before new lobbying restrictions went into effect on January 1, 2008, as well as rumors that he was tangled up in the Scruggs tobacco scandal, Lott began his own lucrative career in Barbour's footsteps as a lobbyist. Most of Lott's clients are big defense contractors like Lockheed Martin and Huntington Ingalls Shipbuilding, a company that just so happens to have a large shipyard on the Mississippi Gulf Coast in Lott's hometown of Pascagoula. And he had every reason to want Cochran to remain in the Senate. "Over the years, we had to fight for funds and contracts," Lott said in a television ad for Cochran. "Senator Cochran has the power and the experience to protect the Gulf Coast. Without Thad Cochran, we could lose some of these important facilities."[43] Or, more precisely, Cochran is needed to protect Lott's new lobbying career.

And the web's lust for power and money knows no bounds, even if it means lobbying on behalf of foreign businesses, banks, and even governments, and against American interests. Thomas Jefferson once said that businessmen, what he termed "merchants," "have no country. The mere spot they stand on does not constitute so strong an attachment as that from which they draw their gains."[44] This could easily apply to lobbyists. Haley Barbour has no loyalty to the country, only to his own pocketbook. He cares not where he makes his gains, so long as he makes them. He is no stranger to international lobbying, nor does he seem to have any moral qualms about it. He has ties to many tyrannical regimes such as Gambia, Qatar, Lebanon, and Iraq, while he and Trent Lott are even connected to our old Cold War foe.[45]

A resurgent Russia, led by Vladimir Putin, has been on the move in their old stomping grounds in Eastern Europe and the Crimea. In response, the US has countered with sanctions against Russian companies. Those companies—whether actually Russian or Americans doing business in Russia—need lobbyists, and for assistance they turned to US lobbying firms, and two Mississippians in particular: Trent Lott and Haley Barbour.

Lott's firm got involved with a Russian bank that was hit by US sanctions, the OAO Gazprombank, which is controlled by Putin's Kremlin. The firm made more than $450,000, with Lott making off with $300,000. Chevron hired the BGR Group, led by Haley Barbour, to help their cause in Russia. As reported by Bloomberg:

> A Chevron project in Kazakhstan sends oil through Russia via a pipeline in which Kremlin-controlled OAO Transneft is a major player. Chevron and its lobbyists were able to convince U.S. officials to spare Transneft, which is subject to financial penalties, from more onerous restrictions that would have prevented U.S. companies from doing business with it, according to three people familiar with the matter who asked not to be identified.[46]

For Lott and Barbour, money is far more important than American national security interests.

Barbour also had his own dealings with a Russian bank, one that was tied to Iran's nuclear program. Even though Haley once called Iran the world's greatest threat to peace and stability, his BGR Group lobbies for the Russian Alfa Bank, which provided much of the financing for Iran's first nuclear reactor. What his exact connections are to the bank or to Iran's program is not known, but we can gain some understanding from the actions of Thad Cochran. In March 2015 when forty-seven Republican Senators sent a letter of warning to the Iranian government, Cochran was one of the few who did not sign it. Instead he urged a more cautious approach, a position more in line with President Obama. This happened, mind you, after Barbour's all-out effort to save Cochran's seat in the US Senate. So was Thad Cochran really Mississippi's senior Senator, or was it Haley Barbour?[47]

One of Barbour's main foreign cash cows is Mexico. Whether we want to admit it or not, the Mexican government favors sending floods of illegal immigrants into the United States each year. Many of these foreign workers never intend to assimilate into the US but work, make money, and send a lot of it to relatives back home. In fact, Mexico receives billions of dollars every year in this very lucrative, yet unofficial, "foreign aid program." They also want their citizens to be able to work and travel in the US without harassment, and even gain a path to citizenship, essentially giving them the rights of dual citizenship. To help push that objective, the Mexican government enlisted the support of the BGR Group.

From August 2001 to December 2002, the Mexican government paid Barbour's firm more than $400,000, some $35,000 a month plus expenses, to assist with the specific issues of "immigration/human capital" and "treatment of Mexican citizens who cross the border." When asked about such a thorny issue, as he prepared for a possible presidential run in 2012, Governor Barbour lied about his involvement, blaming it on Lanny Griffith. Yet the *Los Angeles Times* uncovered documents that proved Uncle Haley was equally tasked to assist in the endeavor and willingly did so. And the main issue the BGR Group worked on was to lobby for a bill creating a path to citizenship for the nation's illegal immigrants, essentially the advocacy of amnesty.[48]

With such vast amounts of money, principles no longer mattered it seemed. The cash had such an allure, far more than any political advancement, because it killed Haley's chances for higher ambition. As far back as 2005, in only his second year as governor, Uncle Haley had thoughts of making a run of his own for president, perhaps as early as the upcoming 2008 cycle, although Hurricane Katrina did put a rather large kink in that plan. But 2012, coming after he left the restrictions of the governor's mansion, would be wide open. And make no mistake about it, Haley Barbour would have been a formidable candidate for president, if only for his prodigious ability to raise vast sums of campaign cash, amounts that could make anyone, even "a fat white Southerner" competitive in the race for the White House.

Though there were other issues that arose, such as his heavy drinking and colorful past remarks about race relations in Mississippi, it was his foreign lobbying as much as anything that killed any plans Barbour had to run for president in 2012 or at any other time in the future. High-level operatives advised him that he would never be able to overcome such a strong liability. Lobbying for domestic interests is bad enough; lobbying on behalf of foreign governments would be inexcusable in the eyes of most Americans and his opponents would most certainly exploit it. Thankfully, Boss Hogg will never reside at 1600 Pennsylvania Avenue.

CHAPTER 4

THE STRANGLEHOLD: HOW THE ESTABLISHMENT KEEPS THE GRAVY TRAIN RUNNING

We've seen how Haley Barbour has a stranglehold on politics in Mississippi. But in the words of Matt Kibbe, then the head of Freedomworks "The Barbours don't represent Mississippians, they represent their lobbying client lists." Never a truer word spoken. In 2014, according to data from the Center for Responsive Politics, the BGR Group raked in over $15 million in fees from its expansive list of corporate clients.[1]

So where does Thad Cochran fit in all this? Aside from being a North Mississippian and an Ole Miss alum, he's Establishment to the core, and perhaps the most important individual in the machine. As chairman or ranking member of the Senate Appropriations Committee, he controls the money and steers it to his favored friends, not to help the state but to enrich his cronies. And he does this in a variety of ways, but mainly through his "bring home the bacon" programs.

With such a vast moneymaking network in place, everyone in the state knew the Barbours would be all in for Cochran before any political war had been declared. And most everyone inside the beltway, as well as inside the state, also knew what Barbour support was really all about—protecting and expanding their empire. "A seventh term for Thad Cochran might mean higher fees for Haley Barbour's lobbying practice," said Club For Growth spokesman Barney Keller. "The

Barbour family wants Cochran in Washington to keep the spending rolling," noted Kibbe.[2]

The 2014 US Senate race in Mississippi wasn't simply about Thad Cochran. Thad was Haley Barbour's lifeline to the appropriations of this country. Barbour and his clients could not afford to lose Cochran's senior position. They were desperate and nothing was going to stand in their way. The Establishment operation, whether in Jackson or Washington, all have business interests that are dependent on primarily on government to make their money. And all need Barbour and Lt. Governor Tate Reeves to keep the money flowing. And they will use whatever means necessary.

Obama's first White House Chief of Staff, Rahm Emanual, now the Mayor of Chicago, once said that the government should "never let a crisis go to waste." In Mississippi, at least under the rule of Barbour, we have another mantra: never let a disaster go to waste. The worst natural disaster in the state's history, and one of the worst in American history, was Hurricane Katrina in 2005. Cochran wanted to be seen as the hero of the Gulf Coast. He was able to steer large amounts of money to help South Mississippi recover from the devastation of the storm. But there was much more going on than recovery work.

Cochran fought hard for unethical no-bid contracts, which allowed much of the work to go to his cronies and those of Haley Barbour, often one and the same. As Keith Plunkett has written, it was "Cochran's long-time engineering cronies who received the large fees associated with readjusting population numbers for water and sewer projects. It was Barbour's niece who bilked the federal government out of money for portable toilets and portable showers, which in turn brought an FBI investigation and fraud convictions. And it was Henry Barbour, despite having no experience in disaster relief, that was named as head of then Gov. Barbour's Commission on Recovery, Rebuilding and Renewal."[3]

Officially at least, Henry Barbour was an "unpaid" executive director of the commission, for which he took "a leave of absence" from lobbying, or so he told a reporter from *Bloomberg*. But his firm, Capitol Resources, had been hired by Government Consultants Inc. to represent them. Government Consultants is "a local firm that advises Mississippi and Louisiana on state bond issues," which would loom large after Katrina. The company paid Henry's firm $65,000 from July 2005 through 2006, "a period that included his work on the governor's commission," while members of Government Consultants "gave at least $27,500 to Haley Barbour's re-election campaign in 2006," for which Henry served as treasurer. But to hear them tell it, there's nothing to see here.[4]

Henry saw his lobbying income rise considerably while his uncle served as governor, from $150,000 in 2004 to $183,000 in 2005, when Katrina hit, and $379,000 in 2006, much of it in Katrina-related business, even though Henry told *Bloomberg* that his firm decided to "not take any new, recovery-related clients" after the storm slammed into the coast, which turned out to be just another Barbour fib. In October 2006, Henry began lobbying for Camp Dresser & McKee Inc., an engineering company out of Cambridge, Massachusetts, that had been a client of Uncle Haley at the BGR Group. Just one week later, seven officials at CDM gave Haley's reelection campaign $1,000 each. If that's not bad enough, Camp Dresser and Waggoner Engineering worked on a $3 million study of water management systems in six counties affected by Katrina, a project that had been a recommendation of the governor's commission, on which Henry sat. In the final quarter of 2006, Henry received $15,000 in lobbying fees from CDM.[5]

And almost none of these very interesting deals were ever adequately investigated. It left question marks in the minds of many Mississippians, including Chris McDaniel. The state was filled with crony capitalism. Special interests saw it. Connected people saw it. And the donor class of the Republican Party was benefitting greatly from the conduct of Haley Barbour. "Democrats have always been corrupt and we have lobbyists that have done it for us," Chris explained in an interview with me. "And all the money provided in these crony deals came largely from the handiwork of Thad Cochran."

When not providing corporations with disaster relief, Thad Cochran, the King of Earmarks, diverted federal funds to cronies to gain hearty campaign contributions. During the 2014 campaign, Timothy P. Carney of the *Washington Examiner* "found $100,000 in donations from D.C. lobbyists to Cochran—with over half of that money coming from lobbyists who work on federal spending bills."[6] A Cochran specialty.

According to the *Washington Post*, in 2009 Senator Thad Cochran earmarked $12 million in spending for Raytheon Corporation, "whose officials have contributed $10,000 to his campaign since 2007. He earmarked nearly $6 million in military funding for Circadence Corp., whose officers—including a former Cochran campaign aide—contributed $10,000 in the same period. In total, the spending bill for 2010 includes $132 million for Cochran's campaign donors, helping to make him the sponsor of more earmarked military spending than any other senator this year."[7]

Cochran claimed the earmarks were "based only on 'national security interests,' not campaign cash." But it is interesting to note that the Defense Department did not want or ask for spending in the areas in which Cochran appropriated the funds. His office spokesman Chris Gallegos responded to the *Post* story, saying, "Senator Cochran does not, and never will, base his decisions on campaign contributions."[8] But how else can this be seen?

Unfortunately, it goes much deeper. In 2008, during Cochran's campaign for a sixth term, the group Taxpayers for Common Sense reported he "received $144,500 in campaign contributions from entities for which he requested earmarks." His biggest donor was shipbuilder and defense giant Northrop Grumman, "which [had] contributed $24,050 to Cochran since 2007."[9]

Also during that same campaign cycle, Cochran "collected more than $10,000 from University of Southern Mississippi professors and staff members, including three who work at the school's center for research on polymers." He tacked onto a defense spending bill "$10.8 million in military grants earmarked for the school's polymer research." The *Washington Post* also reported that Southern Miss, "which would receive $10.8 million in Cochran earmarks, paid $40,000 to a firm that employs Cochran's former legislative director, James Lofton, to help lobby on defense appropriations."[10] But what the *Post* did not point out is that Senator Cochran's daughter, Kate Cochran, is a professor at Southern Miss. This is good ole boy politics and legalized corruption at its finest.

And Southern Miss went to bat for Cochran too, in his campaign against McDaniel. The university has its own political action committee, Eagle PAC, which sent out a fund-raising e-mail that attacked Chris for his votes that were against the wants and wishes of Southern Miss. In recent years, the e-mail read, Senator McDaniel has voted against several major construction projects for the university—he was one of only two votes against a $20 million appropriation for construction of a nursing school, voted against $15 million for USM's business school, voted against $1.5 million for repairs at the Long Beach campus, and voted against $5 million for repairs at the main campus in Hattiesburg.[11] Mississippi's other large university, Mississippi State, which has a top-notch agricultural program to assist the state's large farming sector, also benefitted from Cochran's generosity. Cochran prides himself in his great assistance to farmers and has, in a surprise to some, steered more earmark funds to MSU than any other state entity. In 2007, MSU ranked first in the nation in receiving congressional earmarks with the tidy sum of $43 million. It's no surprise, though, since Mississippi State's President, Mark Keenum, had served eighteen years as chief of staff to Senator Thad Cochran.[12]

Help was coming from all corners for Ole Thad. When pressed about such enterprises, the standard line that the Barbour-Cochran Ring provides is that such government largess brings jobs and economic growth to the state. But such programs never work as they are advertised, and usually do more harm than good:

Barbour and Cochran scored a big victory in 2008 when they brought $580 million in federal money for low-income housing, and then diverted it to an economic development project in the Port of Gulfport, promising 5,000 jobs.

Five years later, the U.S. Department of Housing and Urban Development studied the project and found that the pork project has failed to deliver. "They're still spending money. Money is going out every month and nothing is being done," Glenn Cobb of the Port's Pathways to the Port Jobs Program said on the local Fox affiliate. "It was told to us that they created something around 1,000 jobs," for port workers, but Cobb "found out it was only roughly 50 jobs."[13]

It's never about jobs; that's only the rationale. It's about enriching cronies at the expense of the taxpayers and that's all it has ever been about. It's about getting buildings and monuments named after you. It's about stoking egos and buying a legacy using taxpayers' money. People should be rewarded for creating wealth not transferring it. No one should be honored for how much money they took from other Americans to benefit their constituents.

And how is Thad Cochran rewarded for steering such large sums of money to his friends, cronies, and various associates? Today there are no fewer than 17 monuments to Senator Thad Cochran, some of it programs and scholarships but mainly in the form of government buildings that receive federal funding. There are 10 such buildings named for Cochran on public colleges and universities, including the new "Thad Cochran Student Center" on the campus of Southern Miss. Mississippi State has a "Thad Cochran National Warmwater Aquaculture Center," in addition to its hefty earmarks. There's even a "Thad and Rose Cochran Hall" at the Mississippi University for Women.[14]

With such a lucrative enterprise at stake, the McDaniel challenge to Cochran was a serious threat. The Barbours had no intention of letting their biggest cash cow, Thad Cochran, go down to a movement conservative, so they let it be known before there was even a set match which sideline they and their Tammany Hall-style machine would occupy.

As rumors began spreading about the possibility of Chris McDaniel entering the race, Henry Barbour bluntly stated, "I think he will get his head handed to him and that will be what he deserves. But it's a free country."[15] I felt sure Henry wanted to do the honors himself. Everyone now knew the Barbours would be out for blood in this race, even before the starting gun.

CHAPTER 5

MUDSLINGING MAGNOLIA
STATE STYLE

With the concentration of such an awesome display of force, the Barbour-Cochran camp had no intention of sitting idly by while a young upstart challenged their man in Washington, thus robbing them of lucrative deals at the taxpayer's expense. They intended to use every dollar and every ounce of power at their disposal not just to defeat Chris McDaniel but to destroy him to such an extent that no other conservative ever rose to challenge them again. And in the process of doing so, demonstrated a level of hypocrisy and outright lying that simply defies belief.

But first the Cochran team had to solve two huge, seemingly insurmountable problems. The first was Ole Thad's indefensibly liberal record in Congress, and the second was Chris McDaniel's image as a clean-cut guy with no history of trouble. So to distract from Cochran's record, which he obviously did not want to talk about, and to tarnish the McDaniel all-American boy appearance, they devised a two-pronged strategy for the campaign: Keep Cochran hidden in Washington and use surrogates to attack Chris and his supporters at every turn. In short, they wanted to run a campaign from the sewer.

The first step for any campaign that seeks to engage in gutter politics is to hire opposition researchers, known as "oppo," to dig up dirt. The nastier the better, and they didn't care if it was true or not. Acting as investigators, usually under the guise of media, it's not uncommon for oppo guys to travel to the opposition candidate's hometown and talk to old friends and acquaintances to try to pick up any idle gossip. They will track down old girlfriends and look into any trouble their subject might have gotten into during youthful indiscretions. The campaign can then feed the information to their affiliated blogs and to their contacts in the print and television media.

Chris had told me often, even as far back as early 2012 when we first discussed the possibility of a race against Cochran, that he wanted an issues-oriented campaign, not a mud fest. He wanted to travel the state and speak to the people directly about the issues that confronted us. He wanted to debate Cochran face to face and host joint town hall meetings. Seeing the ideological divide in the GOP before most anyone did, he wanted a campaign that would decide once and for all if Mississippi was as conservative a state as the people liked to boast.

I served as one of Chris's researchers, but we would not engage in the politics of personal destruction, the kinds of ugly attacks, mudslinging, and race baiting that would come to characterize the Cochran campaign. No one on our team traveled to Cochran's hometown of Oxford to dig into any of Cochran's records, as they did against Chris. We were free to examine Cochran's voting records—his earmarks, his spendthrift ways, the huge national debt that he contributed trillions of dollars to, or any legit corruption issues—but nothing else.

Cochran, though, would not place such moral restrictions on his team. We all knew the nasty attacks were coming; we just didn't know when and what shape they would take. And we all knew it was likely they would target not only Chris but those of us close to him as well. Cochran's folks dug dirt on me, hurling racial attacks, smearing me for supporting Pat Buchanan in the Reform Party, and even examining my academic career at Southern Miss, information that had to have come from some of my old professors, which I thought constituted a violation of FERPA (Family Educational Rights and Privacy Act) but I just ignored it. But their main target was always Chris McDaniel and the Cochran-Barbour parade pulled out all the stops. Their oppo guys followed the campaign everywhere. Getting on the bus, getting off the bus. Walking into the hotel, walking out of the hotel. There was always a person recording everything the campaign did. Toward the end of the race there were three individuals. And when they found nothing, they distorted facts, stretched the truth, and simply made stuff up out of thin air. There was nothing out there except speculation, rumor, and finger-pointing.

After discovering very quickly that Chris McDaniel was not a clandestine drunken wife-beater, much to their chagrin, their first stop was to comb through his old talk radio show archives. They even dug up short promos the producers put together to promote the show, which were nothing more than a collection of funny lines over the years.

Over those four years, talking anywhere from ten to fifteen hours a week, Chris covered a lot of stories, some of which were controversial. And over that time period, the number of words he uttered is incalculable, but nothing earth shattering came out of his mouth and much of the more provocative stuff was said in jest, as most all talk radio is known for. But in typical gutter fashion, the Cochran team twisted and took out of context only a handful of minutes, many of them at least a decade old, to try to make Chris look like a bigoted extremist.

In one ten-year-old clip, he joked about the nation's immigration mess and suggested a lighthearted alternative. "Why don't we all immigrate south, let's go to Mexico. . . . You know, a dollar bill can buy a mansion in Mexico."[1]

In another clip, Chris discussed the issue of reparations. "[If] my taxes are going up," he said "I ain't paying taxes." Most Establishment media outlets stopped right there and did not provide the rest of the quote, in an attempt to make him seem racist and unpatriotic.[2] But clearly most Americans do not favor slave reparations and believe it would be a grave injustice to tax current citizens to pay for what bygone generations had done. Furthermore, most Democrats, including Obama and Clinton, have opposed reparations. Yet none of that made the McDaniel hit parade.[3]

In perhaps the most preposterous attempt to smear Chris with his past radio commentary, the opposition jumped on his use of the word *boobies*. Loretta Nall, running for Alabama governor as a write-in candidate on the Libertarian Party ticket decided to have some fun with her anatomy while poking her opposition by offering T-shirts and marijuana stash boxes adorned with a photo of her with in a shirt with a plunging neckline. At the top were the words "More of these boobs." Below that were pictures of the other candidates for governor and the words "And less of these boobs."

Chris decided to have some fun on his radio show and point out the obvious facts. "It's so interesting to see this woman, basically using her boobies . . . I shouldn't have said that . . . using, her uh . . . using her breasts to run for office. And if that's not the most typical Libertarian platform, I have no idea what is."

And that was it, the sum total of the whole episode. Even the liberal site Slate.com slammed the use of that clip as an "unfair hit" on McDaniel.[4] I thought it was perhaps the silliest campaign issue ever raised but it is an indication of the despondency that pervaded the GOP Establishment and the Cochran camp.

But the truth behind the origin of these radio clips was never brought out in the open during the campaign. Chris's radio co-host, Jack Fairchilds, told me exactly how they came to be:

> The radio show was more intellectual than emotional. We were popular, but most of our listeners wanted more excitement; people like controversial statements. Looking back, I guess at times we could be a little boring.
>
> Chris is a dedicated conservative, but he didn't want to offend anyone. I don't mean this as an insult, but he was sometimes too nice for talk radio. People loved him, but we always wanted Chris to be more controversial because being shocking is the best way to market shows and add new stations across the country. We had to encourage him to say things that would get attention because that's just not his nature. He was always firm, but he was never angry or mean about it. He loves people. He never said controversial or shocking things. That was my job.
>
> The attack on Chris for the radio comments was completely unfair. I was his co-host, so the producer and I were solely responsible for the sound bites that were used by the Cochran

campaign, not Chris. The audio they used to attack him was taken from many shows and then heavily edited to appear like he was edgy or controversial. The tapes were altered to make him seem shocking, but he wasn't. Never. We spliced and edited hours of audio to produce the most controversial radio ads we could create. We then used the ads as a way to bring new stations onboard. It was a selling technique set up by our producer to market the radio show. Nothing more.

I was on the radio show with Chris for more than three years. Two hours a day. We had thousands of hours of shows, but there was nothing the Cochran campaign could find to hurt Chris. Instead, they took an advertisement we created and distorted it to injure him. That's all it was.

It was typical of the campaign they ran – lies, distortion, and character assassination. You can't trust those people.[5]

These attacks smacked of desperation on Cochran's part, and yet it never did stick or have much of an impact. In fact, it ended up having the opposite effect on the McDaniel campaign, emboldening our side with even more confidence.

As anyone in the public eye will tell you, if you engage in a lot of public speaking, as politicians and media pundits do, then at times you are going to say things that might not come out right or is not what was actually intended, or, worse still, your comments are taken out of context. "If you live a life on this earth," Chris said, "invariably at some point in your life you are going to say something that could be at least construed to be offensive to *someone* in this country. After all we are so thinned-skinned now."

But the state's establishment apparatus is not so thin-skinned when Haley Barbour says something inflammatory, perverse, or dumb. In 2012, *Politico* headlined his ten "most barbed quotes." For example, after Rick Perry's horrid moment at a GOP presidential primary debate in 2012, when he forgot which cabinet posts he wanted to eliminate,

Barbour commented on it. "You can step on your dick. . . . You just can't jump up and down on it," he said.[6]

"Haley Barbour has said more unusual things than anyone I know," Chris said. "He's said things that would have buried me on day one. Haley makes racial comments and everybody laughs about it. I say *mamacita* and it's a world-ending event. If I had said anything like Haley has said, the Establishment would have thrown me under the bus, and say I wasn't electable. But Haley Barbour is not only electable but worthy of being our hero. It's a huge double standard."

EDUCATION

Another issue the Barbour camp turned against Chris was education. To an assembled crowd in Jackson, he told them exactly what he thought about the issue. "The word *education* is not in the Constitution," he said. "Because the word is not in the Constitution, it's none of their [the federal government's] business. The Department of Education is not constitutional." His remarks drew applause, not boos. In a phone interview with the AP later that same day, Chris told a reporter that he supports education, just not federal involvement in it, mainly because the US Department of Education is completely ineffective, as costs spiral upward and performance moves in the opposite direction. He said the issue of public education should be left to state and local governments where it rightfully belongs. "I think Mississippi, if it's allowed to keep more of its tax revenue, could offset those losses," he said, speaking of the $800 million in federal funds Mississippi receives from Washington each year.[7]

Even though Chris comes from a family of educators (his wife is a teacher) and his children attend public school, the Cochran team jumped all over those comments. Haley Barbour led the attack against Chris using scare tactics to frighten voters. "He's talking about wiping out special education, for autism, physically disabled, mentally disabled, kids who are just slow. That will all be gone if McDaniel gets his way."[8] Barbour's words seemed to be straight out of Democratic talking points. But such was a new position for Boss Hogg. "What I said was the same thing that Haley's always said," Chris told me, "which is a cardinal Republican principle, eliminating the Department of Education. Haley has said it his entire life." But suddenly Haley Barbour had become the chief defender of federal involvement in education. It was nothing more than pure hypocrisy, and the press did not report it. As anyone connected to politics knows, closing the Department of Education had been a part of the Republican agenda going back to Ronald Reagan's 1980 platform, a proposal he specifically called for in his 1982 State of the Union address. It remained a policy of the Republican Party throughout the 1990s, all while Barbour served as RNC Chair, but was later expunged by George W. Bush in 2000 when Establishment forces could finally assert themselves over the old Reaganites.

In fact, in his 1996 book, *Agenda for America*, then-RNC Chair Haley Barbour expressed his disdain for federal meddling in education:

> The federal usurpation of state and local authority in the field of education continues. In 1994, for example, with the passage of a measure called Goals 2000: Education for American Act, the Clinton administration came close to nationalizing American education. The proposed goals, which the Clinton administration insisted were voluntary, specify levels of "inputs" or resources local schools and school districts must meet in order to receive additional federal funding. In reality, of course, these goals are far from voluntary—if a state refuses to submit to the standards, it can lose federal dollars.
>
> While Goals 2000 may have a high-sounding name redolent of academic excellence, it could in certain circumstances actually prevent a school from giving certain kinds of tough, scholastically oriented tests.[9]

Barbour advocated vouchers, charter schools, and other conservative agenda items, all for the cause of "decentralization." It is also interesting to note that Barbour has not changed his mind over the years. In 2012, while considering his own run for president, Barbour advocated abolishing the Department of Education at a breakfast hosted by the *Christian Science Monitor* but stressed that such a position did not make one anti-education. "Being for getting rid of the department certainly doesn't mean you want to get rid of public education. It means getting rid of a federal intermediary so state and local governments can operate without a giant bureaucracy."[10] That is exactly what Chris advocated and what the Barbour machine criticized. O, the hypocrisy.

The ironic thing is, Cochran's record on education was also less than stellar. In fact, Thad had consistently supported more federal involvement in education, although attempting to sell a different version to the general public. In 1979 Cochran voted to create the Department of Education, voted for Bush's "No Child Left Behind," and consistently supported the new Common Core standards. Despite all the federal involvement and money thrown at education, around $13,000 per student, America's schools are in rough shape and our students are falling behind other less developed nations.

VOTING AND ATTENDANCE

Cochran's campaign continued their outrageous assault on Chris by attacking his voting and attendance records in the Mississippi Senate of all things, as well as his personal voting history in Jones County. In an official Cochran campaign press release, and a subsequent ad that hit statewide television, they claimed, "Chris McDaniel has a habit of missing important votes—in critical elections and in his job as a State Senator." Cochran spokesman Jordan Russell said McDaniel "has inexplicably missed voting in some of the most important Republican elections in Mississippi over the past ten years, and his own voting record in the State Senate is just as bad."[11]

But this was just more lies and deception that we had to untangle. In the 2014 legislative session there were a total of 722 votes recorded in the official Senate record. Senator McDaniel missed thirty-one, totaling just 4 percent, which is not a bad record of attendance considering he was also working full time as an attorney and had a full-time family life with a wife and two small boys. Ironically, we discovered that Senator Cochran had missed about 3 percent of his votes, which was especially troubling given that he does not have a full-time job or small children, and does not even live in Mississippi but resides mere blocks from the US Capitol building. He shouldn't miss any votes.

We also thought it very interesting that Cochran's campaign chose the issue of absenteeism to wage war on Chris, given Cochran's life in Washington DC. They jumped on McDaniel for the one and only time he campaigned out-of-state. He traveled to Kentucky to speak at a FreedomWorks conference that was held on behalf of Matt Bevin, then in a battle with Senate Republican Leader Mitch McConnell. Yet Cochran "spent 230 days in Mississippi over a two-and-a-half year period, between April 1, 2011 and Sept. 30, 2013. . . . That rounds out to about 92 days a year, or one day for every three he spent elsewhere." On the other hand, Senator Roger Wicker, Mississippi's other US Senator, during the same two-and-a-half year stretch "spent a total of 491 days there . . . or more than twice as much time as Mr. Cochran." In addition, "Wicker's travel home cost taxpayers $50,958.25, while the Cochran travel tab came to $85,535.31 for 28 fewer trips back to Mississippi." With such a great disparity in cost, it was almost as if someone were traveling with Cochran on each trip. And as we would find out later that's exactly what it was.[12]

As for the Cochran camp's obsession with McDaniel's personal voting history in Jones County, specifically his votes in elections over the past decade, we found such a depiction more than ludicrous. Cochran's team, trying desperately to show that Chris was not a reliable Republican, erroneously claimed that he had voted in the Democratic primary in 2003 when Haley Barbour was running for governor as a Republican and that he skipped both the 2004 and 2008 presidential primaries altogether.

In reality Chris voted for Barbour in 2003, though the records showed that he did not, which could have been a simple mistake on the part of the circuit clerk's office. But a lot of folks in Jones County did not vote in the Republican primary in 2003 because Barbour faced only token resistance and because most people wanted to make their voice heard in a very hotly contested race in the Democratic primary for sheriff. At the time, most local county officials were Democrats but now almost all are Republicans, and the one person who pushed many to switch parties was none other than Chris McDaniel. He expanded the party the right way.

As for the 2004 and 2008 presidential primaries, George W Bush was unopposed in 2004, and neither US Senator was up for re-election and there was no primary in the Fourth Congressional District, so a lot of folks didn't bother to vote, myself included. In 2008, the McDaniel campaign obtained a signed affidavit from Jones County Circuit Clerk Bart Gavin, along with the official voting records, which showed that Chris did, in fact, vote in the Republican presidential primary that year, thus proving yet another Cochran lie. But the fact that a young Democrat named Thad Cochran cast a vote for Lyndon Johnson for President in 1964 was not included in any campaign releases from Cochranland.[13]

The real story of just how the Cochran camp came into possession of McDaniel's voting records should have been a prime media focal point, but, like everything else, it wasn't. From all indications, the records did not come from oppo guys but from Secretary of State Delbert Hosemann. It was discovered that Hosemann allegedly used his official position to conduct opposition research in November 2013, about a month after McDaniel's announcement, when Hosemann himself was ambitiously eyeing the Senate seat and considering a run, but only if Cochran retired. Throughout the fall of 2013, it looked as though Cochran might throw in the towel and Hosemann would have to face off against Chris McDaniel, so he began gathering his ammunition.

When the story broke, Hosemann himself denied the allegation but Circuit Clerk Bart Gavin revealed that one of Hosemann's employees came to the courthouse in Jones County to get the records and when he didn't get prompt service, because of a federal holiday, he phoned the secretary of state, who intervened. "Delbert called one of my election commissioners and complained I wasn't giving his man the information he needed," Gavin said.[14]

Hosemann tried to defend himself by arguing that his employee, Nathan Upchurch, was on leave and not on the clock. "I don't keep up with what my employees do on their time off," he explained. But if that were the case, why did he call Gavin to complain? Again, Hosemann had a ready explanation when pressed. According to an AP report, Hosemann "did get word at some point that Upchurch was being told the clerk wasn't there and no one could help him, so he called an election commissioner he knows to see if she could help." So, by this telling, he was just offering gracious assistance to a "friend."[15]

That probably should have been the end of it, but the politically ambitious Hosemann, who has salivated after Cochran's seat for years, also responded with a political attack of his own, questioning why Chris didn't want people looking at his voting record. The better question is why was a public servant getting involved in a political race by peering into the records of a candidate for public office?

SUDAFED "SCANDAL"

After examining specific votes in the State Senate, Cochran's team seized on Chris's opposition to a bill that would require a prescription to buy Sudafed, or any allergy medication that contained pseudoephedrine, the key ingredient in the manufacture of methamphetamine or crystal meth. They even put out a television spot alleging that Chris sided with meth users and druggies. It was a shameless ad but coming from the Cochran "stink tank," we weren't surprised. In their press release on the ad, the Cochran campaign stated, "News reports have highlighted how effective the anti-meth production legislation has been in Mississippi as a 'huge victory for drug enforcement in this state.' Statewide syndicated columnist Sid Salter recently wrote, 'Mississippi was among national leaders in an initiative to do something proactive to impede the manufacture of methamphetamine in Mississippi—an enterprise that had reached epidemic proportions prior to the courageous 2010 act of the Mississippi Legislature in adopting key legislation to make meth manufacture substantially more difficult in the state.'"[16]

The meth bill was an interesting cause. With Mississippi in the midst of a major meth problem, the state legislature, with the support of Governor Phil Bryant, passed the law that required the prescription. McDaniel's opposition, as well as that of other principled conservatives, was based on two factors: support of working families and the side effects such a policy would cause.

For one, the new law placed an undue burden on lower and middle class folks by requiring them to leave work, go to the doctor—which would be another expense—and then buy a more expensive prescription medication, when all they previously had to do if they had a slight cold or an allergy flare up was to go to Wal-Mart and buy a box of Sudafed off the shelf. Furthermore, with over-the-counter sales banned, there would be absolutely no way to track the sale of Sudafed to meth heads. When they could buy boxes of the pharmaceutical at the local Wal-Mart or corner drug store, it would make it easier for law enforcement to track who purchased it and who might be making meth. The law would drive people to purchase the drug out of state or promote small "shake and bake" operations. According to one report from a top law enforcement officer in Jackson, the problem is not going away. "Meth use is still prominent as it always has been. We're seeing the higher grade of meth coming from Mexico. They have the super labs, which refines the product to the purest form, and it's demanding. Which is coming from Mexico and being trucked into the United States," said Lt. Crieg Oster of the Hinds County Sheriff's Office.[17]

If the policy is so good, wondered Chris, why have neighboring states not followed suit? The only other state that took Sudafed off the shelf at that time was Oregon, which did so before Mississippi and also has had little effect. And actually Oregon's problems began to mount after they restricted Sudafed, something Senator McDaniel looked into before making his decision on the bill. News reports in Oregon show a surge in violence after Mexican drug gangs moved in with their "higher grade" meth. "*The Oregonian* has learned that Mexican cartels, including the powerful Sinaloa and the brutal Los Zetas, have infiltrated almost every corner of Oregon. At last count, authorities were aware of no fewer than 69 drug trafficking organizations selling drugs in the state, nearly all supplied by cartels."[18]

Did these Mexican drug gangs just happen to pick Oregon for its natural beauty? Or is it because there is a void in meth production? The answer is obvious. And it's a problem that has concerned the DEA in Mississippi. "Drug cartels are trying to infiltrate different states and are setting up cell heads as distributors," said Daniel Comeaux, the top DEA agent in Gulfport. "That's what we are seeing here."[19]

So, in reality, with this Sudafed policy it seems that the government sided with the major drug pushers and against working families in Mississippi. McDaniel's major concern was the effect on families and, taking a long-range view of the situation, the future of the state. But

Cochran's team was only concerned about his re-election to the US Senate.

TORT REFORM

Some of the worst attacks against Chris in the 2014 Mississippi Senate primary came from the Barbour-led Mississippi Conservatives political action committee (PAC). In one dishonest mailer they alleged that Chris supported tort reform and caps on damages while in the state legislature, which was true, but then reversed himself and argued that such limits were unconstitutional in a 2012 court case, which was untrue.

Mississippi Conservatives PAC erroneously claimed that Chris, in his capacity as an attorney attempted to get the judge presiding in the case to rule Mississippi's tort reform law unconstitutional, specifically the section placing a cap on economic damages. They claimed that in 2012 Chris represented a client suing an oil and gas company, a case that saw a final judgment of $36 million. The judge did rule the damage cap was unconstitutional. Before an appeal, the case was settled out of court.

But here are the facts: Chris was not the lead attorney in the case. In fact, it wasn't his case, nor was it even his motion. It belonged to another attorney in his firm, Gene Hortman. It was Hortman who made the claim of unconstitutionality, not Chris. Although Chris did not participate in any of the legal arguments, the discovery, or any major aspect of the case but merely assisted Hortman, since he was listed as one of the attorneys on the case, that was enough for the Barbours.

True to its mudslinging nature, the PAC hurled a derogatory legal slur at Chris, referring to him as a "personal injury lawyer," to make him seem like a sleazy, money-hungry ambulance chaser. But, once again, the truth was far different. As a State Senator, Chris had consistently voted in favor of bills to reform the legal system by punishing those who repeatedly file frivolous lawsuits and to limit attorney fees, not something an "ambulance chaser" would ever support. Even Sam R. Hall, a former executive director of the Mississippi Democratic Party admitted "McDaniel supports the tort reform measures already enacted in Mississippi and has spoken in favor of additional tort reform measures." Hall also called the attacks on McDaniel's record as an attorney "disingenuous" and "stale."[20]

A personal injury lawyer files lawsuits against companies seeking damages on behalf of clients. But almost all of Chris's work is in *defense* of companies and against the very trial lawyers the Cochran campaign claimed he was. In fact, he belongs to several prominent defense attorney organizations, such as the Federalist Society, the Defense Research Institute, the Mississippi Defense Lawyers Association, and the Mississippi Claims Association. His law firm, in which he is a partner, has a long history of defending major corporations from lawsuits.

Senator Cochran, on the other hand, has consistently sided with Democrats and trial lawyers throughout his time in Washington. He has voted to kill attempts to limit attorney fees or to institute any kind of tort reform legislation. He's also raked in hundreds of thousands of dollars in campaign contributions from trial lawyers over the years, thus proving that this attack was as baseless, deceitful, and hypocritical as you will ever see in politics.

KATRINA PORK

Perhaps the biggest and longest lasting assault against Chris McDaniel came on the subject of federal funding for relief after the devastation wrought by Hurricane Katrina in 2005. Chris gave an extensive interview with a reporter from *Politico*, a leftwing news organization created as a counterweight to the *Drudge Report*, and his words were twisted and taken out of context by the reporter in question but also by the media in Mississippi, many who are allies of Thad Cochran. Of course the Cochran team ran with it. They claimed he wasn't for Katrina relief, but in reality Chris always supported aid for the victims. The line the Cochran camp used against him was when asked by the reporter if he would have voted for the Katrina relief bill if he was in Congress, McDaniel said he would "have to see the details of it . . . because if it's filled with pork . . . I would have a serious problem with that."[21]

Seeking to make political hay out of the comments on such a touchy and emotional subject, Cochran's allies pounced on McDaniel. Once again Cochran supporter Haley Barbour struck first. "I don't think any person from Mississippi would dream somebody running for senator in our state would not have enthusiastically supported that," he said. "Our delegation worked their fingers to the bone and I think this is the most important legislative achievement of Sen. Cochran's career."[22]

When the attacks began, Chris clarified his position on his Facebook page: "Just to be perfectly clear, I support disaster relief efforts for massive tragedies like Katrina, and I've told the media that on several occasions. However, fraud, waste, abuse and misspent funds must never be allowed. The disaster relief MUST reach the intended beneficiaries, and we MUST be responsible with taxpayer dollars."[23]

Chris most definitely was sympathetic to the plight of those affected by the storm. He also suffered through the storm like everyone else in South Mississippi. In fact, twelve people died in Jones County, the most of any county other than those on the Coast. Chris had damage to his own property; Thad Cochran did not, for Katrina did not reach as far as Washington. But concern for taxpayers and a principled stand against corruption did little to stop the inevitable media blitzkrieg, with Cochran's minions in the press getting in on the act too. Columnist Sam R. Hall, who had defended Chris on tort reform, wrote in the *Clarion Ledger*: "Really? You want to be a U.S. Senator from Mississippi, and you don't automatically and emphatically answer a question about Katrina aid with, 'I absolutely would have supported federal aid to rebuild Mississippi after the most devastating national disaster of my lifetime!'"[24]

Sid Salter, who bragged about riding in a helicopter with Senator Cochran surveying the enormous damage, wrote that the "questions confronting Mississippi voters are whether they want a senator who knows destruction and devastation when he sees it and actually has both the power and the influence to bring unprecedented aid and help with all deliberate speed – and most importantly, does he have the willingness to do so?"[25]

Geoff Pender, also of the *Clarion Ledger*, wrote that "any Mississippian that faults Cochran for doing all he could do to help his state in its hour of need needs to have their head examined." We found Pender's remarks very interesting, since back in 2007 he must have needed his head examined too because he criticized the profligate spending in the Katrina aid package, marveling at the price tag of $23.5 billion. There was enough cash, he said, "to give each man, woman and child in the three southernmost counties $68,500 apiece." It's a system "fraught with waste and fraud and waves of red tape." He rightly pointed out, for example, that the "U.S. Government Accountability Office estimates FEMA lost $1 of every $6 to 'fraud, waste and abuse' for the first $6 billion it spent after Katrina."[26]

Fox News, in a piece called "Hurricane Pork," looked deeper into some of the most ridiculous spending associated with Katrina. "A Republican Study Committee audit discovered that millions went for 'peace' and 'diversity' workshops, a 'yearlong celebration of trees, gardens and other healing places,' theater workshops, anger-management classes and multiculturalism programs to discuss who we are and why we are here.' . . . Evacuees got a free massage or acupuncture treatment. Group counseling sessions and medical checkups were also available, as well as yoga class in the morning and live music—roving mariachi bands, rock 'n' roll acts, singers with acoustic guitars—at night."[27] And it was this corrupt use of taxpayer dollars that Chris wanted to stop.

To Cochran, Barbour, and the mighty defenders of the status quo, that kind of spending is just part of the system, at least that's how they defend it. Or, to borrow from Pender, "Closely monitoring Katrina spending would be akin to closely monitoring the number of grains of sand on the Coast's beach."[28]

Without oversight, waste, fraud, and abuse will certainly occur, as it does with most any government program. Due to mounting pressure and outrage, the government investigated various acts of fraud and arrested, convicted, and punished many, including Barbour's own niece-in-law, Rosemary Barbour, whose company, Jackson-based Alcatec LLC, was found guilty of fraud in a contract with FEMA and ordered to pay more than $350,000 in penalties and damages.[29] Perhaps that's why Uncle Haley and the Cochran gang were so quick to pounce on Chris's advocacy of transparency and oversight; they don't want the light of truth shined on any government programs that their cronies, and relatives, benefit from.

But the real question is what Chris *actually* said in the course of that entire *Politico* interview. Earlier in the discussion he responded to a specific question about hurricane relief, in which he said: "I think everyone generally would agree that [disaster relief] would be a function of the central government under the circumstances [of a major storm like Katrina]. I think where the big disagreement comes is with so much pork and so many special projects that almost never benefit the intended beneficiary. It's one thing to have hurricane relief. It's quite another to use that relief bill to engender favor with supporters or . . . special interests." From there he went on the say that hurricane relief is "a function of the government, it's going to happen, and we are going to do our part to make sure that people are safe and their property is safe. . . . Let's take care of the people that have been affected by the storm."

The controversial part of the interview, where he questioned the merits of the relief bill, was in response to a specific query that concerned the general nature of the spending process, about the big, bloated budget bills floating out of Congress these days filled with pork-barrel projects. The process is controlled by insiders. It's controlled by lobbyists who pack the bills with pork and projects to basically purchase votes. It is an irresponsible way of governing.

What Chris was actually calling for was a reform of the whole system of congressional appropriations, not an end to disaster relief. But shockingly, none of these points were mentioned by the media nor did they bother to contest the accusations leveled by Cochran's political allies. It was as shameful and dishonest a job of reporting and campaigning that you will ever see.

PAC ATTACK

During the 2014 election, Chris received support from conservative organizations like Club for Growth, Madison Project, and FreedomWorks because of his commitment to limiting the scope of the federal government. Cochran's cronies used this to their advantage, alleging in yet another hypocritical attack that outsiders were attempting to buy Mississippi's Senate seat and control Chris should he win the race. Cochran campaign spokesman Jordan Russell said Mississippians had a choice to make. "Do they want Sen. Thad Cochran, a good man, that always put what is best for Mississippi first, or Chris McDaniel, a trial lawyer politician that is manipulated, bought and paid for?"[30] Russell deceitfully claimed that "only 8 percent of (McDaniel's) campaign donor support has come from inside Mississippi."[31]

The McDaniel camp hit back with facts, pointing out that his campaign received more than 75 percent from individuals, not political action committees and special interests. Cochran's support, on the other hand, came mainly from PACs and large contributions from individuals, many from the Washington DC-Virginia region.[32] Cochran didn't care where the money came from. In March 2014, the Podesta Group, run by liberal John Podesta, who worked for both Presidents Clinton and Obama, held a fundraiser for Cochran in Washington. It was a high-dollar affair at that, nothing that the common man could afford—$1,000 a plate for individuals, $2,000 for PACs.[33] When Chris demanded Cochran explain his relationship to Podesta, he received only silence, the oft-used Cochran tactic.

The Barbours didn't care where they had to go to get campaign cash either. It flowed into the Henry-run Mississippi Conservatives PAC from a variety of sources. According to Jeffrey Lord at the *American Spectator*, donations came in from both political parties, which illustrated "in stunning detail how the establishments and donors of the Republican and Democratic parties intermingle." Lord continued:

> Thirty-seven people have donated to Mississippi Conservatives 51 times—and 36 of those donations were for more than $5,000. Let's just talk about these high-rollers. A full 55 percent of them have either 1) given money directly to prominent Democrats; or 2) given money to other PACs from which it seems to have flowed to Democratic candidates. Yes, you read that right. More than half of the high-dollar donors to this so-called Mississippi Conservatives group had previously given money to help elect Democrats. And not just the distant past,

but recently—including Senate races targeted this very year by the GOP.

Public records tell the story, and examples of the first occurrence — direct donations to Democrats—are easy to spot. Donors to Mississippi Conservatives have also in the past written checks to Hillary Clinton, Harry Reid, Dianne Feinstein, Mary Landrieu, Kay Hagan, Mark Pryor, Chris Dodd, and Michael Bennet, among others.[34]

We also found out that a lot of outside money was coming into Barbour's Mississippi Conservatives PAC. Anti-gun nut and former New York City mayor Michael Bloomberg gave $250,000, as did Sean Parker, the former president of Facebook who also believes in gutting the Second Amendment. Karl Rove's Super PAC American Crossroads gave $160,000 and the Main Street Partnership added $100,000. Super PACs supporting Texas Senator John Cornyn and Mitch McConnell gave $50,000 each, while those supporting Bob Corker and Rob Portman donated $25,000 a piece. Missouri Senator Roy Blunt's PAC chipped in $5,000. There was no shortage of money so long as Haley Barbour was part of the gang. The same Haley Barbour, mind you, who said this: "We are not going to let a bunch of people from Washington or New York dictate who represents Mississippi in the U.S. Senate."[35]

RACE CARD

The 2014 Mississippi Senate race was not a case of "pot meet kettle," a phrase that denotes both parties are equally engaged in mudslinging while one is either in denial or lying about it. The mudslinging was purely one sided. Chris did not engage in such despicable behavior; Haley Barbour and Thad Cochran did. They were the pot *and* the kettle. In fact, they were throwing everything including the kitchen sink at McDaniel to destroy him. The question was not "Who is Chris McDaniel?" The real question was "Who is Thad Cochran and Haley Barbour?" Sadly the mud would only get deeper as things took a turn for the worse.

And by worse, I mean the race card, or in our case the white supremacist card. A week after the announcement, I got a phone call from Chris. "How does it feel to be on the national news?" he asked with his familiar chuckle. I was quite shocked. *Me on the national news?* I thought. Perhaps it was something good.

But it wasn't. As it turned out, Tim Murphy, a "reporter" from *Mother Jones*, the fanatical left-wing rag based in DC, had written a hit piece on Chris and had dragged me into it, a case of guilt by association, the first of many in the campaign. It portrayed me as a neo-Confederate conspiracy theorist fanatic who just so happened to be a longtime aide and friend to Senator McDaniel.

The piece, entitled "GOP Senate Candidate Addressed Conference Hosted by Neo-Confederate Group That Promotes Secessionism," was soon picked up by other news outlets, including MSNBC, prominently featured a photoshopped portrait of Chris standing with his arms-crossed and looking defiant in front of a Confederate battle flag. It alleged that we had ties to a white supremacist group that hosted a conference earlier that summer that featured both of us as speakers. Murphy also took some older columns of mine and took snippets out of context to make me look like a fanatic. Coming from the fringe Left I guess I shouldn't have been surprised. I just didn't expect it quite so soon in the campaign.[36]

The conference in question was the Southern Heritage Festival, a small gathering showcased in a Baptist church in the eastern part of Jones County. It's an annual event hosted by the Jones County Rosin Heels, the local chapter of the Sons of Confederate Veterans, an organization dedicated to the memory of Southern soldiers who lost their lives in the War Between the States. They are not racist or devoted to the destruction of blacks. Anyone who says otherwise is simply not telling the truth. And although there are those in the group who promote secession, that is not something I have ever advocated, although I do maintain that state secession is legal.

Right out of the box I had to ask myself a pertinent question: Just how did a reporter in DC find out about an obscure conference in rural Jones County, Mississippi? The answer couldn't have been more obvious: Cochran's team must have fed it to him. Though it was knocked around in the press for a few weeks, Chris McDaniel did *not* attend the conference. I know because I did.

Amazingly, those in the Establishment that were hell-bent on tearing us down threw the Sons of Confederate Veterans at us, even though many prominent Mississippians belong to the organization and have spoken at their events. Governor Phil Bryant and former Senator Trent Lott are members, and both have attended SCV events as keynote speakers. Chris once spoke at an SCV state convention in 2012 when he filled in for Governor Bryant, who could not attend. As for the SCV itself, it has a federally recognized charter, is tax-exempt, and by federal definition can't advocate racist ideology, activities, segregation, or the like.

Later in the campaign, Chris canceled a speaking engagement at a pro-Second Amendment event hosted in aptly named Guntown, Mississippi, when news broke that one of the event's vendors, though not a sponsor, was a notorious white supremacist and racial separatist that sold "white pride" merchandise. Hinging on the racist storyline, the pro-Cochran Establishment website *Y'all Politics* attacked McDaniel for accepting a speaking engagement in the first place.

The head honcho at *Y'all Politics*, Alan Lange, wrote that in politics "the company you keep matters."[37] However, when it was discovered in 2015 that one of Cochran's Washington aides, who had been with the Senator for more than thirty years, was arrested in a "drugs-for-sex" scheme—which interestingly enough included possession of meth— *Y'all Politics* did not feature a similar headline, even when Cochran did not immediately fire the aide in question, tactics we come to expect from the liberal media.[38]

Despite the attacks, McDaniel didn't run away from the media the way Cochran did. He stood in the center of the ring and took their best shots, all while Cochran hid in Washington and, in one of his rare appearances did, in fact, run from the media. When a reporter from CNN wished to speak to the Senator, his dishonorable staff lied and told her that Cochran would be right out, all while they were pulling the big switcheroo, having him exit out of a different door and climb into a different car. Yet Chris McDaniel was the bad one. Welcome to the Mississippi Senate Primary 2014. It would only get worse, much worse.

CHAPTER 6

"NOW IS THE TIME":
MCDANIEL ROLLS ACROSS MISSISSIPPI

Under such intense political heat and scrutiny, it would have been easy for a less courageous candidate to throw in the towel, and many had stayed out of such races altogether because they did not want to face the Barbour Machine, but Chris McDaniel never batted an eye at the atrocious negative attacks coming his way on an almost daily basis. He even had a little fun with all the negativity, once telling an audience, "If I could walk on water they would say it was because I can't swim." But at no time did he ever fire back at Cochran and his team in the dastardly manner in which they had repeatedly shot at him.

Instead, Chris stayed on message in a two-pronged offensive: bashing Cochran's atrociously bad, and very liberal, voting record while advocating a true conservative message. He wanted to be another Barry Goldwater, leading a revival of conservatism nationwide. "You can't lead a conservative resurgence from Maine; you can't lead a conservative resurgence from Massachusetts or California. But, by George, you can lead one from Mississippi," he said to rousing applause.[1]

CONSERVATVE VS LIBERAL

Being a leader in a conservative movement from Mississippi would certainly include taking an aggressive stand against a liberal onslaught that's been ongoing for decades. In fact, I would argue that Chris McDaniel, as a State Senator who by 2014 had done more to fight back against an encroaching federal government in seven years in office in Jackson, Mississippi than Thad Cochran had in more than forty years in Washington. His lawsuit against Obamacare and his numerous bills designed to block federal power in Mississippi were far more than Cochran had done since 1973. In interview after interview, especially with the Barbour and Cochran minions in the press, Chris asked a simple question of his own: "Can you name one fight Cochran has led against Obama?" Stunned silence was the usual response.

The campaigns were a study of contrasts. Though both candidates were in the same party, the ideals of the GOP have gotten muddled to say the least. Jay Cost of the *Weekly Standard* wrote: "[Cochran] is a classic example of the disconnect" between the Establishment and the average voter. "He has been in the Senate for nearly forty years. To what lasting conservative triumph is his name attached? I cannot think of any, nor can I think of any fight against the liberal agenda in which he was a crucial ally." (It was the same point Chris raised repeatedly on the campaign trail, and to which no one had any answers.) "Instead, his claim to fame—as he proudly advertised during the campaign—was leveraging his seniority to steer government largesse to Mississippi." And although the Republican platform is a message of smaller government and "has been the gist of the party's message for nearly 80 years," he continued, "Cochran is not in D.C. to fulfill these promises. His purpose is to perpetuate what Theodore Lowi once called 'interest group liberalism.' He is the modern equivalent of the Gilded Age spoilsman; he parcels federal resources to well-placed factions that, in turn, help secure his reelection. This runs directly contrary to what the Republican party promises to do."[2] This is exactly who Thad Cochran really is.

In contrast Chris McDaniel came down on the side of the party's genuine principles, a philosophy of "true conservatism" he called it. Many Republicans portray themselves as conservatives, especially on the campaign trail, but don't always govern that way, just as Jay Cost had written. In recent years, they haven't governed that way at all. "We've seen this before," Chris told Jonathan Strong of the *National Review*. "Whether it's Eisenhower–Taft or Goldwater–Rockefeller or Reagan–Ford—this is a continuation of that fight. I'm a Reaganite. I'm a conservative. I believe in liberty. And like a lot of Mississippians, I'm frustrated. We're not heading in the right direction."[3]

For Chris McDaniel, conservatism has a definite set of principles, and those ideals—limited government, federalism, low taxes, no debt, free enterprise, and most importantly an unyielding adherence to the Constitution as crafted by the Founding Fathers—must be followed in order to rightfully identify as such. "In my soul I believe I'm first and foremost a Jeffersonian," Chris said in the *National Review* interview. "I admire Taft, of course. I admire Goldwater. Reagan, obviously. I'm very interested in Austrian economics, whether it be Hayek or even earlier philosophers like Bastiat—philosophers that value freedom as opposed to statism." Cochran believed in none of those things, never spoke of conservative values, and his record proves it.

Yet that didn't stop Cochran's minions like the hapless Stuart Stevens, a Mississippian in name only who helped run Mitt Romney's 2012 presidential campaign into the ground against the worst president since Jimmy Carter. Stevens called McDaniel "not particularly conservative," while praising the spendaholic Cochran as a man who has "a history of reducing spending when he was chairman of the Appropriations Committee" and blocking all attempts to give amnesty to illegal immigrants, none of which is true. This was the same Stuart Stevens who soon after helping Obama secure a second term got a job writing for the *Daily Beast*, which no self-respecting conservative would go near, and used that left-wing rag to trash a member of his own party.[4]

AFRAID TO DEBATE

The Stevens-Barbour-Cochran brand of conservatism, however, is nothing more than a set of ideals that were just slightly to the right of Barack Obama, which does not make one a true conservative in the historical Jeffersonian sense or in any sense for that matter. And Chris continuously pointed to the ideological contrast, using hard-core evidence, such as Cochran's atrocious voting record, including the fact that the long-time Senator had voted with Obama 50 percent of the time. If he were so proud of his record of achievement and his brand of "conservatism," then why would he not agree to a debate? There were certainly many opportunities for the two candidates to meet face-to-face. Chris himself extended several invitations, even with personal letters, but Cochran refused. Television stations offered to moderate statewide televised debates, which Chris quickly accepted, yet Cochran still refused to attend.

When finally pressed by a reporter on his refusal to debate, Cochran replied, "I'm not running to be a member of a debate team. I'm a candidate for the US Senate." That he was in the midst of a political campaign, or that the Senate itself is considered the world's greatest debating society, seemed to have escaped his notice after more than forty years in politics. "There's no special reason why I should debate him," he told a *Washington Post* reporter. "I don't know what the debate would prove that everyone doesn't already know."[5]

There was plenty for everyone to know. Even the *Clarion Ledger*, the state's major newspaper, and certainly no bastion of conservative thought, editorialized that the people of Mississippi deserved a debate between the candidates. "Part of our democracy is the open and frank discussion of ideas. This is vital in the election process between two viable candidates who have legitimate differences in political philosophies. . . . Cochran's camp has given no reason. They just flatly refuse to debate," which is "wrong," the editors wrote. "Being unwilling to debate a credible candidate is unbecoming of a member of the U.S. Congress who purports to represent the democratic process by which our leaders are chosen. Cochran . . . should give voters the opportunity to watch democracy in action and to witness the debating of ideas and policies that matter most to our country."[6]

But Ole Thad, "the quiet persuader," was not persuaded. To the *Associated Press*, in an incredibly feeble and contradictory answer, Cochran revealed why he did not want to debate Chris. "I don't know what there is to debate. He obviously is going to criticize my record of service. We disagree on some of the issues. And there are probably some things that we can agree on. But he's obviously, you know, trying to make me look bad by things he's saying about my performance in the Senate."[7] So there was something to debate after all.

Yet, truth be known, Thad Cochran and his handlers feared a debate for two reasons. First, Cochran was simply afraid of having his voting record criticized and exposed on statewide television, which told us that our work on his record was having an effect. There were simply things he could not and would not discuss in front of a mass audience. The Cochran campaign knew what we knew: Even on his best day, Thad could not defend his record. "I would have debated him anytime, anywhere," Chris told me. "But they didn't want a debate; they wanted to hide behind their money, power, and influence." Why Cochran had the support he did, being a candidate who refused to debate his opponent, was beyond me and a lot of other conservatives.

There was a second reason Cochran didn't want to debate. It was called the Reagan Effect. In 1980, Jimmy Carter had based his entire campaign, not on his dismal record, but on making Ronald Reagan look like a dangerous, radical, extremist who couldn't be trusted with presidential power. Listening to the Carter message, one could reasonably conclude that Reagan must have possessed horns, a pointed tail, and carried a pitchfork. Yet after their lone debate that fall, when Reagan wiped the floor with the president, people around the country realized that this Reagan fellow was not dangerous, not extreme, and certainly not radical. The debate had a humanizing effect, if you will, and completely obliterated the Carter message. Cochran's team had the same fears. Chris McDaniel, a young, energetic, dynamic candidate, on statewide television, in contrast to an older, feebler, and not always lucid senior senator, would come off as rational and in line with the thinking of most Mississippi Republicans. The Carter mistake could not be repeated. It was simply too big of a risk to take.

Instead the Cochran team sent out their press spokesman, Jordan Russell, to "debate" Chris by disgracefully crashing a press conference in front of the state capitol building in Jackson. Chris had called the press conference to discuss a number of issues, namely his decision to support Senator Mike Lee's Conservative Agenda. While he was pointing out the fact that Cochran wouldn't "defend his liberal record," but, instead, hid "behind false attack ads" at his home in DC, Cochran's mouthpiece, standing on the edge of the gathered reporters, jumped in with campaign talking points. Russell claimed Chris and his campaign was lying, that it was Chris that skipped votes, that Chris didn't want to support the Katrina victims, and that Chris wanted to increase taxes. All bald-faced lies. And Chris McDaniel was having none of it. When

Russell criticized him for calling Cochran a liar in response to Cochran campaign attack ads, Chris didn't back down and gave as good as he got.

Despite the childish tactics, Chris marched on with his grassroots campaign, traveling the state for months and meeting with the public in a variety of venues—college campuses, town halls, restaurants, factories, fairs, festivals, and public speeches—to talk about the problems in Washington and his solutions for them. In March, he launched a four-city Town Hall Tour designed to discuss the issues with a different policy topic in each city. He invited Cochran to join him but again was turned down. During a ten-day stretch in April, he visited eleven counties and traveled a total of twenty-five hundred miles, crisscrossing the state.

GRASSROOTS EFFORT

Chris never seemed to slow down. Said policy advisor Keith Plunkett, "I've logged thousands of miles on the road with him. He can hardly contain his energy at times and after hours on the road during extended trips I've had him demand for me to pull over at the next exit just so he can get out of the vehicle and walk around. We took to calling him 'Sparky.'"[8]

In the final week of campaigning before the June 3 primary, he engaged in a twenty-five-stop statewide bus tour he dubbed the "Five Promises Tour." Those five promises were: fully repealing Obamacare, enacting term limits on members of Congress, supporting a balanced budget amendment and getting control of spending, family and business tax reform, and fighting cronyism and enacting more free-market based legislation. "We were working so hard, fourteen to sixteen hours a day," Chris said to me in an interview. "There was no sleep. We would pull into a hotel, get to the room and start writing speeches and sending out emails. We worked constantly around the clock. I was sleeping 3-4 hours a night tops. Never stopped. It was tough for us. Despite all our work raising money, Thad Cochran in one night on Capitol Hill with Mitch McConnell raised nearly one million dollars in a single evening. For us it would have taken two to three months of nonstop calling every day to raise that kind of money. It just shows you what you are up against."[9]

That's why Chris has always favored term limits. His experience in the race against Cochran and the Barbour Machine only strengthened that resolve. People claim we have term limits with every election, but if incumbents can raise a million dollars in a single night, then it doesn't matter what your message is. They are going to define your message for you. In the home stretch they had way more money. Rumors were coming out of the Cochran camp that they spent $700,000 in the last two weeks of the campaign simply identifying voters. Yet the McDaniel campaign was spending just $50,000 on radio. And that's why we need term limits. People who say we have them already with periodic elections have never run a race against a machine like Barbour's.

COCHRAN IS OUT OF TOUCH

Closer to the primary, Cochran, despite his vast machine support, knew he needed to be in Mississippi more because Chris McDaniel was having a real impact. One of the things he touted about himself was his vast seniority, a message we would hear a lot as June 3 approached. It was really the only play he had, that his service to the state "has been effective for the people of Mississippi."[10] Seniority was always how smaller, and poorer, states like Mississippi got anything at all. It had been that way since Reconstruction. Southern states had no chance to elect a president or vice president for decades after the War Between the States, so they concentrated on gaining seniority and controlling major influential congressional committees, thereby controlling the flow of cash and goodies.

To counter the Cochran seniority strategy, Chris stuck to principles and his theme of true conservatism—limiting government, cutting taxes and spending, and paying down the astronomical national debt—and contrasting that with Cochran's acquiescence in running up that debt. So it was debt, debt, debt, and more debt. The times had changed and he understood that better than most. "The people of our state are waking up," he told the *Wall Street Journal*. "They understand that Washington has to be changed. They understand there's no way to change Washington unless we change the people we send to Washington. And Senator Cochran, though I respect him, he has not been the conservative vote that we've asked him to be. . . . The people of the state are finally seeing that. They have awakened to his real record and they are ready for change."[11]

As to the issue of seniority, Chris did not think it was nearly as big of an issue as in elections past. First, he argued, "[s]eniority is not what it used to be. No one in the state can name a single charge that Senator Cochran has led against Barack Obama. What good is seniority if he's not willing to fight? Secondly, with a country like ours that is $17.5 trillion in debt . . . the idea that seniority will enable him to bring home additional moneys seems a bit unreasonable and frankly immoral. At some point the adults of this country have to understand this debt issue will eventually crush us. Seniority doesn't mean anything in that context."

It was a powerful and very persuasive argument, one that Chris would love to have put directly to Cochran on the debate stage. But poor ole Thad was having enough trouble of his own simply speaking to small groups. In one memorable speech, he talked of his youthful days in Mississippi, growing up on a farm and "doing all kinds of indecent things with animals." Huh? The blogosphere had a field day with that one.[12] This clearly was the reason why he would not debate, or, more precisely, why he was not allowed to, and it explains why he had been hidden in the first place.

On three separate occasions during his few days on the campaign trail, Cochran showed just how out of touch he was with average citizens, as well as conservatives, when he said the Tea Party movement "is something I don't know a lot about." In two of those instances, one to *Washington Post* reporter Robert Costa, he channeled his inner Obama. "Was it Will Rogers who said all he knows is what he reads in the paper?" he asked. "Well, all I hear about the tea party is what I've read in the paper."[13]

But there was more, including a flubbed answer on one very important issue, perhaps the major issue in the whole 2014 national campaign—Obamacare. When asked about it, instead of repeating his own campaign line that he did not vote for it and has voted to repeal it "more than 100 times," he said it was "an example of an important effort by the federal government to help make health care available, accessible and affordable."[14] Was this confusion or a Freudian slip? Given his past record, including support for federal health care regulations and control, and seeing his time on the stump this go around, it could have been either one.

And confusion was a very real possibility because there were a few serious memory lapses that caused some to rightly question his capacity to continue serving in the Senate. In one of the most well publicized incidents, according to Molly Ball, a reporter for *The Atlantic*, less than thirty minutes after finishing an interview with the senator, he approached her, "held out his hand" on his way out of the building, and said "Hello, I'm Thad Cochran," as if he didn't know her.[15] Then there was the time he got lost going to a Senate Republican luncheon in the Capitol building in DC, where he had served for more than forty years. At his advanced age of seventy-six, it's certainly not uncommon to have memory issues, and we certainly did not want to be seen as smearing an old man, but when someone seeks to serve the public, particularly in such a high office, we have every right to question his ability to do so effectively, especially when incidents arise such as these.

But as amusing as those instances were, they were still just side issues. The biggest and most important subject, as far as we were concerned, was Cochran's record of service. When all was said and done, the combination of Chris McDaniel as a candidate and Cochran's record would bring the aged senator down. But when the race began in October 2013, the task did look daunting. On the surface at least, Cochran's poll numbers reflected a very positive image that one might expect in a state with a long-serving senator, and those lofty numbers had always scared away any serious competition. In fact, the state's media apparatus labeled him "unbeatable" on many occasions.

UNBEATABLE BUT VULNERABLE

When Chris did announce his candidacy, the *Jackson Free Press* headlined, "Senator Chris McDaniel to Announce Beginning of End of Political Career." The paper believed Cochran's "conservative street cred is solid, but he has been criticized for being insufficiently right wing" and would "probably hold on to the position until he gets good and damn ready to step aside." McDaniel, the author noted, might just "be displaying a bit of bravado to run for a statewide office in 2015 as the kid who had the cahones to lock horns with Thad."[16]

It's not like Chris didn't know any of this. Everybody in Mississippi knew that Thad Cochran was considered unbeatable. At the start he had a higher approval rating than any politician in the country. He was unbeatable. But Chris knew his issues and his philosophy were not unbeatable. He knew the discussion was essential so Mississippi Republicans could finally decide what it means to be a Republican. People had to know that there is a clear distinction from being a conservative and being a Republican.

The campaign felt that we were facing a historical moment because we felt like Thad was vulnerable and certainly far from unbeatable. Our team believed that when the voting public saw the specifics of Thad's record, and we could contrast that with Chris's record and stance, then Cochran's support would begin to plunge. Although we certainly had nothing remotely close to Barbour's money and vast support, our goal was to get Cochran's atrocious voting record published on as many blog sites and in as many state newspapers as we could. His record was indefensible, and Cochran's team knew it, which was the sole reason for the negative attacks. They would distract, deflect, and talk about anything under the sun, anything, that is, but Cochran's votes in Congress. That and their propagation of false polling data was a mainstay of their strategy.

In the fall of 2013, the Cochran team released a poll showing Cochran ahead by twenty-four points. By the spring, that same poll, which they pushed around the state, showed him ahead by seventeen points.[17] But the negative attacks and mudslinging continued.

When we asked ourselves why the Cochran team would continue the mudslinging if they really had such a great lead, we came up with a couple ideas. One possible reason was that they wanted to not only defeat McDaniel but bury him, like LBJ buried Goldwater, as a warning to any future conservative challengers. The second reason was more likely: The polls were not representative of the state. The Cochran surveys were tilted heavily toward North Mississippi, which has but a third of the state's overall population. Chris's home base, the Pine Belt, which is home to some of the state's densest Republican turf, was hardly represented at all. It was one of the most dishonest polls I've ever seen, meant only to discourage Chris's supporters. However, as distorted as the poll was, since it was slanted heavily in favor of North Mississippi, it was obvious that Chris had gained seven points on Cochran right in his home territory. That was good news for us, something that was unsurprisingly lost on most of the state's media._

WHO ENDORSED WHOM

To compound Cochran's troubles, Chris began collecting major national endorsements from all the main Tea Party groups, such as Tea Party Patriots and Tea Party Express. The Senate Conservatives Fund, the brainchild of former Senator Jim DeMint, backed him with ads. Other conservative organizations also came to his aid, including FreedomWorks, Club for Growth, Madison Project, Family Research Council, Gun Owners of America, and the American Conservative Union, which flatly refused to endorse Cochran because he was the lowest rated Republican in the Senate. Chris also received endorsements from conservative icons including Sarah Palin, Rick Santorum, Sean Hannity, Mark Levin, Glenn Beck, Laura Ingraham, Phyllis Schlafly, and Gary Bauer. Celebrities like the former game show host Chuck Woolery and several members of the Duggar family of *19 Kids and Counting* also joined the effort.

The Barbour-Cochran team constantly emphasized this false point, that McDaniel's support was almost exclusively from outsiders, including both endorsements and money, while Cochran's support was almost exclusively from inside the state. "The McDaniel campaign emphasizes the outside celebrities who are involved in MS to politically help themselves nationally, not because they are trying to help MS. . . . This is out-of-state money, celebrities and political gunslingers versus leaders who live here, love the state and want to do what is best for Mississippi, not some national political agenda."[18] But once again that was far from the truth. In fact it was the exact opposite.

Cochran had no big name "conservative" endorsers, or at least not any he would dare mention. He, like Barbour, could only point out that all the state's large newspapers and major elected officials, Establishment to the last man, had endorsed him, as if that were something to brag about. That was simply a case of not understanding one of the key features of this race—an anti-Establishment mood. And Chris did get a lot of support from Mississippi conservatives and even from one of the biggest names in Mississippi Republican politics. In what can only be described as a political coup, former Yazoo City mayor Jeppie Barbour, the older brother of Haley Barbour, and father to both Henry and Austin, threw his support to Chris. "I am for McDaniel," Jeppie said, "because Congress spends too much money and Senator Cochran is right in the middle of spending and borrowing money. I resent my grandchildren having to pay for these politicians to party. I am ready for a change."[19]

Cochran could always count on the support of the Establishment, including the Barbour Machine with their money and questionable tactics, but he also had his own mountain of outside help. According to OpenSecrets.org, Cochran raised more than $1.8 million from PACs, with "business-based PACs accounting for more than $1 million" of that total. In all, by June 3 Cochran had raised some $4.4 million to Chris's $1.5 million.[20]

Another notable factor revealing Cochran's liberal leaning was when the US Chamber of Commerce joined in supporting the aging senator. Though the Chamber is business-oriented and considered a Republican organization that supports GOP candidates for the most part, it is far from being an advocate for free enterprise and capitalism. It has become so bad that Mark Levin has renamed it the "Chamber of Crony Capitalism," because that's exactly what it is.[21]

The Chamber, for instance, supported the $700 billion bank bailout, the lifeline to Fannie and Freddie, Obama's auto bailout, the Obama stimulus bill, Common Core, and opposes the repeal of Obamacare. In 2013, it spent $52 million lobbying on behalf of amnesty for illegal immigrants. It also supported unfettered global free trade, including many of the worst trade deals, as bad as those have been for the American economy. With positions like this, it was predictable that Thad Cochran would be their guy. The Chamber spent big money, around $500,000, in ads attacking McDaniel, usually with the same tired old stuff that the Barbour slime machine had thrown throughout the campaign, calling Chris the "personal injury lawyer."[22]

FINAL STRETCH

As the campaign moved to the final stretch, the daunting task of winning the primary was beginning to look like Cochran's problem, not Chris's. After all the attacks, the lies, the deceptions, the mud and nastiness, Chris was not only still standing but in the lead. Conservative stars were coming out in support, enough money was flowing in, and even the *Washington Post* had its eye on the race, placing it in the top ten primaries to watch. What would Cochran and his rascally team do now? They began plotting yet another strategy as June 3 approached, a plan that would inform the public of the awful prospects that could very well await them if they kicked Ole Thad to the curb.

This new effort received a boost by GOP state party Chairman Joe Nosef, who is actually a cousin of McDaniel through marriage. Nosef accused conservatives and the Tea Party of being fanatical, and claimed that could hurt the party in the general election in November. Nosef told Janis Lane, the president of the Central Mississippi Tea Party that if they continued to divide the party by supporting McDaniel, then Democrats would capture the seat in November. Yet the "neutral" Nosef never, at any time, urged Barbour to knock off the vicious mudslinging directed toward McDaniel, which would certainly hurt Republicans if Chris won the nomination.[23] Cochran's camp pushed this Nosef narrative, saying that if Chris won the race and the Senate seat, he would only embarrass the state because he was too radical and too extreme, and the conduct of his campaign had only demonstrated, not assuaged, those facts. They pointed to Chris's radio comments and said his policy prescriptions were too conservative and would end up closing the state's public schools, dangerously slash budgets, and deprive minorities of their voting rights.

This new attack line was in complete contrast to their previous argument, that if Chris McDaniel were elected he would have no seniority in which to get anything done, unlike the ancient Cochran. So how was he supposed to tear down all of civilization yet have no power to do so?

Most Republicans, if not most Mississippians, stood on true conservative principles, which was once the party's platform. "They call us radicals but there was nothing I said, not a single word I said that wasn't at one time or still is a part of the Republican platform," Chris told me. "So you had the Republicans self-indicting their own platform."[24] It's not radical to want to balance the budget. It's not radical to want true constitutional government. That's all Chris was calling for and he stayed on that message for seven and a half months. And that message was resonating with the electorate.

With Chris's message taking root, the Cochran team called for yet another change in strategy. In a new contradictory tactic, which came to signify Cochran's entire campaign program, his team emphasized that the young Chris McDaniel was unlikely to win in November but if he did manage to pull off the unthinkable and capture the nomination, he could also endanger Republicans across the country because his very presence on the ticket, with his inflammatory rhetoric, would drag down the whole party. His bombastic speech might work in Mississippi but wouldn't fly in New Hampshire and elsewhere, thereby hurting those candidates.

Republicans believed they stood a great chance to take control of the Senate from Harry Reid and the Democrats, who had taken it as part of their resurgence back in 2006. Surveys in various battleground states revealed that it just might happen, although it would likely be a close one. Every single state mattered in 2014, even those very strong red states like Mississippi that had always been taken for granted. And control of the Senate, they said, may very well come down to the race in Mississippi. So there was no need to take chances and Chris McDaniel, claimed the Cochran team, was one big, unnecessary chance. "They use the notion of 'electability' to their advantage," Chris said. "How can I drag the party down but people like John McCain can drag it up? And Scott Brown up in New Hampshire made a comment that I was going to hurt him. But I was worried about Scott Brown hurting me!"[25] Mississippi always sends a more conservative Republican Senator to Washington than Maine or New Hampshire does. If Mississippi Republicans were like Maine Republicans, there'd be no point in having conservatives at all. We are supposed to be more conservative in Mississippi, our people are more conservative, but that's not the way the Establishment sees it. They use conservatism *against* the candidate and then libel and slander them.

The Cochran-Barbour Clan began using the same tactics as the Democrats by scaring voters into believing that only Thad Cochran could retain control of the seat and ensure Republicans of a chance to flip the Senate and stop the Obama agenda. And, just before the deadline to file paperwork to run in the Senate primary, Travis Childers, the former Democratic congressman from North Mississippi, decided to throw his hat into the ring. He saw the handwriting on the wall, a likely McDaniel win, and believed he had a better shot against the more conservative upstart. Although he would face a minor candidate in the Democratic primary, it was clear the fall matchup would be Travis Childers versus either Cochran or McDaniel.

Cochran's campaign continued to attack Chris on his very conservative issues, saying they would turn voters off in the general election. This is the Establishment strategy. They smear conservatives in the primaries; then once those smears take hold in the public consciousness, they use those same smears to persuade the public that conservatives are unelectable. Republican strategist and lobbyist Hayes Dent told the state press, "I'm scared to death that we'll lose this in the fall" with McDaniel. Mississippi Conservatives PAC spokesman Brian Perry assured voters that Childers "can win" the race against McDaniel. With Republican friends like that, who really needed any enemies?[26]

The GOP Establishment was in step with Democrats and the liberal media, which was spouting the same vile invective. One Democratic strategist told the *Los Angeles Times* that Mississippi was "not as red and conservative" as some believe.[27] "If Republicans fumble and nominate McDaniel, we'll be ready to catch the ball," said Rickey Cole, head of the state Democratic Party.[28] Former Mississippi Governor William Winter, a Democrat, said a McDaniel victory "would confirm the worst stereotypes about Mississippi," a racially charged statement made to the *New York Times*, which ran a number of anti-McDaniel articles designed to push a certain narrative used by both Democrats and Establishment Republicans. Jonathan Weisman of the *New York*

Times called McDaniel a "major headache" for the Republican Party. "Already on Wednesday, Democrats were quietly expressing glee and moving to elevate the McDaniel candidacy," he wrote, "hoping to make him this campaign cycle's equivalent of Missouri's Todd Akin, whose provocative comments on rape created problems for Republicans around the country in 2012."[29]

There was only one small problem with this particular line of attack. Travis Childers was not a very strong candidate, no matter how much Democrats and Establishment Republicans tried to pump him up. Sure, he'd won two US House races in the First Congressional District in 2008—a special election in May of that year to replace Roger Wicker, who Governor Barbour had tapped to replace Trent Lott in the Senate, and then election to a full term in November. But 2008 was a heavy Democratic year, led by the Obama surge and widespread disenchantment with Bush and the Republicans, even in solidly red Mississippi. Childers, running as a pro-life, pro-gun, conservative Democrat, won easily in both races against Gregg Davis, the mayor of Southaven, a man who was later convicted of embezzlement and fraud in 2014 and sentenced to state prison.

In 2010, however, it was a different story in a very different political climate. That year, when Childers ran for a second full term, the year of the Tea Party-led swell, he lost by more than thirteen points to a state senator, the late Alan Nunnelee. So Travis Childers, who was not well known around the state, lost his own bid for re-election in his home district by thirteen points to a little known member of the State Senate. Yet, they tried to convince the state that Childers could beat Chris McDaniel in a statewide race even after a Rasmussen poll came out in March 2014 that showed McDaniel with a twelve-point lead on Childers, who was managing just 35 percent support.[30]

Somehow the media managed to use the poll to push a false narrative and to try to boost Childers in the public eye. Cochran "has a 60 percent combined approval," wrote J. Paul Hampton, in the *Sun Herald,* citing some anonymous source. Chris was at 43 percent, which is, Hampton reminded readers, "slightly less than President Barack Obama at 44 percent."[31] It was nothing more than transparently political yellow journalism.

Columnist Sid Salter tried his best to help Childers more directly, boasting of his chances in a general election by hearkening back to a bygone era: "Childers is a highly credible candidate for Mississippi Democrats. Childers was legitimately a so-called 'Blue Dog' Democrat—the political descendants of the 'Boll Weevil' Democrats."[32] The Blue Dogs, though, like the old boll weevils, have long since been exterminated.

It was all sheer "liberal logic," and well as desperation, and we had a laugh about it. But it was no laughing matter to the Establishment. In fact, unbeknownst to most people, the GOP Establishment, in Mississippi and in Washington, would much rather have a Democrat in office than a strong, independent-minded conservative like Chris McDaniel. As Alexandra Jaffe wrote for *The Hill*, national Republicans would be "in a tough spot and forced to decide whether they'll embrace a controversial nominee they've spent months trashing."[33] It's my belief that had Cochran lost to McDaniel, the GOP Establishment would have thrown their support, at least covertly, behind Childers. At the very least, their support would have been lukewarm toward McDaniel. The NRSC (National Republican Senatorial Committee), whose strategist Brad Dayspring had already attacked McDaniel and would do so again in a very big way, gave very timid responses at times to questions about future support of Chris if he won the nomination. And judging by some of the rhetoric during the primary fight, one could reasonably conclude they would rather have a moderate Democrat than Chris McDaniel. This would ensure the status quo is forever maintained— open borders, job-killing global free trade, and money flowing in all directions.

But the charge that he could not win in November did not bother McDaniel, who told me one evening on his back patio just before the vote, "I'm not worried about Travis Childers. Not one bit."[34] And there was solid reasoning behind his confidence. Childers and the Democratic Party had big problems in Mississippi. The last Democrat to win a US Senate seat in Mississippi was long-time Senator John C. Stennis, who won election to his first term in 1948 and his last in 1982 against Haley Barbour. So, as George Will pointed out, Mississippi has not had "a freshman Democratic senator since Harry Truman was president."[35]

Of course Stennis, being a throwback to the old Democratic Party, made this fact meaningless.

The last serious candidate the Democrats ran in a US Senate race in Mississippi was Ronnie Musgrove who, incidentally, was the state's last Democratic governor and had won his gubernatorial race in 1999 not by majority vote but by election in the state House of Representatives when no candidate that year received a constitutionally required majority. After a disastrous, and fiscally irresponsible, term in office, he lost his re-election bid to Haley Barbour in 2003. The last Democrat to win a governor's race with a majority vote was Ray Mabus . . . in 1987, when Ronald Reagan was president.

"Mississippi was not going to send a Democrat to Washington as a United States Senator, and everybody knows it, and every poll we took showed it," Chris told me. "But they praised Childers as an electable Democrat. But Childers couldn't even win his own hometown district. He got blasted by Alan Nunnelee, who was an unimpressive candidate. That would be like me losing South Mississippi and thinking I could win statewide. Mississippi wasn't going anywhere. We were either going to be a liberal Republican state or a conservative Republican state but it was going to be Republican."[36]

Indeed the Democratic Party in Mississippi appears to be dead for all practical purposes. Their bench is depleted, with Attorney General Jim Hood being the only statewide elected official, and he's not wildly popular and could probably never win any other office. Of the four congressional districts, three are solidly in Republican hands. The Fourth District in South Mississippi, once held for two decades by Democrat Gene Taylor before his loss in 2010, probably as strong of a Democrat as one could find in Mississippi, has shifted so far into the GOP column that Taylor switched parties in 2014 and sought Tea Party support in his only hope of regaining his old seat. With voters not trusting his switchover, he lost badly in the primary against Congressman Steven Palazzo, who had defeated him in 2010.

In a face-off against McDaniel in November, Childers would have some serious problems when policy issues came up. While he did not support Obamacare, he said he wouldn't vote to repeal it either, and he backed the trillion-dollar stimulus. Travis Childers, stood little chance, if any at all, to win in Mississippi. The *Weekly Standard*'s John McCormack did not give Democrats a chance at all. *"C'mon, this is Mississippi we're talking about,"* he wrote. "The state is much more Republican than Indiana," referring to the Richard Mourdock debacle in 2012. "If former Democratic governor Ronnie Musgrove couldn't win during the Obama wave of 2008, could any Democrat win in 2014? McDaniel's radio show comments that have surfaced to date–cringe-inducing but not utterly jaw-dropping–are not bad enough to bring him down."[37]

Patrick O'Connor wrote in the *Wall Street Journal*, "Despite other Republicans' attempts to fan concerns about Mr. McDaniel's viability in the general election, Democrats will have a hard time winning this Senate seat, even under the best circumstances. The Democratic candidate, former Rep. Travis Childers, lost his congressional seat by a double-digit margin in 2010."[38] And Nate Cohn of the *New York Times* wrote, "There just might not be a pathway to victory for Democrats in Mississippi, even if Mr. McDaniel wins the nomination and runs a weak campaign."[39]

Sean Trende, of *Real Clear Politics*, wrote that "Childers would have to fundamentally remake the political dynamics of the state to win. I won't say that's impossible, but it will be difficult."[40] While Alexandra Jaffe, in *The Hill* blog, wrote, "Mississippi often favors Republicans. And McDaniel's supporters point to the 2008 Senate race, when former Gov. Ronnie Musgrove (D) lost to Sen. Roger Wicker (R) by double digits in a favorable year for Democrats, as evidence they'll hold the seat regardless of their candidate."[41]

Even those we could fairly conclude are smart folks in Mississippi knew what would happen in a match between Childers and McDaniel. The pro-Cochran rag *Y'all Politics* gave Childers little chance. Frank Corder wrote, very early in the race, that the "political environment is certainly worse for Democrats in Mississippi now, thanks in large part to their national party leaders and folks in new media exposing their ties that bind. The Mississippi Democratic Party simply doesn't have anyone that can legitimately win statewide." The head man at *Y'all*, Alan Lange, tried to trash McDaniel by saying that such a race would be close and certainly "not a gimme for Mississippi Republicans (think

Christine O'Donnell)," but he did concede, in the same paragraph, that Childers was not a strong candidate. "The best state Democrats could do was find a guy that four years ago got beat by 15 points . . . in his own district . . . as an incumbent." Such was the political schizophrenia that often pervaded the Establishment's work.[42]

Even Henry Barbour, of all people, said Childers did not have much of a chance against Chris. "The political environment favors McDaniel," he said, "and sometimes it's hard to overcome the political environment, one that's sick of Washington."[43] And a political environment in Mississippi that's sick of the Barbours and their machine, an operation constructed solely for the purpose of trashing a good man and saving their kingdom. Forgetting all the mud, the lies, and the junk, that is what this race was really all about. At its most basic level, the tremendous fight that raged across the state pitting the Barbour machine against the people was an epic battle for the soul of the party. This race was ideological every bit as much as it was anti-Establishment and anti-incumbent.

For the Barbours and Thad Cochran, it was about maintaining the corrupt status quo, to continue influence peddling and lining their pockets with a grip on power and one hand in the treasury. For Chris, it was about bringing reforms and clean government to advance the lasting interests of the people, not personal gain. Everything was looking good for our side because we believed we had the best candidate with the best message. "Chris has a vision for this country, and he inspires people when he offers it," said McDaniel's colleague, State Senator Michael Watson from the Gulf Coast. "Mississippi loves its incumbents, but we also love to elect young, energetic senators. It's Chris's time now."[44] We all felt it. But before the vote on June 3, as the Barbours saw it all slipping away, they took advantage of an unfortunate incident to try to change the entire game. And they almost succeeded.

CHAPTER 7

A GRAND POWER PLAY:
THE TRUTH ABOUT THE
"NURSING HOME CAPER"

L ate one evening on April 20, 2014, a wannabe investigative journalist named Clayton Kelly, apparently in possession of an entrance pass, walked through the doors of St. Catherine's Village, a senior living facility in Madison, Mississippi, for the sole purpose of photographing Rose Cochran, the wife of Senator Thad Cochran, as she lay helpless in her bed, suffering as she was in the final stages of Alzheimer's disease.

It had been a long-held secret that Cochran had a mistress in Washington, a female staffer named Kay Webber, all while his wife remained at the nursing home, her permanent residence since the year 2000. Many Mississippians, though, did not completely understand the story beyond mere rumors. Most people, particularly those who were not "in the know" politically speaking, might have naturally assumed the public photos of Thad and Kay attending swanky events were those of Mr. and Mrs. Cochran, as the caption of many erroneously stated.

With the encouragement and active assistance from three other conspirators, Kelly wanted to prove to the state, once and for all, that Cochran was, in fact, married and his dalliances with Ms. Kay constituted an illicit affair. The best way to do that, Kelly reasoned, was to show Mrs. Cochran in the nursing home, juxtaposed with pictures of the Senator and the "other woman" in a crudely made Internet video uploaded on his blog. He probably thought such an expose might swing the contest heavily in McDaniel's favor or, in shades of Woodward and Bernstein, might even force Cochran from the race. At the very least, he wanted credit for breaking the story and exposing Cochran as an adulterer, which wouldn't go over well in the Buckle State of the Bible Belt. As he told police investigators later, he wanted to break the story and become a great political journalist. In fact, he thought his escapade was in the mode of a journalist, protected by the First Amendment.[1]

Within hours of the video being uploaded on April 26, members of Chris's campaign were informed of it. "I received a group text the night the scandal first hit," policy advisor Keith Plunkett told me. "I didn't think much of it at the time, and I don't even remember who initiated it. The video just sounded like some kid doing something stupid to me. My response was for us to sit tight, prepare for a possible statement and talk in the morning. The next morning we did a conference call and told all volunteers to put the word out through social media and such, if anybody knew this guy tell him to take it down. It was foolish and uncalled for. That's not representative of what we were trying to do and it is not representative of Chris. A few hours later the video was nowhere to be found. In fact, I've never watched the video to this day."[2] Nor have I.

The disgusting video was nowhere to be found because campaign manager Melanie Sojourner immediately went to work to get the video removed. At 8:54 a.m., on April 26, Sojourner sent out a campaign-wide email: "HELP... someone has created a video about Thad and Kay. It must come down ASAP. Does anyone know where this came from? Please, get this stopped. These volunteers are going to cost us this race over this one topic if it doesn't get stopped. If I find out anyone associated with our staff had anything to do with this it is immediate grounds for dismissal. We have to know we cannot engage in these attacks."

Staffer Scott Brewster replied within minutes, "I don't know him or how to reach him but it came from a guy named Clayton. Not sure if it's his first or last name. I can try to reach him. Want me to try?" Other staffers chimed in with offers to scour Twitter and other social media platforms to find the offending person and get the video pulled. Word filtered down through the grapevine, and the video disappeared soon after it was posted. Sojourner sent out another campaign-wide email a few hours later: "I'm being told he's been contacted and handled. Let me know if y'all see anything else. Please continue to monitor and scrub throughout day. Regional Directors ... Please make sure you have gotten word to all your volunteers. I want to know why this started! Who pushed for it?"[3]

It took nearly three weeks to sort that out. But the video was down just a few hours after it was uploaded on the Internet. And everyone went back to work. End of story, or so the campaign thought.

Kay Webber began working in Senator Cochran's DC office in August 1981, just two and a half years after his first election to the Senate. How long they have known each other beyond that has not been determined. What is known, however, is that Cochran and Webber were much closer than the typical working relationship, as the two have been spotted on numerous occasions in DC-area restaurants and at social functions. Cochran's campaign spokesman, Jordan Russell, bent over backwards to assure the public that Kay Webber was not in an intimate relationship with the Senator. She "is a member of the staff and a trusted aside, and any other suggestion is silly gossip."[4]

But was it really just silly gossip? Chris did not want to venture into the Cochran-Webber affair, at least as far as adultery was concerned, and specifically told me to focus instead on the issues at hand, just in case I got any ideas. And I must admit, it was mighty tempting. But lucky for us, as the campaign unfolded, more and more came out about this unusual relationship.

On the website Legistorm.com, which is a non-partisan, for-profit company that researches, verifies, and publishes information about members of Congress and congressional staff, as well as Cochran's official Senate webpage, Webber is listed as an executive assistant and director of special services, but just what those "special services" actually are, one can only speculate.[5] With this special relationship, two legitimate campaign issues emerged very quickly: Webber's expensive Washington home and the extensive travel that both she and the Senator engaged in for at least a dozen years.

First, despite the limitations imposed by thirty-three years on a congressional staffer's salary, which at the time was just over $70,000,

Kay Webber owned a home just blocks from Capitol Hill that in 2014 listed for more than $1 million, and perhaps as much as $1.7 million. Furthermore, as early as 2003, just three years after his wife was placed in the nursing home, Cochran began listing the Webber house as his primary residence, even on Federal Election Commission forms and other documents. And Webber's financial statements also list "rental income," presumably from her "boss" who was living in the basement, or so he and his campaign contended.[6]

The house itself is not a concern; the financial wheeling and dealing that it took to obtain it is. Erick Erickson at *Red State* reported:

> According to individuals who have reviewed the transaction, when Webber purchased the house, she had a co-signor on the home who was a donor to Cochran and who listed her own occupation as homemaker. So a congressional staffer making $72,000.00 and a homemaker who donated to Cochran went in together and bought a million-dollar home.

> That homemaker's husband, William Shows, was the head of the Pearl River Valley electric cooperative. Electric cooperatives have been the number one source of campaign contributions to Thad Cochran over the years. Sources tell me the homemaker's husband also sat on the board of the bank that helped finance the transaction.

> That would be Trustmark Bank, which is currently having FEC trouble over a campaign loan to benefit Cochran.

> Likewise, Trustmark's CEO, Richard Hickson, contributed to Cochran's campaign in 2000, 2001, and 2007. In 2008, Trustmark got $215 million in TARP funding from the federal government.

> Now, here's the real kicker. Ms. Webber and Mrs. Shows bought the house for $1 million with, it appears, $200,000.00 down and a $800,000.00 mortgage in 2001. At the time Ms. Webber's

congressional salary was less than $100,000.00 a year and Mrs. Shows, who only had a 1% interest in the home according to individuals who have seen the paperwork, listed her occupation as a homemaker. A year after the purchase, Mrs. Shows gave Ms. Webber her interest in the home making Ms. Webber the sole owner.[7]

So Webber got help in securing a home loan by a member of the board of directors of Trustmark Bank, the same bank that is connected to Thad Cochran and, during the 2014 Senate campaign, gave a questionable loan to the Barbour-backed, Cochran-supporting Mississippi Conservatives Super PAC. William T. Shows, the husband of the woman who cosigned for the loan, served on the bank's board. It might also be noted that William T. Shows is the brother of Ronnie Shows, a former Mississippi congressman and longtime state politician.

More questions came when it was discovered that Shows was dropped from the loan about eighteen months later, in October 2002, and the loan was refinanced with Webber as the sole owner. But how would this be possible if her financial condition did not change? Her salary did conveniently increase from $72,000 to $91,000, but certainly not enough to warrant re-financing a million-dollar property. However, Cochran moved into the house sometime in 2003 and began paying Webber "rent," supposedly to live in what they contended was a basement apartment. Unless his rent payment to her was astronomical, it's quite likely the re-financing was the result of pure cronyism.

And the house must be quite a swanky place, because it was used as a fund-raising venue, which may also have been illegal. Aside from fund-raisers on behalf of Cochran, two others were held at the Webber House: One for Sheila Jackson-Lee and another for Charlie Rangel, both very liberal Democratic members of Congress. Why allow fund-raisers for these two? And why was this not investigated by the FEC as an obvious violation of the Hatch Act? Webber, as a federal employee, is barred from political activity. But, as this Senate race showcased, the Establishment doesn't play by the rules.[8]

Most Mississippians believed Cochran's main residence was in Oxford, and no one really thought anything of it. But to a reporter for

Politico in 2012, he said he visited Mississippi eighteen times a year. That seemed a rather strange answer, as if one was discussing visits to grandma's house, and was far less than other members who "went home" and not simply "visited" the states they happened to represent in Congress. The fact is Washington was Thad Cochran's home and had been for decades.[9]

When he wasn't "home" in DC, or "visiting" Mississippi as a guest, Cochran was jetting around the globe with Ms. Kay, his trusty aid for "special services." *Breitbart*'s Matthew Boyle did an exhaustively researched piece in which he discovered that, according to the *Congressional Record*, "where trip details including cost are listed, Webber has traveled with Cochran at taxpayer expense to 42 countries across five continents since 2002," on at least 33 separate trips. He continued:

Cochran and Webber traveled eight times to France, five times to Italy, four times to Israel, and twice to Japan.

The full list of countries they traveled to includes: Italy, France, Brussels, Ireland, the United Kingdom, Belgium, Hungary, Russia, Norway, Germany, Spain, Portugal, Greece, Malta, Austria, and Czech Republic in Europe; Colombia, Brazil, Paraguay, Uruguay, Argentina, and Chile in South America; Guatemala, and Mexico in North and Central America; Japan, China, Kyrgyzstan, Malaysia, Vietnam, Hong Kong, the Republic of the Philippines, and South Korea in Asia; Turkey, Jordan, Israel, Azerbaijan, Oman, and United Arab Emirates in the Middle East; to Morocco, Egypt, Cape Verde, and South Africa in Africa.[10]

Government watchdog groups found the trips strange indeed. Bill Allison of the Sunlight Foundation called the excursions "a little unusual," especially given that Ms. Webber has no experience or expertise in foreign affairs. "Generally speaking, when you look at these types of Congressional travel, they will–if they bring somebody–bring a person who knows the subject matter. They won't bring the same person over and over again." Tom Fitton of Judicial Watch added that the trips were peculiar. "We've investigated these CODELS [congressional delegations] and many tend to be wasteful junkets, so it is fair to ask about any frequent fliers," he said.[11]

Cochran spokesman Jordan Russell defended the Senator's actions by pulling out his ever-handy liberal playbook. "This is sexist," he said. "Why are they questioning her qualifications? All members of Congress have aides that travel with them. If a male had been working with him for thirty-three years, would that be questioned?"[12] But we countered that if Senator Cochran had been living with the male aide in question, and attended many functions with him, then yes it would have been questioned also. Of course Russell did conveniently forget to mention that on some of these trips, Webber attended "spouse" activities with other congressional wives, making it a strange liaison indeed.[13]

Nor did Russell disclose why the Senator and his female aide traveled to California to explore the vast wine country. What legislative business a Mississippi Senator had there is unknown. Legistorm provides scant reasoning on the purpose of the trips. All it says for the California trip, dubbed a "Report on activities in the California wine industry," was "To conduct a fact-finding program on issues of importance to the wine industry."[14] And what issues those might be and how they relate to Mississippi, since the state doesn't grow grapes of any kind, is not known, nor was it disclosed anywhere else. But any reasonably minded, honest adult can conclude what trips to the California wine vineyards, by two adults living in the same house, actually entailed. Sadly, though, Mississippi's taxpayers, many of whom could never afford such a trip, worked hard so that Thad and Kay could enjoy a multitude of these types of junkets. And that became the central aspect of our focus.

Since it involved public funds, making it fair game according to our campaign guidelines, I did my own research. The first bill Thad Cochran ever co-sponsored in the House of Representatives in January 1973 was HR 2364, an act "to prohibit travel at Government expense outside the United States by Members of Congress who have been defeated, who have resigned, or retired."[15] The reason for this proposed piece of legislation was to end a corrupt practice, whereby members who were ending their congressional careers, either by choice or by force, were taking overseas excursions, usually labeled "fact finding missions," on the taxpayer's dime, a nice little "reward" before leaving office. Unsurprisingly, the bill failed.

I found it very interesting when looking at the trip data that Thad and Kay had visited eighteen different foreign countries from January 1 to September 30, 2013. This is significant because it was widely speculated around the state that Cochran was planning to retire and not run for a seventh term. At one point in the campaign he told a *Washington Post* reporter, "I thought it was time for me to retire. I thought I'd served long enough."[16] So, since he did not announce that he was indeed running again until November 2013, this looked like a career-ending trip blitz for the couple, and just more evidence that Cochran's words and actions were never in agreement.

As for the juicier details, Cochran's supporters and campaign cronies tried to allege that we smeared the great Senator with allegations of an affair with Webber but the McDaniel campaign never, at any time, brought up the 'adultery' issue, refusing to even mention the word. Unfortunately there were supporters around the state that took to Twitter and Facebook to put the adultery issue in the spotlight but the McDaniel campaign moved to snuff those out immediately.

But even though Jordan Russell and other members of Cochran's team "lied like gentlemen" to hide the relationship, once calling any suggestion that the association was anything other than professional "outrageous and offensive and the dirtiest form of politics," events eventually showcased their fibs and proved our side right once again. On December 12, 2014, a little more than a month after the end of the fall campaign, Cochran's wife, Rose, died. Strangely enough, Cochran brought his "special services" aide Kay Webber with him to the funeral in New Albany, Mississippi, where Mrs. Cochran was buried, and the next day, as unbelievable—or sickening—as it sounds, the two of them were spotted in town shopping for jewelry.[17]

Five months later, on May 23, 2015, Thad Cochran and Kay Webber were married in Gulfport, Mississippi, although his staff in Washington lied about it for weeks, as rumors of the planned nuptials began to leak.[18] The whole sordid tale of Thad and Kay was either

Mississippi's political Lie of the Century, or one heck of a whirlwind romance. But as Occam's Razor holds, the simplest explanation is usually the right one. The available evidence is all the proof anyone needs at this point to verify that Thad Cochran dumped his wife in a nursing home in 2000, lived permanently in Washington, and carried on an adulterous relationship with a member of his staff with whom he shared a home and whom he later married mere months after his wife's death.

As the campaign moved into the final month of May 2014, the word was getting around about this "special relationship" between Thad and Kay, and more specifically the obvious financial corruption involved, as well as the taxpayer funded trips, so nothing else was really needed to provide proof of Cochran's major character flaw. The best thing the McDaniel campaign could do at this point was to simply let the matter be and allow the people to draw their own conclusions. As for Chris, he was riding high, climbing to the lead in the polls, winning on the issues, so nefarious hanky-panky was uncalled for, and just plain wrong in a campaign for US Senate.

On the night of May 16, nearly four weeks after Clayton Kelly snapped the infamous photo of Rose Cochran, and nearly three weeks after he uploaded his crude video, Kelly found himself in handcuffs and on the way to jail. Early the next morning, around 7 a.m., I received a campaign-wide e-mail, which included the vast volunteer network, from campaign manager Melanie Sojourner. She was blunt and to the point: "No one talk to the media about it and if anyone associated with the campaign had anything to do with it, then that individual would be fired or, in the case of unpaid staff and volunteers, disassociated."

I was completely in the dark and a bit shaken by the news. I had never heard of Clayton Kelly or about any video, since I had been out of state for a couple of weeks. Immediately after reading the e-mail, I Googled "Clayton Kelly" and nothing came up about any arrest. About two hours later, the Internet was humming with news of the apprehension. This gap led to speculation and accusations that the McDaniel campaign must have been involved since Sojourner, as campaign manager, knew about Kelly's arrest before the media did.

It got worse when the Cochran campaign released the audio of a voice mail Melanie left very early on the morning of May 17 to Cochran campaign manager Kirk Sims, whose wife, if you recall, works for the influential law firm Butler Snow. In the wake of the arrest, Melanie reached out to Cochran's camp to assure them that no McDaniel staff member had anything to do with the photograph or the video. She wanted to personally assure Sims that the McDaniel team was in no way involved. It was a courtesy call and the right thing to do. When Sims did not answer, most likely a deliberate act on his part, she left a voice mail for him. Sims then released the recorded message to the media in an attempt to twist her words and use them against us.

Keith Plunkett also characterized it as sleazy. "The problem was the people running the Cochran campaign were not respectful or responsible people. They would have used anything they could to injure Chris, whether it was true or not."[19] And that would include releasing a personal voice mail about an unfortunate political incident.

Initially the McDaniel campaign team, including Melanie Sojourner, were, like me, also in the dark as to what exactly was transpiring in Madison County. "At the time I left my message to Kirk," Melanie told me, "I absolutely had no idea that there was any connection between the arrest made on May 16th and an Internet video that had briefly circulated on social media a month earlier. After all, I actually had never seen the video and still haven't seen it to this day. All I was told was that it was a video about Thad and Kay. The arrest on May 16th was of a guy taking a picture of Mrs. Rose Cochran. I had no idea the two were connected."[20] It would take some time for all the sordid details to emerge.

Later in the day on May 17, after more details broke, the McDaniel campaign released its own statement about the incident. "The McDaniel campaign found out about the break-in when a local political blog posted about it at 11:40 p.m. last night. Senator McDaniel has denounced the break-in and called Senator Cochran to extend his condolences. It is unconscionable for the Cochran campaign and the liberal media to use the act of a sick individual to lob despicable accusations."

As for the phone call to Cochran, the so-called "last gentleman" Senator never returned McDaniel's call. In fact, throughout the months-long campaign, which lasted from October 2013 to June 2014, Cochran and McDaniel never spoke. Not one single time. That's how shielded the Cochran team kept their man and another indication that Thad was no gentleman at all. But Chris did discuss the incident with the media and did a number of interviews on the day of Kelly's arrest. He didn't duck the media firestorm; he addressed their questions, as a true leader should do.

A few days later it got much worse. On May 22 police from Madison arrested three other men—John Mary, Richard Sager, and Mark Mayfield—in connection with the nursing home incident. This was no longer a lone-nut theory. And that's when I got a sick, sinking feeling down in my stomach. *This madness could very well end the campaign right here and now*, I thought. All the hard work everyone was putting in was about to be thrown away in an instant by this incident. I felt so bad for my friend.

Although we had nothing to do with the insanity, that's not the story we would get from the media in Mississippi or across the country. They were only interested in filth and pushing such a juicy tale as long as they could. In fact they tried to have it both ways: Making Chris McDaniel part of the conspiracy but, at the same time, wanting to know the connections he must have had with Kelly in order to get the video removed so quickly. Yet of this media narrative no one ever asked the most basic question: If Chris had been a part of this shameful conspiracy to smear Thad Cochran, why would he have wanted the video taken down mere hours after it was uploaded?

Soon fear spread among the many staffers and volunteers of the McDaniel campaign, who were frightened that the authorities, as well as the Cochran camp, which, unbeknownst to us at the time were working hand in hand, might try to falsely tie one of them to it. It took on the aura of a witch-hunt. Who would they go after next in their zeal to tie McDaniel to the scandal? Would this be another McCarthy kangaroo court where the slightest connection, with no real evidence, would be enough to hang one of us?

The possibility became even more realistic when the judge in the case set very large bonds for each of the conspirators: $250,000 to $500,000. "People charged with murder can get bonds less than

$250,000," said Merrida Coxwell, Mark Mayfield's lawyer.[21] And all of this was over a simple picture. Only Mayfield had the funds to post bond and John Mary was released without any jail time because of medical conditions. Kelly and Sager remained in jail for at least a week, with Sager held on the highest bond, a half a million dollars. Everyone suspected that they were squeezing these two for more information on a high campaign official or any connection to McDaniel, real or imagined.

The media, though, was ecstatic over the ordeal. In fact, the very day news hit about Kelly's arrest, the *Clarion Ledger*'s story contained a photo of Kelly and McDaniel together, which had been taken at a campaign event. They also dug up photos of McDaniel together with Mark Mayfield and John Mary. Politicians take thousands of photos with supporters and no one does a background check on any of them. But none of that mattered at this point.

Though the media couldn't help but to compare Chris with Richard Nixon and the scandal that brought him down, the truth is Watergate in the Magnolia State this was not. Like so much in this campaign, the state's media never reported the real truth behind this incident. Nothing was as it seemed. We were about to see a grand political scheme, a shameful power play perpetrated by Cochran and his cronies.

The real story of the infamous Mississippi nursing home caper was not the incident itself but the Cochran campaign's use of the "break-in" for political purposes, in essence politicizing the abuse of Rose Cochran for Thad Cochran's own gain. Clayton Kelly was charged with exploitation of a vulnerable adult, but it was Thad Cochran who was truly guilty of that charge. His was not the action of a loving husband, an honorable gentleman, which he and his friends always claimed he was, nor was it the actions of a strong candidate with a robust campaign holding a commanding lead over a hapless opponent. Even though the Cochran camp had been releasing polling data for months, some even showing Cochran up as many as seventeen points, they were, in fact, behind in the race, and their desperation in the wake of the nursing home incident is proof positive. The truth is, Thad Cochran and his team knew of the photograph at least as early as the day the video hit the Internet on April 26 but held the information nearly three weeks before notifying the police.[22]

When asked by reporters about the violation of his ailing wife's privacy, Cochran's only answer was that it was "bizarre." What was bizarre, though, was Cochran's response to the photograph and the video. This was an incident that if it had involved any honorable family in Mississippi or anywhere in the country, the police would have been called on the very day it happened. Rather than call the police, Cochran contacted his personal lawyer, Donald Clark, who works at Butler Snow, the firm of Barbour and the elites. Clark later told *Breitbart* news that when he learned of the incident, he "gathered appropriate background information on [Cochran's] behalf and looked at his options for both civil and criminal remedies. That resulted ultimately in our contacting the appropriate law enforcement authorities on his behalf and turning this matter over to them." To the *New York Times*, Clark said that he and the campaign "did not delay our response to this incident due to any political issues or timing." He told *Business Insider*, "We believed a crime may have been committed and we immediately notified the City of Madison Police Department." But that was simply not true.[23]

First, we know for an absolute certainty that the police were not the first authorities notified about the incident. In addition to his lawyer, Cochran also contacted Madison mayor Mary Hawkins Butler, not the police. Second, the Cochran campaign admitted to the press, from spokesman Jordan Russell's own mouth, that they knew of the video the day it hit the Internet on April 26. And third, we know the campaign waited nearly three weeks before contacting the "appropriate law enforcement authorities" because, according to the Madison Police Department's own news release about the Kelly arrest, they did not receive information about the nursing home incident until May 15. So that conclusively proves that it was at least nineteen days, essentially three weeks, before the *appropriate* authorities were, in fact, notified. It was simply more lies and deceit from Thad Cochran and his "righteous" campaign staff.[24]

We all knew that Chris McDaniel had nothing to do with such a dastardly deed. It was completely out of his character and contrary to his life thus far. And after the Cochran camp's all-out oppo research, they knew that too but waited nineteen days before releasing the information for two reasons: political timing and to try to determine McDaniel's liability. They wanted to see if there was some kind of connection to the conspirators—even if they had to make one up. A constant media pounding might throw enough question marks in the minds of a sufficient number of people to persuade them to switch their vote or stay home, either of which would benefit Cochran. But despite all their lies and "explanations," when Cochran decided to wait for the perfect time to strike at McDaniel, it ceased to be a criminal matter and became a political opportunity. They did not see it as the terrible act it was but as an opportunity to turn the race, and that's exactly what they did. It was political opportunism at its very worst.

Breaking the story in mid-May was Cochran's "October Surprise." If Cochran had gone to the police in April when the photo was taken, arrests would have been made and the press would have broken the news with more than a month of campaigning still ahead, thereby allowing McDaniel sufficient time to get his message out and salvage his campaign. Holding on to the information for three weeks pushed it closer to the primary vote on June 3, which would make it much harder for Chris to weather the ensuing political firestorm. The Cochran-Barbour squad was looking for a knockout blow against their most dangerous challenger.

The second part of their strategy was connecting Chris to the black bag job. One of the first things Cochran's camp wanted to know was just how McDaniel's team knew about Kelly's arrest before the media reported it. And the "neutral" party hacks let it be known what they thought about the incident, throwing out all vestiges of objectivity. Brian Walsh, who once worked as a spokesman for the NRSC but was a consultant to Cochran, tweeted, "If the McDaniel camp had no involvement in [the] Cochran incident how did they know about the arrest before everyone else?"[25]

The answer was simple: Many people knew of the arrest before the media reported it. *Jackson Jambalaya*, a well-known Jackson blog run by the legendary "Kingfish," who has numerous connections with the police and the criminal courts, reported the arrest the night before at approximately 11:40 p.m.[26] Sojourner picked it up from there, as did a great many others. It just didn't hit the mainstream media until the following morning. As Melanie told me, "That night, well after midnight, I ran across the article posted to *Jackson Jambalaya*. I remember my heart just sank and I thought, 'What the heck! This is maddening. Who is this person? Are they crazy? Who would do something like this?'"[27]

But it was the involvement and subsequent arrest of John Mary that gave the Cochran camp the strongest connection they needed to make a case that McDaniel was involved in the "break-in." Mary had been a frequent guest cohost of *The Right Side Radio Show* for several years, sitting alongside Jack Fairchilds. Jack had been the original sidekick from the show's inception until 2007 when Chris left to began his career in the legislature. With Jack moving up to serve as the show's main host, numerous cohosts filled the number two spot, including me, Lewis Garvin, and later on, John Mary, known by his radio name "John Bert."

At times, Mary had filled in for Jack as the main host, and I had been on the show as his cohost numerous times. Armed with this information, the Cochran camp made the false claim that John Mary had been McDaniel's cohost on *The Right Side*, which was a bald-faced lie. Chris McDaniel had never, not even once, sat on the same show with John Mary. This was a disingenuous deceit crafted deep within the bowels of Cochran's snake-pit campaign.

Richard Sager, originally from Vicksburg, listed his home address as Laurel, where he was then living while teaching and coaching soccer. When Cochran's camp discovered Sager was living in Jones County, they concluded that Sager must have been a close "friend" of McDaniel's and ran with it. They produced a despicable ad—probably when the photograph emerged—that alleged McDaniel's direct ties to the conspiracy. It was one of those rare occasions in history where the Left and the Establishment Republicans were on the same side. They were working in collusion with one another to defeat the conservative. And we saw that time and time again in every press report. They were doing everything they could to tie it to the McDaniel campaign, all while we were doing everything we could never to even mention the word *adultery*.[28]

Richard Sager, who was arrested for his involvement in the plot, told me explicitly that the McDaniel campaign was in no way involved in the scheme. "The campaign had absolutely nothing to do with it," Sager said. "We didn't want the campaign to know about what we were up to and worked to keep it quiet. Basically we went rogue." In fact, Sager conveyed to me an important aspect of the case that seemed lost on everyone—the police had the phones and computers of all the suspects. Had there been a connection with Chris McDaniel, "they would have found it."[29]

The campaign was in the clear; there was never any doubt of that, but the damage had been done. It cost us eleven points in four days. Although we bounced back some, instead of being up by eight points down the final stretch, the campaign now found itself three points *down*. It was a huge turn of events, but the most tragic aspect of this terrible deed was the fate that befell Mark Mayfield. Although I never met him or spoke with him, I've never heard anyone say a negative word about him and his lone e-mail to me, a complimentary note sent a few weeks before the incident, was quite gracious. He seemed to be a genuinely nice guy who was passionate about his country and wanted to help reform the government. But after his arrest he fell into a deep state of depression and according to rumors had lost most of his legal clients. It was too much for the man to take. On Friday, June 27, 2014, just days after the primary runoff in which Chris ultimately lost to Cochran, Mark Mayfield committed suicide in the garage of his family home near Jackson. The battle of Mississippi had now spilled blood.

CHAPTER 8

THE VICTORY: JUNE 3, 2014

Thad Cochran had never lost a race in his political career, from his first campaign for the US House in 1972 until his election to a sixth term in the Senate in 2008. But on June 3, 2014 he tasted defeat for the first time at the hands of a young state senator with none of the money, power, privilege, or name recognition Cochran had, all while fending off the onslaught of negative attacks by the Establishment machine and their appalling use of the nursing home scandal. But the aftermath of the primary vote would provide an opportunity for the Cochran-Barbour team to once again deceive the public and hide evidence of vote malfeasance.

In the wake of the nursing home trickery, Chris made a brilliant political move that took the steam right out of Cochran's deceptive sail – he invited former Alaska governor Sarah Palin to come to Ellisville, Mississippi one week before the vote. The good people of Jones County loved Sarah Palin, and with Jack Fairchilds working tirelessly to organize an effective ground game, her appearance would give us a huge boost in the heart of the Pine Belt where we needed it most.

Of course on the day Governor Palin arrived no one was surprised to see the Republican Establishment in Mississippi attacking her as hard as Democrats did in 2008, referring to her as a "loser" and making other nasty remarks on social media. This only showed their true colors, as well as their desperation. And since no one of Palin's stature had traveled to Mississippi in support of Cochran, his despicable campaign resorted to attacking any messenger who came to help Chris.

People came from far and wide to see Governor Palin as she spoke at Jones County Junior College in the very heart of Ellisville. It was an overflow crowd, and Palin delivered as usual:

> We need to elect those who can undo a lot of what's been going on in Washington these days and to re-establish that foundation upon which America was built—that foundation that Chris McDaniel believes in and has lived out, that foundation based on freedom and right priorities when it comes to budgeting your tax dollars and where they will be spent. . . . We know that Chris is running for the right reasons. I wouldn't be here today if I didn't believe that. Of all these candidates we want to support and elect into office, Chris is running with a servant's heart and that's what we need in the United States Senate. Mississippi, we are proud of some of the good guys in the Senate like Ted Cruz and Mike Lee—we promised them reinforcements. Mississippi's effort in that is to send Chris McDaniel to the United States Senate in service to this great country.[1]

But she also talked about all the negative stories, namely the nursing home scandal, then roiling the campaign. "Those are distractions meant to take your eye off the ball," Palin said. "What the media's doing is that same old noise—that blah, blah blah, white noise in the background. The intention is to distract," something she had a lot of familiarity with. "I think I do know what the [McDaniel] family is going through on this journey," she said. "The family wants to be strong. And they need to have from you all a hedge of protection provided by a prayer shield so that they remain strong because the journey is in fact on June 3 just beginning for your next United States Senator Chris McDaniel."[2]

Palin was the talk of the Pine Belt for days, completely wiping out discussion of the nursing home incident and throwing the Cochran campaign off its game. In fact, the whole scandal seemed to be losing steam, having little effect on hard-core McDaniel supporters and not as much on undecided voters as the Cochran camp wanted. But talk was over. It was now the moment of truth. Time to vote.

On Election Day we were all nervous, to say the least, with questions racing through the mind of everyone. What would happen? Would we win it tonight? Or would the presence of a virtually unknown third candidate, Thomas Carey, push the race into a runoff? A runoff would mean three more weeks of work, which I relished, but it would also mean more attacks and mudslinging. These thoughts were on my mind as I walked into the Hattiesburg Convention Center that evening hoping that the gathering of supporters would soon turn into a victory party.

Rather than sit in the stress-filled war room, with the ever-present smorgasbord of Rolaids and Pepto-Bismol, Jack and I worked the crowd talking to old friends, eating catered food, and watching the returns roll in. The excitement only grew as things were beginning to look solid for our man in many key counties, including quite a few in North Mississippi, notably Desoto, which Cochran expected to carry but was losing badly.

As we watched the vote totals shift back and forth for a few hours, as they always do on election night, we soon began to notice that something was amiss in Hinds County, in Jackson, the bastion of Republican boss Pete Perry. The returns in Hinds steadily rolled in until the count reached 60 percent. Then they miraculously stopped and remained at 60 percent for hours, well into the early morning.

As a historian I well knew that they were likely pulling the oldest political trick in the electoral book. Throughout American history, political shysters always held back a few precincts where they exercised complete dominance so that if a race were nail-bitingly close, and their candidate was behind, the shortfall could be closed with a few "extra" votes in those precincts. The most notable case where this happened was Lyndon Johnson's great "victory" in Texas in 1948. This was likely what was happening in Hinds County, especially given the fact that Chris had topped the 50 percent threshold statewide at the exact point when the count suddenly stopped. Cochran was staring an outright defeat squarely in the face. Jack looked at me and said what we were both thinking, "Pete Perry's up to something!"

Pete "the Cheat" Perry, as he was known, the boss of Hinds County, reminded me of Boss Tweed of Tammany Hall, and it was not just that they both had a pudgy physique. William Marcy Tweed was perhaps America's most notorious political boss, which is really saying something. He pocketed taxpayer money, broke laws, and stole votes by the wagonload. He once skimmed millions off the construction of a county courthouse that was originally estimated to cost $250,000 but ended up with a price tag of $13 million, a massive amount in the 1870s. But Tweed met his end with the rise of reformer Samuel J. Tilden, who saw to it that the old political boss died in prison.

Although Perry isn't in the same category as Boss Tweed when it comes to smarts or cunning, he certainly deserves the same fate. Chris McDaniel was our Samuel J. Tilden, who could bring down the established order in Mississippi. That was the goal anyway. The Establishment saw him that way too so he had to be destroyed one way or another. And Boss Perry would do his part.

Like most political bosses, Perry has spent a lifetime working in government in a variety of capacities, holding various patronage jobs in the administrations of Reagan and the first George Bush. His positions in the bureaucracy were due to nothing more than his political connections. His most well-known station was as state director of rural development in the USDA, a $150,000-a-year job that requires a presidential appointment and, at least since 1989, the blessing of Mississippi's senior Senator, in this case Thad Cochran. Perry's performance, though, was less than stellar, to put it mildly, as he was fired in 1983 for completely mismanaging the office. Consider for a moment just how hard it is to get fired from a federal bureaucracy for mismanagement. Yet Perry managed to do just that. But that was not the end of the story. Months after he was canned, Perry was caught in the USDA office rifling through files late on a Sunday night. Apparently Perry somehow forgot to turn in all of his keys upon his dismissal.[3]

Pete Perry was not Cochran's only bad move in recommendations for appointments to the state director job, though. Don Barrett had to leave after he extended a $9 million loan to the secretary and girlfriend of his brother-in-law. And Nick Walters (absolutely no relation to the author) was indicted by a federal grand jury for a conflict of interest. He was attempting to get a rural development loan for a hospital in

Natchez but had a financial interest in the facility. He also lied to investigators about it, adding further charges. And what's more, he'd already been under scrutiny for lavish travel expenses. Mississippi corruption and cronyism knows no bounds.[4]

And that corruption would extend to vote theft. Boss Tweed once said, "As long as I count the votes, what are you going to do about it?" This seemed to be Perry's attitude in a nutshell, especially on this important election night.

Hinds County is a liberal Democratic stronghold in general elections. Obama carried 72 percent of the vote in 2012. But it's also a fortress for Thad Cochran in GOP primaries, because he's more leftist than traditional Republican and because Pete Perry is the county GOP chairman, not to mention the often-overlooked fact that one of the five county election commissioners is Connie Cochran, Thad's own sister-in-law. Therefore, it's not unusual for Ole Thad to get two-thirds of the vote, and of course it's a prime location to create new votes and to simply keep counting until the total comes out the "right" way.

After the crowd dispersed, and as midnight approached, Jack and I drove over to the hotel that housed the "war room" and sat in on a meeting of the campaign's extensive staff, minus the candidate and the campaign manager. The focus of the meeting, headed by Dane Maxwell, then serving as the campaign's director of operations, was Hinds County. And everyone knew what this meant. There was simply no way Cochran would win the primary that night; he had to hope for a runoff. Chris still could, so the Cochran-Barbour machine had to hold McDaniel under the 50 percent threshold, and that's where Perry was likely earning his hefty pay, which we will detail later.

Before the meeting broke up, Dane asked Scott Brewster, the campaign's coalition coordinator, to drive up to the Hinds County courthouse to "see what's going on." With numbers still trickling in, it was obvious that officials were still hard at work "counting" votes to make sure McDaniel remained at 49.5 percent, thus pushing the race into a runoff. Dane never said anything about busting through the doors or going in a window, much less tampering with ballots. The mission was simply to see what was transpiring at the Hinds County Courthouse.

Joining Brewster were Tea Party activist Janis Lane and a member of the Southern Baptist Convention, Rob Chambers. Not exactly the Watergate Five. Lane, in fact, phoned Pete Perry seeking his explanation as to why, after the midnight hour, 100 percent of the votes still had not been counted in Hinds County. She also wanted to let him know that the trio was headed to the courthouse. Perry did not answer the call, so she left a voice message and they proceeded to the courthouse to get some answers themselves.

When they arrived, they were "directed by uniformed personnel" to a door that was propped open. They entered the building thinking this was the way they were to go to where the officials were counting votes. When they let the heavy door shut behind them, it knocked over the prop and magnetically locked, trapping the trio inside. With no way out, Lane called Pete Perry for help. "Eventually a Sheriff's officer showed up and opened the door to let them out."[5]

When asked by the press why the three were in the courthouse, Boss Perry was his usual sanctimonious self. "I don't know. I know I wouldn't walk into a courthouse at 2 o'clock in the morning by myself or with somebody else and just walk around inside the building. I'm not going to go into a public building just because somehow or another I happened to find a door that was unlocked," said Perry, apparently with no sense of irony given his own "undercover" work in his former USDA office.[6]

This led to yet another flurry of activity by the media. The *Daily Beast* read: "Mississippi Tea Party Goes Watergate." The Ben Jacobs piece essentially described the McDaniel campaign as the second coming of Nixon and the plumbers.[7] Others followed suit at such a rapid-fire pace, the Cochran's slime team was having a field day. Cochran campaign spokesman Jordan Russell took to the airwaves to push a false narrative with a media that was becoming increasingly anti-McDaniel. "They cannot keep themselves out of trouble with the law," he said. "This is a campaign that is out of control." He went on to describe Chris's campaign as one full of criminals. "We've had two separate criminal investigations in one campaign. Is this the kind of person that we want representing our party?" he said. "It is astonishing that the same people who are up to their eyeballs in four felons breaking into a nursing home are also up to their eyeballs in potentially breaking in somewhere else again. And this time they can't deny that a paid staffer is involved. At some point you got to say enough is enough. How many more arrests of allies and McDaniel team members before we can say this has gone too far?"[8]

In the end, after two investigations into the strange courthouse caper, no criminal charges were filed against the three McDaniel supporters because there was no criminal activity. The district attorney and the Hinds County Sheriff both exonerated Brewster, Lane, and Chambers of any wrongdoing. But this was yet another case of the Cochran team pushing a false narrative to keep any prying eyes from seeing exactly what they were doing with the ballots in Hinds County. Though they accused McDaniel's people of seeking to tamper with the ballots, in truth that's exactly what Boss Perry was up to his neck in. Even Hinds County constable John Lewis was well aware of Perry and his vote counting ways. "I was a strong advocate for the McDaniel campaign to send somebody down there that night to oversee Pete Perry," he told a local Jackson affiliate. "I don't think Pete Perry should go unsupervised counting an election." Lewis also admitted to the press that the door of the courthouse that the trio entered was, in fact, broken so there was no way they could get themselves out.[9]

In truth, there were no criminals on Chris's staff, on the campaign payroll, or close to the candidate. In fact, anyone of questionable character was shunted aside, and a number of people were. However, that is not the case with Cochran and his close associates. On June 23, the day before the runoff vote, police arrested Lee Ellis Blair, a paid Cochran campaign staffer, field representative, and member of the Desoto County GOP executive committee, for deliberately stealing and destroying McDaniel campaign signs the day before the runoff vote. For his actions, he was let go. "He's fired," said Jordan Russell in an e-mail to *Breitbart*. "Unlike Chris McDaniel, we don't tolerate that type of behavior."[10] But which McDaniel paid staffer had ever exhibited "that type of behavior," or had been arrested for anything at all, he did not say. There were no criminals, and Russell knew that. He was just lying again.

Owing to the corrupt culture of Mississippi, criminal acts have reached Cochran's DC office. Ann Copeland had been an aide to Thad Cochran for nearly three decades but was tangled up in the Jack Abramoff scandal in 2009. While working for Cochran in DC, Copeland swapped legislative favors for tickets to concerts, including the pop group NSYNC, Paul McCartney, and Green Day; hockey games; ice-skating events; $25,000 worth of meals; and even the circus. She worked hard on behalf of one of Abramoff's biggest clients, the Mississippi Band of Choctaw Indians. Abramoff, in return, rewarded her. "She gets everything she wants," he wrote in one e-mail.[11]

So just what did Abramoff get in return for all those gifts? Senator Thad Cochran went to bat for the Choctaws, writing a letter to the Secretary of Interior on their behalf and later placing a hold on an Indian gaming bill the Choctaws did not like. For his service to Abramoff's clients, Cochran "received about $82,500 from Abramoff, his lobbying partners and tribal clients between 2001 and 2004, including roughly $8,000 in the period around which the letter was sent." Cochran's staff, however, always maintained that actions taken by the Senator would have transpired without any gifts to Copeland.[12]

Cochran did not fire Copeland because she resigned just as the dragnet closed in on Abramoff and the whole sorry mess. She pled guilty to "conspiracy to commit honest services fraud" and was sentenced to seventy-five days in a halfway house and seventy-five days of home confinement.[13]

The Copeland scandal was not the only trouble in Senator Cochran's office. Since his 2014 Senate campaign ended, another longtime Cochran staffer, Fred Pagan, who managed the Washington office, was arrested by federal agents from the Department of Homeland Security with over 180 grams of meth and a "date rape" drug in a package mailed from China to Pagan's home. He later confessed to police—though he pled not guilty to the charges—that he was involved in a drugs-for-sex scheme. Cochran did not immediately fire him, even after it was reported that he had confessed to police. Initially, he was only suspended for his mishap, which had been ongoing for some time.[14]

And most of the criminality associated with the machine was of a violent nature. Haley Barbour's son, Haley Jr., the same son who served as a lobbyist for the Southern Company while his father was governor and was instrumental in the Kemper coal plant fiasco, was arrested and charged with assault for a fight in a DC bar after he punched a man in the face apparently for inappropriately touching his wife. Though after the police came, Barbour's wife never told them about any touching.[15] Perhaps someone insulted the honor and dignity of Boss Hogg?

Though never arrested, campaign manager Kirk Sims was also involved in a scrum at the famous Grove on the campus of Ole Miss while serving as Governor Bryant's chief of staff in October 2013. With Johnny Football and Texas A&M in town, things must of gotten a bit heated, especially after the Rebels dropped a second straight close one to the Aggies. It's disputed who was actually engaged with Sims but suffice it to say, this is not the conduct of a Southern gentleman or a top-level aide.[16]

As far as fights by politicians are concerned, even though he had nothing to do with the Cochran campaign, former congressman-turned-lobbyist for his mistress's company, Chip Pickering, was arrested in 2008 after getting into a fistfight with a soccer coach at his son's match in Madison, an episode that, running alongside his other tomfooleries, further deflated many Mississippians who thought he might be different from the usual lot.[17]

The media, and those who profess a love of democracy, should have been focused on the shenanigans that were going on in Hinds County, but the only focus was on the non-story of the courthouse "break-in" and Jordan Russell's spin. This is how corruption is perpetuated by way of the media, both in state and nationally. And with an Establishment man as secretary of state, Delbert Hosemann, no one would ever question the discrepancies, much less investigate them. Nor would Attorney General Jim Hood.

Even though Chris had not secured enough to win outright on June 3, he did best Thad Cochran by a half of a point, 49.5 to 49 percent, with Thomas Carey, now a footnote in Mississippi history, gaining a half a percent, anti-incumbent votes that most likely would have gone to McDaniel thereby putting him over the top. Though the beleaguered challenger had fallen just a handful of votes short of outright victory, the GOP Establishment was stunned. How could this have happened? And given the very recent history of runoff elections, incumbents generally fair far worse. To win, Cochran would have to take dirty campaigning to new heights. And that's exactly what the "Gentleman Senator" did.

CHAPTER 9

THAD THE KEYNESIAN:
COCHRAN COURTS DEMOCRATS

After the loss on June 3, Cochran's team knew they were up against the wall. In situations like this the incumbent, especially well-known Establishment candidates forced into a runoff, almost always lose and sometimes the defeat is huge. Ted Cruz actually lost the primary in his US Senate race in 2012 to the Establishment's handpicked candidate, Lt. Governor David Dewhurst. In a field of nine candidates, Cruz finished in second place but was more than ten points behind Dewhurst. Yet in the run-off a few weeks later, picking up the support of the other anti-Establishment candidates, Cruz won nearly 57 percent of the vote to capture the nomination easily. So prospects for Chris, who was coming to be seen more and more by conservatives as Mississippi's Ted Cruz, looked bright.

One Republican strategist, Ford O'Connell, said as much to the *Christian Science Monitor*. "In a runoff it is hard to see how McDaniel is not a slight favorite, as his supporters are driven by something Cochran's aren't—excitement," he said. "Runoffs usually entail a much lower turnout. Therefore the candidate whose core supporters have more intensity tend to win."[1] And Cochran's team knew that uncomfortable fact, so it was back to the drawing board to craft new plans for the three-week runoff campaign. His team already knew they had a lot more ground to cover, given their performance up to this point, which was made all the more troubling if the 1.5 percent from Thomas Carey was factored in for McDaniel. Just those few voters would put the challenger over the top. But when new polls began emerging in the days after the primary, the anxiety for Cochran quickly turned to panic. A survey on June 8 showed Chris with a slight lead, but a poll a week later, on June 15, gave him an eight-point lead. The next day a poll indicated a lead of twelve points for McDaniel. The seat was clearly slipping from Cochran's grasp, and his loss on June 24 could be huge indeed.[2]

Understanding the dire situation, much of the Establishment finally came out to help save the aged Cochran. Many Republican Senate bigwigs on Capitol Hill attended a lavish fundraiser hosted by Senator Mitch McConnell at the National Republican Senatorial Committee (NRSC), including Cochran's Mississippi colleague Roger Wicker, but also included Senators Lisa Murkowski, Rob Portman, Lamar Alexander, Orrin Hatch, Chuck Grassley, John Barrasso, John Thune, John Cornyn, Bob Corker, Susan Collins, Kelly Ayotte, Dean Heller, and Richard Shelby.

Politico received a copy of the invitation McConnell sent out. "Our friend Thad is in a battle in the coming weeks that will have a very real impact on our fight for the Majority," the invitation said. "You have helped all of us in the past, and we need your help for him now. It is critical that he has financial resources now, and we are going to make sure he has them." McConnell asked his fellow GOP Senators to contribute $5,000 to PACs and make $2,600 in personal contributions, the amount allowed by law. Other guests were asked to contribute $2,000 and $1,000 respectively.[3]

According to *Breitbart's* Matthew Boyle, who waited outside the event to get some feedback, the fundraiser was not all that enthusiastic, especially since Cochran did not even show up to his own event.

A Republican staffer told Breitbart News the mood inside the room—in which both Wicker and McConnell spoke—was somber. There was "a lot of looking at shoes," the staffer said, and "a lot of people anxious to get out the door." When Wicker and McConnell spoke, the staffer said, "what they didn't say was stunning."

"Thad's name was only mentioned once," the staffer said, and there was "no talk of what he had done, or what he would do… The silence was deafening."

Around 6:20 p.m., a different fund-raiser attendee walked outside to sarcastically inform another who was just arriving: "You're missing all the great speechifying in there."[4]

Many of the attendees refused to speak with Boyle, giving no response to questions about their support for Cochran. Rob Portman of Ohio reminded Boyle that he was the vice chair of the NRSC and so he would be supporting his "friend" Thad, who he said was a "good conservative and he's been great for Mississippi."[5] In all, the fund-raiser netted Cochran's camp a million bucks in less than one hour.

Washington moneymaking was one thing, but the home front was the real problem for Ole Thad. So to gin up some excitement at home, Cochran invited the top half of the GOP ticket in 2008, Senator John McCain, to attend rallies on the Gulf Coast and in Jackson. McCain used his family ties to Mississippi and his and Cochran's veteran status—both served in the Navy—as a reason to discuss the vital issue of veterans, an important topic in Mississippi.

The McCain appearance was strange because in 2008 Cochran had expressed his doubts about McCain's ability to be a good president. "The thought of his being president sends a cold chill down my spine. He's erratic. He's hot-headed. He loses his temper, and he worries me."[6] That was the same year that Cochran said Obama would make a "good president." For Katherine Skiba of *US News and World Report*, the "gentleman" Cochran's vile invective against McCain not only violated Reagan's eleventh commandment not to speak ill of a fellow Republican, "he spat on it."[7] Chris, on the other hand, never criticized any fellow Republican's character or temperament but instead countered by pointing out that McCain and Cochran had together spent seventy-two years in Washington. "That's a long time, and a long list of appropriations," he said in a campaign e-mail.

The biggest star to speak on behalf of Cochran was former NFL quarterback Brett Favre, who normally gives money to Democrats, but cut a supportive television ad for Cochran, which proved one of our main points – Democrats always had a lot of respect and admiration for him. "I've learned through football that strong leadership makes the difference between winning and losing," Favre says in the ad. "And when it comes to our state's future, trust me: Mississippi can win— and win big with Thad Cochran as our strong voice in Washington. Thad Cochran always delivers, just like he did during Katrina." It was a theme we would see repeated throughout the runoff campaign: all the good things Cochran has done for Mississippi.[8]

But it was the backstory to the Favre ad that caused controversy. Before he left the governor's office, Haley Barbour, like Bill Clinton, had his own Pardongate scandal, forgiving 208 convicts, many of them violent offenders, in a move that angered much of the state and for good reason. Many of the pardons were unreasonable by anyone's standards, including the pardon of fourteen murderers.[9] Here are just a few:

David Glenn Gatlin reportedly drove nine hours to shoot and kill his estranged wife, Tammy Gatlin, while she held their infant son. He also shot her friend Randy Walker, who survived.

Anthony McCray was convicted of killing his wife, Jennifer McCray, after the two had reportedly been arguing at a cafe. He left, returned, and shot her once in the back.

Bobby Hays Clark was convicted of manslaughter for shooting and killing his former girlfriend, Veronica Conner.

Paul Joseph Warnock murdered his girlfriend, eighteen-year-old Carol Ann Hall by shooting her in the back of the head while she slept.

Michael Davie Graham stalked his ex-wife, Adrienne Klasky, for three years before he finally shot her to death with a 12-gauge shotgun while she waited at a traffic light in her car.

Clarence Jones murdered his ex-girlfriend, twenty-two-year-old

Carla M. Smith. Smith had filed multiple assault and trespassing charges against Jones before her death. Jones waited for her in her apartment on New Year's Day and killed her by stabbing her twenty-two times.

Victor C. Collins was convicted of fatally beating his girlfriend, Peggy Campbell, with a tree branch. Her body was later found in a pile of leaves.

Jimmy Lee Avera shot and killed his estranged girlfriend, Tabitha Ann Sparks, age twenty-four, while she was pregnant, and while her two children were at home with her. He fired eleven shots at her, including one that struck her in the back as she tried to run away.

Just looking at the gender of these vicious criminals, and that of their victims, it seemed Haley Barbour was conducting his own personal war on women, saving many men who had savagely killed their girlfriends or wives. There were other pardons, of course, even some granted to women, but one pardon in particular caught everyone's eye. Scott Favre, Brett's brother had been convicted of drunk driving and vehicular manslaughter in 1996 when a friend, Mark Haverty, was killed in a crash after a night of drinking. Scott was sentenced to fifteen years in state prison but the judge suspended fourteen of those years and ordered one additional year of house arrest.[10]

In 1997 Scott Favre was arrested again, this time for driving with a suspended license. The judge revoked his parole and sentenced him to thirteen years in prison, but he served just sixty-seven days when it was determined that he had been wrongfully arrested. Despite Favre's past, Governor Barbour granted the pardon and effectively cleared his record. So was the Favre ad payback? Quite likely it was, since Brett Favre had never appeared in a political ad before.[11]

But their biggest play was a political Hail Mary. Having failed to convince the state's Republican voters that Chris was a danger, more like a dreaded resurgence of Richard Nixon, or that their man in Washington was a conservative, in a final bid for victory the Cochran team decided to use Thad's progressive record, as well as his seniority, to their advantage. The Cochran campaign began making major inroads into Democratic territory to seek additional support, a concerted effort that included a push for moderate to liberal whites and a despicable race-baiting campaign aimed at blacks that began just days before the vote on June 24 in the hope that Chris would not be able to counter it. Thad, the former Democrat who was still a good friend to those in his old party, had no concern with this new tactic. It must have felt like coming home to him, since he only opportunistically switched parties in 1972 in order to run for Congress. He could now shed his Republican opportunistic sheepskin and run the campaign he wanted to run. Before he had tried to compete with Chris on conservative virtues; now he could dump all that baggage once and for all and tout Keynesian economics, epitomized by his bread-and-butter policy – earmarks. In fact, Thad Cochran is known as the "King of Earmarks," usually tapping hundreds of millions per year for political projects. So, instead of hiding this liberal spendthrift record, they began to flaunt what Cochran had done for the state in his four decades in Washington.

The latest theme ran something like this: Without Thad Cochran, there would be no roads, bridges, or military installations in Mississippi, and the election of Chris McDaniel, an extreme budget cutter, would end it all, even though, as they had previously argued, Chris would be a freshman US Senator and would have no seniority to do anything.

Annual federal largess is massive, no doubt about it. Washington spends an enormous amount of money on a variety of endeavors, some constitutional, most of it not. And Mississippi, like a lot of other states, gets a big portion, particularly for the defense industry. "I hope to be able to continue to use my influence in Washington to be sure that we get our share of the federal dollars that are available to help us," Cochran told one reporter.[12] And where would those dollars go if not Mississippi? To other states, of course. So why should we needlessly let that happen? This was the main question they posed to Mississippi voters.

And that federal support for the state was enormous. In fact, almost 46 percent of the state's entire budget came from the federal treasury, ranking Mississippi first among all fifty states in federal aid as a percentage of state revenue.[13] For every dollar the state's taxpayers sent to Washington, more than three came back in one form or another. So Cochran simply alleged that if McDaniel replaced him, every cent of federal money would immediately disappear, because only Thad Cochran could get it. "My opponent says he's not going to spend money like I spend money," Cochran told reporters. "Well you not gonna have any roads and bridges and we're not gonna have a lot of things that are essential to our economic betterment and growth opportunities if you follow his plan and cut all these programs."[14] This argument was completely liberal but also completely narcissistic: There will be no infrastructure or economic growth in Mississippi without Thad Cochran in the US Senate.

Cochran also began hurling insults Chris's way to get his point across, using words right out of the Democratic playbook. In one instance he told a reporter, "We're confronted with an opponent of mine who has no experience in public office at this level."[15] To another reporter Cochran grew nastier, claiming that McDaniel was an "extremist" who would be "dangerous" if elected, because the state has "a lot of federal initiatives, and if he's going to cut the budgets, we're going to be the state that suffers the most. To me, that's unthinkable."[16] When defending his spending habits, Cochran's ace-in-the-hole, his sharp elbows always came out in full force.

Remarkably, later on in the campaign Cochran tried to claim he had never attacked anyone during the race. Whether this was a lie or just another memory lapse, we couldn't be sure. And just four days before his latest round of assaults, Haley Barbour, in describing his good friend Thad Cochran, said, "He campaigned like he's always campaigned. He's a true gentleman. He never says anything bad about his opponents or anybody, for that matter."[17] Whether this was more of Haley's lies or the fact that they were not on the same page, again we couldn't be sure.

Cochran always focused on his results in procuring federal funding. "We try to make sure Mississippi's voice is heard in Washington, is effective for our state and produces the results that you have right here in this state," he told a crowd in Gulfport. It was an issue, though, that always bothered me, as it did a great many Mississippi conservatives.

But many pseudo-conservatives bought into it. Josh Mars, a spokesman for young business leaders, told the *Washington Post's* Dan Balz that keeping Cochran was a must. "He has done more for Mississippi than any other representative, senator, governor in the past, and I think it is imperative that we keep this man where he's at to keep Mississippi moving forward."[18]

Moving Mississippi forward with results was the new Cochran mantra. "That was the contract," said Marty Wiseman, retired director of the John C. Stennis Institute of Government at Mississippi State University. "We'll send you to Washington, and we'll keep sending you as long as you watch out for Mississippi. Whatever else you do up there really doesn't matter. That's what makes the current race so darned strange."[19]

Why would anyone believe such economic rubbish? We were not, in fact, moving forward with good results. Economically speaking, among the fifty states, Mississippi ranks last, and has since Reconstruction. And it's not as if we don't know that; it's all over the news. With each passing year, stories emerge that showcase the state as the poorest in the country. We usually just take it with a shrug these days, even when other states use it as the butt of jokes, such as Kentucky's Democratic House Speaker, who said "if the Republicans take over the House we will become in Kentucky like ... Mississippi." Or when the Weather Channel described us as the "landmass between Louisiana and Alabama." Or the time in 2006 when New York Congressman Charlie Rangel asked rhetorically, "Who the hell wants to live in Mississippi?" just after attending a fundraiser in the Webber-Cochran house near Capitol Hill.[20]

In 2014, the year of the race, CNBC put together a list of the ten poorest states in the Union, and once again Mississippi topped out the survey because the state's median income is just $37,000, half as much as Maryland, which headed the list of the ten richest states. In a survey by *Yahoo Finance*, published on September 19, 2014, Mississippi remained the poorest state. According to the report, "no state had a higher poverty rate than Mississippi, where more than 24% of people lived below the poverty line. The next-closest state, New Mexico, had a poverty rate more than two percentage points lower than Mississippi.

Other problems the state faced were a high jobless rate and a high proportion of households on food stamps. In 2014, 8.6% of workers were unemployed, the sixth highest rate nationally, while 19.4% of households relied on food stamps, the second highest rate."[21]

It got immeasurably worse when the *Christian Science Monitor* headlined a story in August 2014 this way: "Britain poorer than all US states except Mississippi." Our former mother country has been in the death throes of socialism for decades, which has dragged down its once vibrant economy to the point that every single US state is stronger than Merry Ole England, except our own of course.[22]

Mississippi, as we natives will readily admit, seems to rank last in all the good categories, and first in all the bad ones, which kinda goes hand in hand. And it's not just economic. We are first in obesity; last in public health. We are first in illiteracy, while our public schools rank last. We are first in poverty; last in job production and economic growth. We are first in public corruption; last in efforts to combat it. Or as Steve Wilson of *Mississippi Watchdog* recently wrote, "Reform is always a step behind Mississippi corruption." We seem to always get a smoke detector after the fire, he said.[23] And that goes with every issue.

To reverse this never-ending presence in the economic doldrums, those at the helm had argued for years that more revenue was needed to fix the state's problems, but all the new money from gambling and tobacco, not to mention all the money Cochran had funneled to the state over the decades, which was staggering, yet Mississippi remained last. Awash in cash certainly did not translate into better schools, fewer in poverty, less crime, and declining obesity. And for Mississippi Tea Partiers, this was the real issue. "Thad Cochran has been in Washington, D.C., for over 40 years. The state of Mississippi was ranked 50th out of 50 when he went, and we're still ranked 50th out of 50," said Janis Lane, President of the Central Mississippi Tea Party. "Where are the jobs from that money? Where has that money gone?"[24] Or more directly, into whose pockets has it gone? The donor class that supports the Establishment, of course.

But despite the distastefulness of the facts, Thad Cochran felt the need to argue that he is the only reason Mississippi is not a Third World economic basket case, somewhere in the same neighborhood as Zimbabwe and Afghanistan, and that Chris McDaniel was a great destroyer, somewhere to the right of Genghis Khan. It smacked of egotism, not sound economic policy. How such an argument could work was beyond any of us.

For Chris, there is a reason Mississippi is suffering economically and it's *because* of all the federal spending. "Mississippi is dead last in jobs, education, and nearly every statistical category, and it is a result of an addiction to a federal spending apparatus that stifles economic growth, and a new post office someplace is not going to change things for the state," Chris told me. "These people that tell you that we would suffer without federal dollars are the most shortsighted, selfish individuals in the world. They are saying, ignore $19 trillion in debt, ignore borrowing 43 cents out of every dollar, ignore the downgrade of American treasuries, ignore the end of the republic because Mississippi needs a four-lane highway somewhere or needs a new post office someplace. It's mind-boggling. We functioned well prior to being an appendage of the federal government. We functioned well prior to the adoption of the income tax. We will function well afterwards."[25]

But would the state's economy really tumble if we stopped getting all the federal money, much of which was in the form of welfare and food stamps? Could we conceivably get more *last* than we already are? The obvious answer is no. Yet these people think we can keep doing things the same way but get a different result. As Chris said many times during the campaign, the state, with Thad's leadership, has had forty-two years of a failed approach but the Establishment wanted six more.

To drive home his point, Chris consistently cited a study from Harvard's Business School that tore a gaping hole in the Cochran earmark theory. According to researchers, the more federal dollars that are brought home by members of Congress, the more the local economy suffers. Earmarks *hurt* job creation and economic growth rather than assist it. "Part of the problem," wrote the *Wall Street Journal* in citing the study, "is that public money is 'crowding out' investment opportunities for firms. 'Some of our results point towards the role of competition for state specific factors of production, including labor and fixed assets such as real estates,' the authors write. 'Public spending appears to increase demand for state-specific factors of production and thereby compel firms to downsize and invest elsewhere.' They add that 'We also find evidence that the effects are most pronounced in sectors that are the target of earmark spending.'"[26] In other words, Cochran's earmarking is a major reason why the state of Mississippi is still lagging behind economically. But at least his donors are happy.

Chris's plan to reform the system was not harsh in the least. "It's not as if we could come in the next day and rip away all federal dollars, that was never the idea. We were not proposing the end of everything. The idea was a responsible phase-out of things threatening the solvency of the nation and get back to self-government and self-sufficiency," he told me.[27]

The idea is to take the initial steps in what will be a long process of saving the country from fiscal disaster. But politicians don't think that way. They think in terms of two- or four-year cycles, and as long as they are able to deliver the goods it takes to line their pockets, and those of their friends, and get reelected in the process, even if it is with money borrowed from the next generation, then so be it.

But another problem is that our local governments are just as addicted to federal money. The mentality filters down even to the supervisors and the mayors, because they are all beholden to the money. During the campaign, as the McDaniel team came into a city, they usually met immediate resistance—signs would disappear, yet Cochran's would remain; mayors refused to meet with Chris or any member of his campaign, and supervisors wouldn't come around, and all because they were all begging for money from Washington. "It's not the people of Alabama's place to pay for a pothole in Jackson, Mississippi. But that's exactly the system we have created and the supervisors empower that system by addicting themselves to federal money," Chris told me.[28]

This local addiction to federal cash hurt McDaniel in his own home county, at least as far as public officials were concerned. There were three Jones County supervisors who know and like Chris but who worked against him even though they don't know Thad personally, but they liked his ability to keep the federal dollars flowing. They feel that strongly about it. "Why would a supervisor take a trade trip to Washington, DC, for a country that borrows 43 cents out of every dollar spent?" Chris asked. "They are coming home to their people and they are essentially saying, *I don't care what happens to your kids because we are going to get you a new community center.*"[29] Chris Bowen, a supervisor in Forrest County, just south of Jones County, told the *Washington Post* that Cochran was a "statesman," who has "mastered the art of mediating and bringing people together as well as any individual I've ever met."[30] And bringing supervisors together with federal money apparently.

That kind of mind-set is destroying our country from top to bottom, as even states engage in the same reckless spending. In the 2015 Mississippi legislative session, for example, there was a bond bill where tens of millions of dollars were appropriated for a fish aquarium in Gulfport. In various counties around the state there are fire departments and community centers that have been built with state money. The handout mentality is entrenched now and if we don't change that, we will eventually collapse.

Chris's philosophical beliefs and how he would have governed in the US Senate is far different than Thad Cochran's way. Chris believes that no matter how good an idea is if it's not constitutionally within the scope of the federal government to oversee it, then the states should handle it. But that's not what Cochran does. He votes to pass it anyway, with no regard for the sovereignty of the state or the Constitution. And that's dangerous. But that's who Thad Cochran is and that's who Haley Barbour is. They, like John McCain and others, are the greatest symptom of everything that ails this country. Conservatism is rooted first and foremost in the Constitution. And the Constitution must be followed in its purest form, otherwise why would we even have one? Haley Barbour has said that purity in politics is a loser but the Constitution is not a loser.

So it greatly complicates the system of cronyism when reformers like Chris McDaniel emerge ready to tackle the problems, clean up the mess, and move forward with ideas for a freer, less-dependent, more self-reliant and self-sufficient economy, which just might improve things. And when he emerged as a conservative reformer, the machine attacked, denounced, and destroyed. So Mississippi remains seated at the bottom. But, again, at least the donor class is happy.

Throughout the early part of the campaign, the McDaniel message had been repeated over and over again that Cochran was a closet liberal, and now it seemed he was finally admitting it. As he told reporter Molly Ball, before forgetting who she was: "I think my service in the House of Representatives and Senate have shown the kind of senator I'll continue to be, trying to work to help create opportunities for new and better-paying jobs for more and more Americans. To do this, we've got to have good working relationships with the international community, trying to contribute through our politics to peace and security. Prosperity exists because we do have peace and security."[31]

Unsurprising to us, Rickey Cole, the state's Democratic chairman, agreed with Cochran. "If Mississippi did what the tea party claims they want . . . we would become a Third World country, quickly. We depend on the federal government to help us build our highways. We depend on the federal government to fund our hospitals, our health care system. We depend on the federal government to help us educate our students on every level."[32] Of course he did not explain Mississippi's last place ranking in these categories.

Cochran's economic stance mirrored that of the Democratic Party, the same Keynesian economic theory that Barack Obama advocates, which holds that all economic growth is government driven, particularly in down times, and we must keep throwing money at problems or they will only get worse. It was a full-fledged assault on Chris's conservative economic philosophy, which was a throwback to the good ole laissez faire days. And it proved Cochran was not a conservative, but an obstacle to the hardworking people of Mississippi, alleging that they could not build a strong society and a lasting economy without government help, and specifically Thad Cochran's help.

Cochran's new campaign spots touted the "great Senator's" herculean efforts: "Our aerospace industry, shipbuilding, military bases, Thad Cochran's strong leadership makes it happen." And employment was a big part of those industries. "The loss of Cochran would absolutely translate to lost jobs," said one wealthy industrialist from Jones County. Another ad referred to Cochran as a "powerful voice" for jobs in the state, a spot that ran 274 times from June 11 through June 16, roughly 45 showings a day.[33]

Cochran did not worry about insulting committed McDaniel supporters who had already made up their minds or McDaniel-leaning Republicans. He hoped to woo Democrats into pulling the lever for Ole Thad. In this runoff round, with the Democratic primary campaign over, the Cochran camp went all out to persuade those Democrats who had *not* voted on June 3 to vote in the Republican runoff.

It was going to be a tough sell in a very conservative state. They would have to motivate Democrats to cross over and also to contend with a Republican base that was sick to death of Washington, the corruption and cronyism, the liberal ideals, and the rising national debt. One angry voter in Desoto County complained that everyone had their hands out like people at the food stamp office. Another was concerned with what side deals Cochran had to make to get the money sent to the state. And side deals and cronyism is what Cochran is known for, much to the chagrin of conservative voters. "Cochran, known as the King of Pork for bringing federal money to Mississippi, doesn't bring money to the citizens of Mississippi or they wouldn't have been consistently ranked the poorest state for his entire 42-year tenure," said Carol Hill, a retired doctor from the Coast. "He brings federal money home to his crony friends."[34]

But was Cochran's Democratic outreach even legal? In fact, the issue was raised that voting as a Democrat in the Republican primary or runoff was, at least by the letter of the law, potentially illegal. Mississippi has an open primary system whereby voters do not register with a specific party and can vote in either primary but not *both*. However, there is a law on the books designed to prevent crossover voting and keep the primaries somewhat in line with party purity. Under the law, specifically MS Code 23-15-575, Democrats could vote to decide the Republican nominee, but there is one catch: "No person shall be eligible to participate in any primary election unless he intends to support the nominations made in which he participates."[35]

So, at least potentially, if any Democrat decided to vote for Cochran in the June primary or runoff, then they must support him in November, although, as critics pointed out, it is a completely unenforceable law.

However, the intent of the statute is to keep the party primaries pure without requiring a registration by party. But as we would soon see, party purity, adherence to principles, and basic political decency was nowhere to be found with the Cochran Camp and his merry band of political assassins.

CHAPTER 10

RACE-BAITING 2.0

The Cochran outreach to Democrats who hadn't voted in the primaries was bad enough, showcasing his betrayal of party loyalty and primary purity. But their team understood that even a small segment of Democratic voters who had not voted on June 3 might not be enough, especially if McDaniel surged after his win, so the Cochran campaign, and all of its component parts, began to encourage Democrats who *had* voted in the Democratic primary on June 3 to vote in the Republican runoff on June 24, which was, without question, illegal. And the biggest bloc of Democratic voters in Mississippi was the state's large black population, totaling roughly 38 percent of the overall populace.

In his effort to court blacks, Cochran pushed his same economic argument that only he could bring in the vital federal help Mississippi needed, but this time he added support for increased welfare, food stamps, and support for public education, particularly traditional black colleges, in the mix of federal aid he had secured.

As a quintessential Southern state, Mississippi and its political past had always centered on the issue of race. It's no big news to say that it defines our history. As Southern historian Ulrich B. Phillips once noted in his most famous essay, "race is the central theme of Southern history," meaning the maintenance of white supremacy dominated the politics of nearly every state in the South from Reconstruction onward. Fortunately, though, in today's world, unlike the world Phillips inhabited, that is not the case. Blacks vote in Southern elections, hold a wide variety of political offices, and the Ku Klux Klan has been eradicated as a means of political intimidation, despite the best efforts of Hollywood and the leftist media to convince the nation otherwise.

This is particularly true in the state of Mississippi, which has made great strides in race relations in the decades since the upheavals in the 1960s. Segregation had ended by 1970 and schools across the state had mixed student bodies. Chris and I both attended integrated public schools and thought nothing of it. Even in Jones County, home to one of the most violent Klan organizations in the country in the mid-'60s, there was progress. In 1955, well before the tumult that was to come, Jones County Junior College, where both Chris and I attended, and where his father was a professor, defied the state's laws against integration and sent the football team to Pasadena to compete in the Junior Rose Bowl Game against an integrated team from Compton, California, becoming the first sports team in Mississippi's history to play in an integrated game. In 1995, JCJC held a wonderful fortieth anniversary ceremony, bringing together both teams from that historic game for a celebratory weekend, including actor Red West, who played in that bowl game for Jones. ESPN even did a lengthy segment on it, demonstrating how much has changed in Mississippi.[1]

The violent upheaval that came in the '60s was the last gasp of the old guard, which thankfully has passed into history. And over the last fifty years we have worked for racial progress. In the 1990s, the state went after two old vile racists to finally convict them of their racial crimes and put them in prison where they belonged all these years. In 1994, Byron De La Beckwith, Medgar Evers's murderer, was sent to the state penitentiary, where he died in 2001, and former Klan Imperial Wizard Sam Bowers, who was from Jones County, was convicted in 1998 for the 1966 murder of Vernon Dahmer in Hattiesburg. He died in prison in 2006. And when two Hattiesburg police officers were tragically murdered in May 2015, one white and one black, citizens from both races came together to pay their respects to the fallen officers. In fact, today African-Americans hold more public offices in Mississippi than in any other state. With agitators out of the way, we have seen that people can get along and work out their problems. But sadly the agitators on *both* sides of the issue won't stay down for long.

In recent years, race relations have taken a tragic turn for the worst, unfortunately. Even Haley Barbour has had troubles with past racist remarks. It was enough to cause more heartburn for those who considered supporting his potential 2012 presidential bid. Barbour, as before mentioned, ran against John C. Stennis for the US Senate in 1982. Incidentally, the youthful Barbour's 1982 campaign slogan was "A Senator for the '80s," as opposed to a Senator *in* his 80s, as Stennis had turned eighty the previous August. But Barbour obviously had no problem backing a seventy-two-year-old Thad Cochran in 2014. This was just another example of Haley the Hypocrite.[2]

Senator John C. Stennis had been around forever it seemed. After service in the state house, then as a prosecutor and judge, he came to the US Senate by winning a special election to succeed the infamous Theodore G. Bilbo, as notorious as any racist that ever walked the halls of Congress, or anywhere else for that matter. Bilbo, a member of the Klan while in the Senate, was known to discuss race relations in rather crude language and had once proposed an appropriations bill that would spend $2 billion to transport all blacks back to Africa. When Republicans took control of the Senate in 1946, the year Bilbo won election to a new term, they refused to seat him because of the blood-curdling language in his speeches defending white civilization. He died of cancer in August 1947, which kept the dilemma from continuing to hamper the Senate.[3]

Senator Stennis was much more gentlemanly in his nature than Bilbo. But as a US Senator representing Mississippi, Stennis was expected to keep the same viewpoints and he worked to maintain Jim Crow, signing the Southern Manifesto in opposition to the *Brown v. Board of Education* decision in 1954 and supporting filibusters against every civil rights bill as well as the Voting Rights Act of 1965. But by the 1980s, the old arch-segregationist had undergone a serious change of heart and voted to extend the Voting Rights Act in 1982. "I didn't want to go back to all the days of misunderstanding. I didn't want to turn around and go back," Stennis said.[4]

But going backward seemed Barbour's true destination, or at the very least he sought to use racism to defeat Stennis. Some of the Boss's biggest verbal gaffes have been racial in nature, while he has supported causes that upset the black community. Once during the campaign against Stennis, Barbour made one of his most infamous racist blunders, one that still reverberates around Mississippi. When an aide angered him during a meeting, Barbour told the young lad, "You will be reincarnated as a watermelon and placed at the mercy of the blacks."[5]

One black member of the Mississippi House of Representatives, Willie Perkins, who served during Barbour's tenure as governor, said of him: "As far as I'm concerned, he has never done anything as a governor or a citizen to distinguish himself from the old Democrats who fought tooth and nail to preserve segregation." Another black representative, Rufus Straughter, said Barbour "has a pattern, in my opinion, of doing things that are outrageous and insensitive."[6]

And some of those "outrageous and insensitive" things were comments to reporters. In 2010, Barbour told the *Weekly Standard* about his days growing up in Yazoo City during the Civil Rights Movement in the 1960s. "I just don't remember it as being that bad," he said. And Yazoo City has been hailed as one of the only cities in Mississippi that integrated their school system without violence, so that prompted the *Weekly Standard* reporter to ask Barbour why that was the case. "Because the business community wouldn't stand for it," he said. "You heard of the Citizens Councils? Up north they think it was like the KKK. Where I come from it was an organization of town leaders. In Yazoo City they passed a resolution that said anybody who started a chapter of the Klan would get their ass run out of town. If you had a job, you'd lose it. If you had a store, they'd see nobody shopped there. We didn't have a problem with the Klan in Yazoo City."[7]

Although this was clearly a case of Barbour trying to show that Yazoo City would not tolerate the awful violence that the Klan had been perpetrating against blacks throughout Mississippi and the South, it did seem as though he was praising and defending the White Citizens' Councils, which may not have been the official Klan, but it was essentially the KKK in more expensive suits and business attire. In short, the Klan and the Councils had the same goals, white supremacy, but only different paths to getting there. He was forced to walk back these comments before seriously considering a run for president. And it didn't help his cause that in 1988 these former groups seemed to be reincarnated, to borrow from Haley's vast vocabulary, as the Council of Conservative Citizens, and Haley Barbour was a participant in their meetings. In 2003, when running for governor and being pressured about the issue, he refused to ask the CCC to remove his picture from their website.[8]

In early 2011, just a couple of months after his legendary interview with the *Weekly Standard*, Governor Barbour found himself embroiled in a controversy about a state license plate for Confederate General Nathan Bedford Forrest, who was also the first Grand Wizard of the Ku Klux Klan. Derrick Johnson, president of the Mississippi NAACP, called the planned license plate "absurd," ripped Forrest as a "racially divisive figure," and called on Barbour to denounce the plan. "I find it curious that the governor won't come out and clearly denounce the efforts of the Sons of Confederate Veterans to honor Nathan Bedford Forrest. As the head of the state, he shouldn't tap dance around the question." Barbour refused to denounce it. And in 2011 the NAACP actually sued Governor Barbour for a racially discriminatory redistricting plan that had not been pre-cleared by the United States Department of Justice, as required by the Voting Rights Act. So perhaps he really was steamed that Stennis had voted for its reauthorization back in 1982.[9]

Over the years Barbour has shown no signs of letting up. Soon after the 2014 midterms, with race still obviously on his mind, Barbour, on a conference call with clients of his lobbying firm, referred to President Obama's policies as "tar babies," a reference to a character in the Uncle Remus stories, African-American folktales of the nineteenth century, which is considered racially insensitive. He later issued a half-hearted apology.[10]

Thad Cochran is not exactly squeaky clean on racial issues either. He has a long history of associations with segregationists, facts that he admits in his official Senate biography.

As early as 1951, Cochran accompanied his mother as she drove through her hometown of Utica, and helped deliver door to door a campaign tabloid for the [Democrat and segregationist] Paul B. Johnson, Jr. campaign for Governor. His father was a surrogate in the campaigns of Felder Dearman for Highway Commissioner and Jack Tubb for State Superintendent of Education. Cochran often traveled with his father and helped with voter registration for these campaigns.

Later, Thad Cochran became active in other political campaigns on his own. He appeared on television for the first time to endorse Fred Thomas for Sheriff of Hinds County in 1967. He was Hinds County Chairman in Brad Dye's successful race for State Treasurer, and he wrote talking points and issue briefs for [staunch segregationist] Charles Sullivan's campaign for Governor in 1971.[11]

Cochran also refused to sign a Senate resolution apologizing for the failure to pass anti-lynching legislation. Cochran's old colleague and supporter, Trent Lott, did not sign it either.[12] Cochran has also given interviews with neo-Confederate periodicals, including the now-defunct *Southern Partisan* magazine.[13]

So these twin pillars of racial "progress" in Mississippi, Haley Barbour and Thad Cochran, decided to mount a full-fledged race-baiting campaign to destroy, not just defeat, Chris McDaniel, and with him the entire conservative movement. Instead of using intimidation and outright violence to keep blacks *away* from the polls, the Barbour Gang used threats to drive them *to* the polls. They boasted that without Cochran in office, the state's black folks would lose all their government benefits.

By taking this line of attack, the Cochran team made is seem like the wild-eyed, crazy Tea Partier Chris McDaniel, if he won the nomination and the election, would, somehow without any seniority, see to it that Mississippi's blacks would be put out in the street the day after the election, losing food stamps, housing, and educational opportunities. It was the same sickening message Cochran had showcased with whites: *You can't make it without me.* To blacks he took the full Democratic line: *You can't make it without government.* And make no mistake about it, this was an attack not just on Chris McDaniel but on the entire conservative movement.

Race-baiting campaign tactics have been around a long time but it's usually, though not exclusively, done by Democrats to trash Republicans. GOP candidates have certainly used those tactics on Democrats, but they were never to be used on their own teammates. Democrats, though, use it more often. From Joe Biden saying to a black audience that Republicans will "put y'all back in chains," to Obama referring to his grandmother as a "typical white person," or to Dick Harpootlian saying he wanted to send Nikki Haley "back to wherever the hell she came from" so "this country can move forward," Democrats are notorious race-baiters. When a reporter asked Congressman Steve Israel, the chairman of the Democratic Congressional Campaign Committee in 2013, if any of his Republican colleagues in the House are racists, he said "Not all of them, no. Of course not." But then he added the necessary jab, "To a significant extent, the Republican base does have elements that are animated by racism." Yet it is the Democrats that call any prominent black conservative an "Uncle Tom," among other, nastier names.[14]

We're used to such trash from the mouths of Democrats but not from fellow Republicans aiming their vile invective at fellow Republicans. Taking a page out of the playbook of the campaigns of old, including Jimmy Carter's race-filled campaign for governor of Georgia in 1970, this race-baiting hit job on Chris McDaniel and his conservative followers would be littered with racist flyers and push cards distributed in black communities, radio ads aired on black radio stations, print ads placed in black community newspapers, and robocalls directed to black homes. It was a campaign that would hit heavily black and Democratic areas across Mississippi and receive its funding from none other than the Mississippi Conservatives PAC founded by Boss Hogg himself and run by nephew Henry, as well as the NRSC. Both the NRSC and the Barbours, however, vehemently denied any involvement in the race-baiting campaign.

One of the most despicable ads of the campaign, and one of the most vile to ever run in any election, attempted to tie Chris to the KKK. It ran on the day of the vote and came to be came to be known as the "Klan Ad":

This is an Election Day alert. Polls are open from 7 a.m. to 7 p.m. When Congressman Thompson says a group of Tea Party radicals scares him, we should listen. Last week the *Clarion Ledger* was able to tie McDaniel's campaign to an ally of the Ku Klux Klan. And this supporter of McDaniel's campaign was a Klan lawyer. If we stand by and don't go to the polls today, do you understand what we could lose? We could lose food stamps, housing assistance, student loans, early breakfast and lunch programs—and disaster assistance, as well as cuts to Social Security and Medicaid.

The right-wing Tea Party people are saying we are too lazy to care or too afraid to go vote. They say we only want a hand out or something for free. If you didn't vote on June 3 in the Democratic primary, you can vote today. Bring your voter ID. Now that we've heard what Congressman Thompson has said, we know what to do. We are not going to turn back the hands of time.

The voice on the ad was Ruth Harris, a spokesperson for the Citizens for Progress PAC. She claimed responsibility for it and said she and four of her friends somehow managed to scrape up enough funds to buy the radio ads.[15]

The Klan tie-in, though, was just as ridiculous as the substance of the whole ad itself. When former Klan Imperial Wizard Sam Bowers was finally brought to trial by the state of Mississippi, as an American he is entitled to a defense, and as a Jones Countian he hired a local attorney, Carl Ford, who was supporting Chris. That was the extent of the KKK ties.

When the revelations appeared in the press that Harris and her cabal of elderly ladies bought the ads, the Barbours jumped on the news to absolve themselves of any association with such appalling tactics. "I am glad the people really behind this despicable KKK ad have been revealed, because Sen. Cochran's opponents have falsely accused our group and others of running it," Henry Barbour said, claiming righteous indignation. "As I have said from the start, I had zero to do with it."[16] But that's far from the end of the story. Barbour's fingerprints, as well as those of the NRSC, were all over the entire, despicable race-baiting campaign.

To conceal their involvement in this deplorable operation, the Barbours, with their Mississippi Conservatives PAC, funded two new organizations: Citizens for Progress, which was responsible for the Klan Ad, and All Citizens for Mississippi. It was these new PACs that were responsible for the radio ads, robocalls, push cards, and flyers and every smidgeon of race baiting aimed at McDaniel. And, again, these new organizations got every cent of their funding from the Republican Establishment.

According to Aaron Gardner of *Red State*, it was Greg Brand, a Jackson-based political operative and friend of Hinds County GOP chairman Pete Perry, who purchased the Klan Ad, a fact revealed by the manager of the radio station with which it ran.[17] The Jackson-based blog *Jackson Jambalaya* tarnished Brand as a well-known dirty trickster in Hinds County politics. So it's quite obvious he had some connection with Citizens for Progress, or at least got the job of paying for their radio spots.[18]

As for the leadership of the Citizens for Progress PAC, while Ruth Harris served as a spokesperson, it was an Atlanta operative named Mitzi Bickers who actually ran the organization. Ms. Bickers is a black pastor from Atlanta, former president of the Atlanta school board, and a former aide to the mayor, who was brought in specifically by the Barbours. She had previously gained notoriety for a campaign in Atlanta, which operated under the same name that sought to raise local sales taxes. She was forced to resign as the mayor's aide in 2013 after it was disclosed that she filed false financial disclosure forms related to that campaign. So Bickers knew just how to run an unethical, illegal, and despicable campaign operation.[19]

FEC filings prove that Citizens for Progress was the recipient of $44,000 from Barbour's Mississippi Conservatives PAC, with $25,000 specifically going to Bickers. The PAC also paid the Pirouette Company, which Bickers has been affiliated with in the past, approximately $19,660 for robocalls. Henry Barbour has admitted that much, although not about all the specifics. "We hired Mitzi Bickers to do paid phones," he told the *Daily Mail* of London. To the *Daily Caller* he said that he had discussed the content of the calls but had "never heard them." As for Bickers' past, Barbour said he didn't know anything about it because she "was recommended by a Mississippi mayor."[20] For such smart people, they didn't seem to know very much.

The Bickers robocall in question went like this:

Hello neighbors! The time has come to make a stand and say 'No!' to the Tea Party, 'No!' to their obstruction, 'No!' to their disrespectful treatment of the first African-American president. Next Tuesday, June 24, Tea Party candidate Chris McDaniel is in a runoff against Senator Thad Cochran. If we do nothing, Tea Party candidate Chris McDaniel wins and causes even more problems for President Obama. It pushes the damaging cuts in funding to our public education system. With your help we can stop this. Please commit to voting against Tea Party candidate Chris McDaniel next Tuesday. Say 'No!' to the Tea Party.

Even though Henry Barbour admitted that his PAC gave money to Bickers for the calls, Jordan Russell, in another senseless explanation, blamed it all on the McDaniel campaign, calling it "an obvious, transparent stunt."[21] So his explanation seemed to be that McDaniel's supporters wanted to destroy their own candidate.

On the day of the runoff vote, June 24, another notorious radio ad ran in the city of Canton, just north of Jackson, a total of forty-eight times in a twelve-hour period. The ad, also narrated by Ruth Harris and designed as a follow-up to the Klan ad, went like this:

Alright, the polls have been open four hours. You've heard what Congressman Bennie Thompson has said. This election may be more important since we elected President Barack Obama the first time. If someone tells you that by voting today, you cannot vote in November—it's just a Tea Party, bald-faced lie. Are you going to let the clock run out on today? By not voting, you are saying 'take away all of my government programs, such as food stamps, early breakfast and lunch programs, millions of dollars to our black universities.' Everything we and our families depend on that comes from Washington will be cut. Mississippi will never be the same. The question is, will you spend $5 on gas to vote, or allow the Tea Party to send us back to the good ol' bad days? Vote against the Tea Party. Vote Thad Cochran.[22]

Later in the day, Citizens for Progress, with more funding from the Barbours, ran yet another ad practically begging those who had not voted to get to the polls as fast as possible to "say no to the racist agenda of Chris McDaniel and his Tea Party." And who paid for these ads? Again, it was Citizens for Progress. And where did they get their money? Again, from Barbour's PAC.

All Citizens for Mississippi was another PAC assembled to wage war against the McDaniel campaign. It was unethically headquartered out of the New Horizon Church International, a church that enjoys tax-exempt status from the IRS. Located in a strip mall in Jackson, a reporter for the *Jackson Free Press* paid a visit and "found a white sheet of printer paper taped on a door in the complex, reading, 'ALL CITIZENS FOR MISSISSIPPI SUITE 600.' New Horizon's name and logo span across the front of the building strip." Obviously, it was a slipshod operation thrown together at the last minute to fulfill its shoddy purposes. In fact, the organization no longer exists, having served its one-time dastardly deed, but we can only assume that it would be reincarnated if a new threat emerges. The church's pastor, Bishop Ronnie Crudup, ran the PAC. He also served on the Community Advisory Board of Alan Lange's MuniStrategies firm, which is the same MuniStrategies that is the recipient of Cochran largess. It might be noted that Alan Lange also runs the pro-Establishment and fanatically anti-McDaniel *Y'all Politics* website. Pete Perry confirmed to the *New York Times* that Crudup was being paid to help turn out Democrats. "We're working with a whole bunch of different folks," the boss said, "and Crudup is one of them."[23]

Throughout the campaign, Crudup's PAC never registered with the FEC, nor filed any reports on contributions or expenditures, all in clear violation of FEC regulations. Only after all was said and done, and Crudup returned from a fall trip to Africa, did he finally get around to filing his paperwork. But no need to worry, he told Jimmie Gates of the *Clarion Ledger*, because everything "was legal, and none of it was unethical." He claimed to have raised more than $200,000 from a variety of sources, including fund-raisers where both blacks and whites attended, or so he said, but the reports did not show any of that, nor did it show any PAC expenditures for radio ads.[24] Crudup also told Gates that he spent all the money he raised, yet the FEC reports showed more than $33,000 cash on hand. One would expect more from a preacher of the Gospel but not in this garbage heap of a campaign operation.[25]

As for the All Citizens for Mississippi radio ads, there were two of them, one featuring Bishop Crudup:

This is Bishop Ronnie Crudup of All Citizens for Mississippi encouraging every registered voter to go out and vote on June 24. We're in a critical time, which means we must make tough decisions. The issues do not just affect Republicans but they affect every citizen. A victory by Tea Party candidate Chris McDaniels [sic] is a loss for the state of Mississippi.

It is a loss for public education. It is a loss for the health care industry of this state, for the farm families and agriculture. It is a loss for Ingalls and the ship industry, for our military bases.

It is a loss for the citizens of this state in a time of natural disaster, for our public universities and particularly our historically black universities.

A victory for Chris McDaniels is a loss for the reputation of this state, for race relationships between blacks and whites and other ethnic groups. Mississippi can't afford Chris McDaniels. We cannot afford the price of inexperienced, untested, disconnected leadership.

Billions are at stake. On June 24 go out and vote for Senator Thad Cochran. This ad was paid for by political action committee All Citizens for Mississippi.[26]

All Citizens for Mississippi also cut an ad narrated by Pastor Arthur L. Siggers, who, like Crudup, couldn't even get Chris's name right:

> I'm Pastor Siggers, Pastor of the Mt. Olive Baptist Church. These are some tough times, tough times socially, tough times spiritually, tough times economically, and yes, tough times politically. And tough times call for tough decisions. A time when there is an effort to roll back the hand of time. I'm talking about the race for the US Senate between Thad Cochran and tea-party candidate Chris McDaniels [sic]. I know that traditionally we as a community don't vote Republican, but for this special election, we need to turn out in record numbers to push back against this tea party effort. Thad Cochran's record speak [sic] for itself—from hiring the first black staff member in the 70s, to supporting the Martin Luther King Memorial, to supporting the Martin Luther King federal holiday, to supporting black farmers, to supporting Alcorn, Jackson State, Valley State, Tougaloo, and the list goes on and on. I urge you to vote Thad Cochran June 24th. He's been good for Mississippi. He's been good for black folk.[27]

The Siggers ad ran in the Jackson area at least eighteen times.

How were these ads funded? From both the Barbours and the NRSC. All Citizens for Mississippi received $145,000 from the Barbour's Mississippi Conservatives PAC, funding that is well documented in FEC filings, as well as money sent to other groups like Citizens for Progress.[28] But what about NRSC involvement? Records show, according to Erick Erickson at *Red State*, that "the NRSC paid an Alexandria, VA company $13,000.00 for media production and $69,000.00 for media placement on June 20, 2014, with the Mississippi runoff on June 24, 2014." And the records also show that the ads were specifically tagged for Thad Cochran.[29]

Erickson contacted the NRSC and was told by a spokesman that the buy was for web ads, to which Erickson believed was "either a load of horse manure or the NRSC is filled with greater incompetence than we first imagined." But he also discovered something else ominous. "On the exact same day the NRSC paid a media buying company to place its advertising, 'All Citizens of Mississippi' *used the exact same company from Virginia* to place its advertising attacking tea party groups."[30]

Mountain Top Media's Rick Shaftan also investigated the peculiarity and discovered that although there was a cheap, amateurish web video that appeared, and was later taken down, no major television or radio ads "ever aired in Mississippi that was paid for by the NRSC," and no one "ever saw or heard anything that carried a 'Paid for by the National Republican Senatorial Committee' tag," he told GotNews. com. Furthermore, Shaftan discovered that Jon Ferrell, the NRSC's media buyer, purchased the media ads, including the Siggers spot. In fact, according to Shaftan's work, Ferrell placed multiple orders on black radio stations on behalf of All Citizens for Mississippi.[31] Said Shaftan, "We keep finding these racially-charged ads that were ordered by the NRSC's media buyer on the exact day the NRSC's $13,000 for 'media production,' $69,000 for 'media', and $93,000 for 'telephone calls' went in," he told GotNews.com. "And the excuses from NRSC that they used the money to make a giant 'digital only' buy behind an amateurish web video is an insult to anyone with a brain."[32]

So there can be no doubt that funding for this massive media hit job on Chris McDaniel came from the Republican Establishment, some of it from the Barbours and some from the NRSC. These "ugly tactics," wrote W. James Antle III, "bore the imprimatur of the Republican establishment."[33] In fact, seven Republican US Senators contributed $160,000 to this effort—McConnell, Corker, Portman, Hatch, Burr, Blunt, and Crapo. "I can confirm," wrote Erick Erickson, "that the attack ads in Mississippi run by 'All Citizens for Mississippi' were funded by Senate Republicans.... It appears our Senate Republican leaders are willing to risk losing a Senate majority so long as they can get their own re-elected."[34] Rick Shaftan agreed. "I'm more convinced than ever that donations raised from conservatives in the name of winning Republican control of the Senate were fraudulently diverted to pay for racial attacks on conservative Chris McDaniel through this illegal Super PAC. If I'm right, all of these people will end up in orange suits."[35] They should but probably never will.

At least one of these "shady seven" senators, Rob Portman of Ohio, who headed the NRSC and has a PAC that unknowingly contributed to this effort by giving $25,000 to Barbour's Mississippi Conservatives Super PAC, was disturbed enough to speak out about it.[36] When his part was discovered, Portman told the *Cleveland Plain Dealer* that he had "absolutely no discretion" over how his contribution would be used by Mississippi Conservatives PAC but added that he believed "using race as a political issue, as these ads apparently did, was wrong."[37] Wrong perhaps but that was not enough for the party to actually do anything about it, as we will soon see.

As for Cochran's campaign, the NRSC donated more than $45,000 to Citizens for Cochran and in the three weeks between the primary and runoff sent forty-five staff members and numerous volunteers to Mississippi, who knocked on 50,000 doors and made 18,000 phone calls to voters across the state on behalf of Cochran.[38] The NRSC essentially gave their staff the weekend off and then redeployed them to Mississippi to do whatever it took to turn out Democrats for Thad. Keep in mind, the NRSC raises money under the guise that they work against Democrats. In Mississippi they bribed Democrats. This was an all-out effort by Washington Republicans, who were working in the state behind Cochran, yet all the while moaning about outside groups polluting the pristine Mississippi electorate on behalf of McDaniel.

The Barbours had a major role, as has been pointed out, in funding both new PACs. According to a spokesman for the Mississippi Conservatives PAC, Brian Perry, the organization "did contribute to All Citizens for Mississippi," but did not "have any editorial control of what they do. In fact, once we give, we cannot tell them how to spend their money."[39] But that's simply not the whole truth. Why did these new groups—All Citizens for Mississippi and Citizens for Progress—appear all of a sudden? They were not in operation before the runoff. And all of their activity, 100 percent of it, was racial in nature. When you add the media spots in with all the other activity, the robocalls, the flyers, and everything else, it seems like a concerted effort because that's exactly what it was. According to a scathing report by the Tea Party Patriots Citizens Fund, more than 92 percent "of the funding for these racial slurs and race baiting attacks came directly from Henry Barbour's Mississippi Conservatives PAC."[40]

The funding aside, the ads were nothing short of disgusting, as was the effort by the Cochran camp and its moneyed supporters to conceal their involvement. One radio station manager, Jerry Lousteau of WMGO-AM, was unsurprised at the effort. "It doesn't surprise me that people are going to want to hide from this, because that's always the way it is. The candidates want plausible deniability. They say they don't know [who did it] and that's usually a lie." To Lousteau these radio spots were "some of the worst race-baiting ads I've ever seen in this business. Really bad stuff."[41]

In addition to the media ads, at least one newspaper ad appeared in the *Mississippi Link*, an African-American paper based in Jackson. All Citizens for Mississippi also paid for it. The ad, featuring Cochran's smiling face and listing his accomplishments, many of which directly served the interests of the minority community, ended with this request: "The decision on who is going to be our next senator is going to be made in the republican primary. We're asking democrats to cross over and vote in the republican primary to ensure our community's interest is heard." And that interest was obviously food stamps, welfare, Martin Luther King memorials, and black education, not what was best for the entire state or the nation.[42]

There were also push cards and crudely made, grammatically challenged flyers, which sounded to some like a Greg Brand specialty, distributed in heavily black areas. The headline of the flyer read: "The Tea Party intends to prevent blacks from voting on Tuesday. According to the Clarion Ledger, Chris McDaniel & the Tea Party plan to prevent Democrat voting in the Senate runoff on Tuesday between Thad Cochran and Tea Party candidate Chris McDaniel. We know the Tea Party uses 'Democrats' as code for 'African-Americans.' Don't be intimidated by the Tea Party. Let's turn out for all Mississippians and vote for Thad Cochran. Thad Cochran works for Mississippi. Mississippi cannot and will not return to the bygone era of intimidating black Mississippians from voting. We must rise up on Tuesday to have our voices heard on who will represent Mississippi in the US Senate. VOTE THAD COCHRAN."

The flyer had side-by-side photos of McDaniel and Cochran, and underneath a comparison of key votes important to the state's black voters. Cochran, it read, supported the Martin Luther King Memorial, public schools, the Jackson Medical Mall, All Mississippians, and the Farm Bill, which just so happened to be filled with food stamp money. McDaniel, it said, voted against the Mississippi Civil Rights Museum, opposes federal funding of public schools, and opposes SNAP funding in the Farm Bill. He was also involved in the nursing home photo scandal, the flyer alleged, and made racist comments on his radio show, it pointed out.

Of the crudely made flier, Haley Barbour himself felt the need to disavow it very quickly. "I don't know who put it out," he said, telling *National Review* that Cochran's support from Democrats "bubbled up organically," a spontaneous uprising to support the old Senator who always supported them. "Within a week of the first primary some black churches in Hattiesburg started running ads on the radio in Hattiesburg by raising the money themselves," another Barbour "fact" that quickly fell apart.[43]

The push cards were professionally made, complete with a nice picture of a smiling, casually dressed Thad Cochran, though the message they contained was just as sleazy as the flyer. Across the top was a picture of McDaniel aside an image from the '50s or '60s of blacks demanding the right to vote. "The Tea Party Intends to Prevent You from Voting. If challenged, demand your right to vote! Don't let Tea Party representatives discourage you from voting in the Senate run-off on Tuesday, June 24. This election is much greater than political parties and affiliations. It's time for all of us to send the Tea Party a message of strength and unity. We need to vote Thad Cochran on Tuesday, June 24th. Chris McDaniel in Washington, D.C. is a step backward for the state of Mississippi. We've come this far, we can't go back now! Paid for by All Citizens for Mississippi."

The nature of these racial attacks was very hurtful to Chris, feelings he expressed to me on numerous occasions. He's never exhibited any racist attitudes in his life, nor any hatred or hostility to any group of people. In fact, Chris was the only white player on the high school basketball team. He has very close and dear African-American friends.

One of his closest friends was a football star from high school, Glynn Branch. When I spoke to Glynn about his relationship with Chris, and the entire McDaniel family, he had nothing but praise for a man he said was "like a brother to me" throughout childhood. "I was at his house more than mine," he told me. "I ate at his house, slept in the house, and went on trips with his family." And when he was down on his luck and didn't have a way to get to school every day, Chris's father Carlos gave Glynn a truck. "They were good to me. Chris has always been there for me. Anything I needed, he was there. When my dad got sick and was having trouble with the VA, Chris got everything straightened out. If that's racist, I'd like to meet more people like that. But Chris doesn't have a racist bone in his body and I'd stand up in front of a church congregation and say that."[44]

Another of Chris's close African-American friends is Talib Bey, a former basketball coach at Seminary High School who now works in the private sector. In an interview, Coach Bey had nothing but praise for a man he calls a "good friend."

Chris is a special young man and I've known him for years. We played basketball against each other in high school, he at South Jones, me at Laurel. I've also known his family for years, his whole family. His kids are friends with my kids. And I've coached his son in youth basketball.

As for politics, I supported his candidacy against Thad Cochran and will again. He is a great leader and would make a great asset to the government, wherever he chooses to serve. I consider him a 'young gun.'

He's certainly not a racist. It's just that the African-American community needs to get to know him like I do because he is for all the people and will help our community as a whole. He is the right one, whether in Jackson or in Washington. Whatever he needs me to do in the future to help him win, I am committed to doing it.[45]

And it is black community outreach that caused Chris to face some criticism after the campaign as to why he did not try to counter the attacks with an appeal to black conservatives. One major critic was Star Parker, a conservative African-American columnist who wrote of the success of the attacks "despite being executed in broad daylight." McDaniel "knew exactly what to expect" because the "Cochran campaign told him. Yet he remained a spectator through it all. His counter strategy was no counter strategy and just continued what he was already doing: appealing just to Mississippi's conservative white electorate." McDaniel should have known, she writes, that "not all blacks are liberals. In Mississippi's huge black population are many conservative black pastors who want freedom for their flocks. They know that black poverty is not about government money." His campaign "seemed clueless that there were potential allies in Mississippi's huge black population to counter Cochran's liberal assault."[46]

But what Parker, and others like her, did not understand was two things: the overwhelming liberal nature of the counties where the race baiting attacks took place and the timing of them. As for the timing issue, the overall campaign seemed to be going strong on the issues, with back-and-forth barbs about spending and the role of government, but just a few days before the vote, the Cochran camp released the race-baiting torrent. "We didn't get wind of the racial attacks until very late because they waited until the very end to launch the attacks. And that actually violates state law," Chris said. "We have a law on the books that says if you take these types of actions that impugn morality—and racism is one of the most immoral things in our society—if you do that within five days of an election it's a crime. And they did it within two to three days, pushing these attacks and those voters to get out to the polls. They should have been prosecuted but they weren't."[47]

As for the overwhelming liberal nature of the counties, although Parker claimed there were many conservative blacks in Mississippi, the facts dispute that. The hard reality is this: In every Republican primary in the last several decades, African-Americans simply do not participate. "Never have and never will again unless a bunch of money is on the street," Chris said. "In fact it's less than three percent that vote in Republican primaries. When you are trying to unseat a forty-one-year incumbent, and doing it with a new organization and not much money, you've got to focus on *Republican* voters, which is precisely what we did and it's what *they* did for the first year of the campaign. They just lost those voters so they had nowhere else to turn for another group."[48]

Although Parker suggested that McDaniel failed because he did not reach out to the large number of black conservative pastors, and seemingly their "flocks," the truth is, the numbers were not on Chris's side, and he knew that far better than Star Parker. Throughout her polemic aimed at Chris's "failure," she failed to name a single prominent black conservative that would have been willing to stick their neck out in that political climate. Chris's message was aimed at every Mississippian, black as well as white, male as well as female, as all conservatives should do. Cochran's, by contrast, was not. He aimed his message squarely at one particular group of voters: Those who wanted more government, more services, and more access to the hard-earned money of the state's taxpayers. Chris could have used his relationship with Glynn Branch, Talib Bey, and other African-American friends that he has had for many years, but he was too honorable to exploit friendships for political purposes.

If you listen to the Barbours and their litany of lies you would think it was their campaign that acted honorably. Austin Barbour, Haley's other, lesser-known nephew, who had a top job with the Cochran campaign and miraculously did not coordinate any messaging with his brother Henry at the Mississippi Conservatives PAC, said that the campaign "spent a lot of time bringing a conservative message to black voters, as well as to white voters, the old and young, men and women."[49] And that conservative message was the strangest anyone has ever seen: more food stamps, welfare, federal money for state projects, and minority-based spending.

But Henry Barbour tried to steer clear of the issue and act as if his hands were completely clean, as if it never happened. When asked in March 2016 if he would vote for Donald Trump if he became the Republican nominee, the self-righteous Henry said it would be a tough vote to cast. "My expectation has been that I would support the Republican nominee, but I can't support somebody who would divide the country by race. That's unacceptable to me and I think unacceptable to most Americans. And so it would make it very hard for me."[50] This from the same man who helped orchestrate a campaign to smear conservatives as racists, bigots, white supremacists, and affiliates of the KKK.

With garbage like this flying around, it's easy to see why the Barbour's PAC created these new front groups, headed by African Americans, to do the dirty work, so as to appear to have clean hands in all this sickening madness. But their hands are as filthy as any political pigs can get, a point that would be proven soon enough. Yet as unbelievable as it may sound, the race would get worse still, much worse, as more earth-shattering revelations came to light on the very day of the runoff on June 24, 2014.

CHAPTER 11

STREET MONEY

Despite the Cochran campaign's sleazy smear operation, over the next three weeks McDaniel stayed positive and focused on his message of limited government. More conservative stars came out to help the surging challenger in those twenty-one days of furious campaigning between the primary and the runoff. And everyone just knew that Mississippi was poised to do something on a grand scale for the conservative movement.

Former US Senator and presidential candidate Rick Santorum, who won the Mississippi presidential primary in 2012, appeared at a couple of events around Jackson. Santorum had previously endorsed Chris via Facebook, cut an ad for him that aired just prior to the primary vote, and traveled to the Gulf Coast to make a few public appearances before June 3. In that ad Santorum said Chris McDaniel "has been a fighter for our 2nd Amendment rights, the right to life, a fiscally responsible government and stopping Obamacare. He has been a staunchly conservative leader in Mississippi, and I am confident he will bring that dedicated spirit to the US Senate."[1] In his Jackson appearance, Santorum said that Mississippi could begin to reverse its status as a last place state. "I know in Mississippi, you can be the butt of jokes because you're 50th in this or whatever the case may be. But now you can be first."[2]

Congressman Ron Paul, also a former presidential candidate and the face of the freedom movement across the country, traveled to Hattiesburg to speak at a huge outdoor rally. There he told the assembled crowd that his son Rand, serving as a US Senator from

Kentucky, needed help in Washington to save liberty. And he pointed to the large contribution that Michael Bloomberg gave the Cochran Super PAC, Mississippi Conservatives, thus proving a big difference between the two candidates. Why did Bloomberg choose to give to Cochran? "That's the guy that wants to tell you what you can drink and eat. . . . Liberty means responsibility. It means that you can make decisions that are harmful—but in a free society, your mistakes should be your mistakes and not collective and you can't go to the government and tell them to fix the mistakes." But Cochran couldn't be trusted, said Paul, since he's been there so long. "I spent 23 years in Washington, not straight through," the retired congressman said. "I went up in '76—I won a special election. I was there for four terms and that's when I met the opponent that you're campaigning against and I think he's been there way too long, to tell you the truth."[3] And nothing in all those years pointed to any special relationship Cochran had to liberty, only with more government.

In those three weeks, Chris McDaniel was doing things the right way, the honorable way. His message of true conservatism was getting out, money was in the bank to finish the race, media attention at its peak, the ground team in place, so all we needed now was for June 24 to hurry up and get here so we could get rid of Ole Thad and begin making concrete plans to take out Travis Childers, a process I was already deeply planning in my own private war room.

But Cochran's team was as busy as bees as well, though not with putting together a morally decent strategy, as we would soon learn, but one filled with more deception and filth. We knew he was courting Democratic voters, but how would the Cochran campaign get thousands of black Democrats, who are obviously not accustomed to voting Republican, to cross over and pull the lever for a party they had not supported en mass since before the days of FDR's New Deal? It was actually something akin to treason for blacks in the South to support the GOP in modern times. So how was this possible? And, keep in mind, the race-baiting campaign did not begin until a few days before the June 24 vote, so pundits were not thinking in those terms in the days immediately after June 3.

Many experts and commentators around the country, especially conservatives, were skeptical such a risky tactic was even doable. Most expected a McDaniel victory. Ed Morrissey, writing for the site HotAir. com, believed Chris would win handily and wouldn't "be surprised to see McDaniel win by more than 51/49." Others expressed downright skepticism that the motivation of black Democrats was even possible. Matt Lewis at *The Daily Caller* noted the challenge of getting "Democrats to turn out and vote in a Republican runoff election on some random Tuesday in June."[4] Lisa Murkowski and Joe Liebermann, Lewis noted, both used unorthodox strategies to win tight races, but the Mississippi race was a party primary and Murkowski and Liebermann had pulled off their miracles in general elections. What the *Washington Post* had already called the "nastiest primary in the county" was about to get a whole lot nastier with the Cochran chosen method of persuasion.[5]

As soon as the immoral race-baiting ads began hitting the airwaves just days before the vote, and nasty flyers began showing up on car windshields in black neighborhoods, a second prong of the Cochran-Barbour strategy was unleashed. There were serious allegations of very heavy dough, via the Barbour's generosity, being handed out around the state for use as "walking around" money, also known as "street money," claims that turned out to be true. It's the age-old tactic of vote buying, whereby operatives walk around town with large stashes of cash to hand out to potential voters, a nice incentive to see to it that they voted and voted the right way. It's been around since time immemorial and the tactic was always used on Election Day in certain crucial areas.

Most of this money, though not all, was funneled into the hands of several key black pastors, especially in and around Jackson, including Bishop Ronnie Crudup of All Citizens for Mississippi, who was also a friend of Cochran crony Alan Lange. Crudup took in and doled out tens of thousands of dollars in a so-called get-out-the-vote effort. The rest went to Thad's very own operatives to hand out. One young female Cochran campaign worker, Amanda Shook, head of "operations," was given an unusually large amount of campaign cash, receiving payments of $8,000, $10,000, and $15,000. Of course when asked why a twenty-five-year-old woman would be given such vast amounts of money, it was explained away as "get out the vote" funds for the "volunteers."[6] The heavy money, said spokesman Jordan Russell, was a "sophisticated ground game."[7] Initially the Cochran campaign did *not* disclose these cash payouts to the FEC. Only when they were caught did they fess up and blame it on an accounting "screw up" that was amended on later reports. It was just more dishonesty and another effort to avoid scrutiny for their shady campaign, the same operation, mind you, that consistently decried McDaniel's staff as one "full of criminals."[8]

When it was eventually revealed that a lot of these dollars did wind up in the hands of very well-placed black pastors, things got even more interesting and harder to explain for the Cochran Gang. One well-known and connected blogger in Jackson put it this way: "There is a little group of black preachers in Hinds County who um, lets just say get very active in election day politics and might even do it for a fee. Every time there is a local election, there is a race among black candidates to see who can get to 'the preachers.' One reason the church should stay out of politics. It won't surprise me to learn that some of these preachers followed their usual practice as leopards don't change spots."[9] And Hinds County was the main targeting effort.

Kim Wade, a black Mississippi conservative radio host, posted on Facebook that many black pastors throughout the state are on the take. He wrote: "Ok, here the going rate being paid by the GOP for cross over votes Tues. The bag man is dispensing $5000 a pop. Their contact will pay the pastor $2000 cash if instruction to go out and vote for Thad comes from the pulpit. $1000 cash to the pastor if the pastor allows a 3rd party to make the appeal. Individuals are to be offered $25.00 to vote. Most of that money is usually kept by the pastor and his money contact and they just make the appeal to their members. So if you get the appeal this Sunday. You can take it to the bank your pastor is on the take. If your pastor will take money under the table. He'll take it off the top of the table."[10]

Those few rumors alone are enough to make one's blood boil. These Democratic pastors were handed tens of thousands of dollars in cash in five-dollar bills! And no one ever asked anyone in the Cochran campaign what was done with all that money. It's easy to find out, though. The FEC report says one pastor was given $30,000 in cash.

If it's not reported, there are two possibilities: income tax evasion or he gave it out on Election Day. All it would take is a prosecutor to get an indictment for income tax evasion and, it's all but a guarantee, the canaries will start to sing loudly. He'll tell you everything he did with that money. It's that simple, but no one did a thing, because that's how crooked the system is. This is especially true since, as Erickson and Shaftan reported, the NRSC had paid for the All Citizens for Mississippi media spots, and there's no expenditure on FEC reports for any ad buys for All Citizens, so Crudup's money had to have gone somewhere else, either in his pocket or in those of the many other active "operatives."

Keith Plunkett, Chris's policy advisor and a longtime Republican operative in Madison County, received reports of this nefarious activity. "I was getting calls from people all across the state telling me this was going on, and I had one Democrat operative in my home county who has done this a long time flat out tell me he was paid $30,000 to hand out to voters. He paid out half and kept the rest. It wasn't a secret to those of us who have worked in politics for very long. It's happened in this state for decades. What was new was that a Republican was doing it in a GOP primary."[11]

The name that kept coming up as being right in the middle of the whole sordid affair was none other than Pete Perry, the chair of the Hinds County Republican Executive Committee, a county where the Cochran campaign would pick up an additional ten thousand votes in the runoff. As reported by the media, the Mississippi Conservatives PAC, Cochran's fundraising arm run by the Barbours, paid Perry, through his "consulting" firm, $60,000, ostensibly for "get out the vote" services. FEC reports do show a $60,000 payment on June 20, just four days ahead of the run-off, but also another $51,000 that had been paid out on June 10, making the total $111,000 in less than two weeks, a fact the media did not point out. So here was the head of the party in Hinds County taking sides in a contested primary and being paid an enormous sum to crush a fellow Republican.[12]

When the news first broke, Perry admitted that his firm was doing get-out-the-vote work for the Super PAC. When reporters asked state party chair Joe Nosef, he gave the all-too-familiar Obama-style answer, that he didn't know anything about it "until you just told me."[13] So do they really expect us to believe the chairman of the state Republican Party had no idea that a county chair was on the take for more than $100,000 from a massive Super PAC backing the Establishment candidate in a contested party primary for an all-important seat in the United States Senate? He either knew or he was asleep at the wheel.

Perry took the self-righteous road and blamed the story's emergence in the press on the courthouse lock-in incident, trying to paint it as McDaniel retaliation, or something. He told the *Clarion Ledger* that if anyone wanted "to level a suspicion or accusation of what I'm doing wrong, I would be glad to answer it." But that was just another lie. When he was asked specifically about it, just days before the vote, Perry wouldn't specify what the precise nature of his work was "because I don't want the McDaniel campaign to know what we're doing." And that's probably for a good reason, because what he was doing was illegal. Where that money really went no one knows for an absolute certainty, and Perry refused to say. When pressed about it further, he snapped to one reporter, "None of your business."[14] So much for full disclosure.

Cheating on elections is something Boss Perry did often, and apparently did well, according to one well-placed Democrat. The late Claude McInnis, who was a very well respected Democratic operative and served as election coordinator for the Hinds County Democratic Executive Committee before his death in 2015, told *Breitbart* that Perry specifically asked him to help the Cochran campaign cheat. And if you wanted to cheat in Hinds County with Democratic voters, even illegal ones, going to someone like McInnis would be a good place to start.

And McInnis knew Pete Perry very well indeed. As reported by Matthew Boyle of *Breitbart*:

> Charging that Perry 'has never ran a legal election in this state' because 'he was never qualified by the Secretary of State's office,' McInnis alleged that Perry asked him and county Democrats not to share records of who voted in each primary on June 3. The practice—called 'switching the books'—is where, heading into

a runoff, Democrats and Republicans swap poll books that list which voters voted in the respective parties' recent primaries.[15]

Without sharing the books, Boss Perry kept a secret from the McDaniel campaign, withholding who had already cast a ballot in the June 3 Democratic primary, thus making them ineligible to vote in the June 24 Republican runoff. Therefore, Perry insured that potentially thousands of Democrats could cross over and vote illegally in the runoff and the McDaniel campaign would remain in the dark about it.

When the state's top Democrat got wind of what was happening, he did the honorable thing by alerting the McDaniel campaign just a week before the vote. State Democratic Party chairman Rickey Cole, in a message to McDaniel aide Ric McCluskey, accused Pete Perry of paying James "Scooby Doo" Warren thousands of dollars to funnel to black preachers and others to get the vote out for Cochran. "Large sums of cash are being passed around. These guys are old school 'walking around money' vote buyers," Cole wrote. "He is working with Lane (LC) Murray and probably also Greg Brand," he said, referring to the same Brand that others pointed to as the likely culprit of the racist fliers, as well as the 'bagman' for some of the radio ad buys. "It is happening in Hinds County, but they are trying to move black voters in the Delta, Adams, Jefferson, Clairborne too. Need some out-of-state media to put some heavy scrutiny on Pete asap."[16] It might also be noted that the FEC reports from All Citizens for Mississippi also show a $16,000 payment to 'Scooby Doo' Warren, as well as another $19,000 payment to Best Solved Solutions, a get-out-the-vote organization of some type that just so happened to share the same address as Mr. Warren.[17]

Alerting the McDaniel campaign to the danger was certainly good news and a good bet that it was true. What motive would Rickey Cole have to lie? It would only destroy his reputation and that of his party. But Cole's mention of Lane Murray caused another strange incident, as if the campaign didn't have enough of them already. In what Matthew Boyle called "the most insane story of the MS Senate race," Murray, an ex-Klansman and apparent political operative, threatened State Senator Tony Smith, a staunch McDaniel supporter, after Smith posted a screenshot of the Cole allegations on Twitter. Murray called the allegations a "bald-faced lie" and claimed to be supporting McDaniel, though he never said so publicly until asked by Boyle. But why did Murray not threaten Cole since he'd made the allegation not Senator Smith? That showed me that Murray was indeed working for the Democrats and was in no way backing McDaniel. His admission of support was simply a way to keep the KKK allegations stirred up to hurt McDaniel.[18]

In an interview with *Breitbart*, Perry denied directly giving money to 'Scooby Doo' Warren, and said he hoped the money from a Super PAC backing Cochran routed through a company he controls wasn't being used to pay people to vote. But Perry wouldn't explain where the all money from the Super PAC had gone, and 'Scooby Doo' later confirmed that he was being paid to help Cochran. According to *Breitbart*, "Warren confirmed to the *Clarion-Ledger* that he is working for Cochran, and got approval from Washington, D.C., Democrats to do so. 'I called D.C. and told them what was going on with the tea party,' Warren said. But I can't do anything after the 24th because I'm a Democrat . . . Whoever wins will have to deal with me in November." So Warren's statement was an admission that he was working for Cochran to help his cause with Democrats for the June 24th runoff, but then would only pay Democrats to vote Democrat in November. Such a principled man.[19]

Matthew Boyle of *Breitbart* then interviewed Perry and asked him if he believed payments were being made for votes, to which he replied, "I certainly hope not" because he'd "been against that all my life since the 60s." He'd "seen it done and I'm totally against it." He continued with his campaign of denial, "It's not going on now that I know of. And I certainly hope it's not going on either side. Everybody will come out against it too–the governor, lieutenant governor, me, Joe down the street from me will probably come out against it. I hope it's not happening and I don't know if it's happening on the Cochran side and I hope the McDaniel side isn't doing it either."[20] It could hardly be reassuring to hear this from a man caught rifling through files at the USDA weeks after he was terminated from his job and whose name has been floated around as being at the center of just about every vote-stealing scheme in Mississippi in recent decades.

With the Mississippi press, though, Perry became more defensive and indignant, seemingly suffering from the same severe case of psychological projection that had to be affecting Jordan Russell. "I know that everything that Claude McInnis said in his interview with *Breitbart* was not just a lie, everything he said was a damn lie," he told the *Jackson Free Press*. "He made that up. . . . He [McInnis] wouldn't know an honest election if he saw one. The election in Hinds County was running proper. It was fine. We had 500 poll workers around the county working in 118 precincts, and they were doing their job." So by saying McInnis "wouldn't know an honest election if he saw one," was Perry admitting he knew that elections in Hinds County were dishonest? That would seem to be an admission of sorts because nowhere has Pete Perry ever called out the Democrats for running a dishonest operation in Hinds County. Crooks, you see, don't generally rat out other crooks. Of course what his definition of "proper" and "doing their job" was is open for interpretation. To borrow a line from a contributor at *Red State*, the whole thing "reeked of flop sweat."[21]

Another pastor that made serious allegations against the Cochran team was Stevie Fielder, who claimed that he received money in envelopes to hand out in exchange for votes. Independent journalist Charles C. Johnson broke that outrageous story on his GotNews.com website in a devastating piece that also connected Cochran campaign manager Kirk Sims to the scam. "They said they needed black votes," Reverend Fielder told Johnson in a phone interview. Saleem Baird, Cochran's minority outreach leader, was put in charge of the operation. Baird, who worked for Senator Roger Wicker before joined Cochran's campaign, was once arrested for running an illegal strip club in Jackson while in Wicker's employ, yet the charges were later dismissed and he remained on Wicker's staff. In text messages, Baird told Fielder to "give the fifteen dollars in each envelope to people as they go in and vote. You know, not right outside of the polling place but he would actually recruit people with the $15 dollars and they would go in and vote." Fielder said Baird was in charge of the effort statewide, and he, Fielder, was to get $16,000 for his vote-buying efforts, but was "stiffed" in the end by Baird.[22]

Complicating the matter, though, was the issue of Johnson paying Fielder for his story, what the provocative journalist called "checkbook journalism," which is certainly nothing new or out of the ordinary. The press also tried to say that McDaniel spokesman Noel Fritsch paid Fielder for the story, which was nothing more than a lie to discredit the McDaniel campaign, Johnson, and Fielder. But Johnson hit back with hardcore evidence in the form of photographs of Fielder holding up his phone showing text messages from Baird saying the money was going to be in envelopes and asking Fielder to e-mail him at his official campaign email address, saleem@thadforms.com, with his personal information.

The multiple text messages from Saleem Baird to Stevie Fielder read:

> June 21, 2014, 12:33—"I'm wirking [sic] my way that way I'll get with you that's a guarantee."

> June 21, 2014, 3:12—"I'm heading back from Brookhaven to Jackson but I can tell them to release those funds to you. Send me individual names and amounts along with home address to saleem@thadforms.com and I'll have money separated in envelopes at the office waiting for you."

Were those messages made up out of thin air? Did Noel Fritsch hack Saleem Baird's phone and create them? The obvious answer to both of those questions is no.

So, seeing the texts as legit, why did money need to be separated in envelopes? To hand out to people, of course. The Cochran camp, after they first called the whole thing a hoax, pointed to Baird asking Fielder for a home address, presumably for those campaign "volunteers" the money-filled envelopes were going to be handed to. Why, Cochran's people asked, would Baird want addresses for people who are being paid to vote? But why did they first call it a hoax? Like the rest of this sordid campaign, any confusion could have been solved if just one single prosecutor, or a reporter, simply asked to see Baird's phone or his phone records, or subpoenaed them in an investigation, which would have made it very easy to prove any malfeasance on his part. But in the days after the story broke, Baird was nowhere to be found. He apparently had bugged out of the state. How convenient.[23]

The Cochran campaign initally called the Fielder charges "baseless and false," but finally had to admit to hiring Fielder after the Johnson story broke. They claimed to have hired him for the get-out-the-vote effort that Perry was in charge of in Hinds County. The issue took on a new twist when Fielder later reversed himself and recanted his story, which came about only when Mississippi attorney general, Democrat Jim Hood, began investigating the matter. Hood's aim was not to investigate the allegations of Cochran spreading street money all over the state, but to see if the McDaniel campaign had paid Fielder to lie. So no one could really blame Reverend Fielder for taking back his comments. And Hood never did even consider investigating the Cochran campaign, nor did the media. It was dirty pool and the press was complicit.

CHAPTER 12

THE "DEFEAT": JUNE 24, 2014

With the all-out race baiting ad blitz and the allegations of street money all over the place, it didn't take a genius to figure out what was likely to happen within days of June 24. Everyone felt sure the other side was about to pull out all the stops to make sure Cochran got over the line. We were watching as closely as we could, but because the McDaniel campaign was seriously outgunned in money and muscle, several groups backing Chris—the Senate Conservatives Fund, FreedomWorks, and the Tea Party Patriots—sent election observers to monitor the polls. That caused a serious backlash from the Establishment, Democrats, and their affiliated groups, who complained of voter intimidation and suppression. "We'll be on the lookout," said Derrick Johnson, president of Mississippi's NAACP.[1] "There is no authority in state law for a PAC or other outside group to place 'election observers' in Mississippi polling place," wrote secretary of state Delbert Hosemann and attorney general Jim Hood in a joint memo, sharing their sudden interest in the integrity of the election system.[2] Both officials said they would deploy poll watchers to monitor the vote, as well as monitor these outside monitors. But we soon realized that we needed monitors for the monitors of the monitors.

State party chair Joe "Neutral" Nosef seemed to side with Cochran and the Establishment on the issue of poll observers. "I've talked to almost every lawyer with a bar number in Mississippi," he said, in an unbelievable boast to MSNBC's Chuck Todd, "and one thing that seems to be clear is it's nearly unenforceable," speaking of the law that prevents Democrats from voting in Republican primaries, which was one target of the vote watchers. "So the last thing that I want is a bunch of out of state people questioning randomly, or worse, people who are trying to vote today."[3] But Ken Cuccinelli, a former Virginia attorney general and head of the Senate Conservatives Fund, had a different take. "The laws in Mississippi are unusually open to poll watching from the outside. We're going to take full advantage of that and we're going to lay eyes on Cochran's effort to bring Democrats in. . . . And of course, if they voted in primaries, that's illegal."[4]

Jonathan Capehart of the *Washington Post* wrote of Cuccinelli's effort in a vile racial attack, saying "He is either ignorant of or couldn't care less about Mississippi's violent history of blocking blacks from the ballot box. My bet is both apply." The New Jersey born and bred Capehart, who knows far less about Mississippi than he claims, tried to tie the deaths of the three civil rights workers—Mickey Schwerner, Andrew Goodman, and James Chaney—murdered by the Klan near Philadelphia, Mississippi in June 1964, a year before Byron de la Beckwith murdered Medgar Evers, to the McDaniel camp wanting to ensure there was no foul play at the polls. Black conservative Lloyd Marcus, who supported Chris and appeared at rallies with him, took Capehart to task in the *American Thinker*, claiming the comparison was "beyond the pale of low-rent race-baiting politicking." It was, said Marcus, "deplorable, divisive, racist, and evil."[5]

After all the deceptiveness and political maneuvering to this point, Chris just wanted to ensure simple fairness in the process. "We just want fair elections," he told the press. "As chairman of the Senate Elections Committee, I've always just wanted fair elections. . . . The Republican Party has a primary for Republicans. That's the way it's designed. And that's the way it's supposed to be. I am a Reagan conservative. I'm not ashamed of that. Senator Cochran, however, has shown his true colors. We knew him to be a liberal Republican. By reaching out to liberal Democrats, he has confirmed what we have always known—that he doesn't have our best interests at heart."[6]

On June 24, the day of the runoff vote, Chris received an endorsement by the future President, Donald Trump, by way of Twitter. "I hope voters in Mississippi cast their ballot for @senatormcdaniel. He is strong, he is smart & he wants things to change in Washington,"

Mr. Trump wrote. This came early in the morning and was a nice little boost for what would turn out to be a very trying day.

In the end, the Cochran liberal message of fear mongering with food stamps and welfare expansion, aimed at black Democratic voters, as well as his extralegal campaign activities, won the day. There was a major increase in voter turnout, something rare in runoffs. In fact, there has not been an increase in voter turnout in a runoff in any Senate race in thirty years. We knew early on that things were not looking good for our campaign. We were getting reports all day of incredible surges in turnout in non-Republican areas and were getting calls about boxes with hundreds of votes where there are usually no Republican voters. We got a report that hundreds of Democrats were voting in a Democratic stronghold in the city of Hattiesburg. Keith Plunkett was also getting the same reports. "The day of the runoff I began getting precinct reports in from across the state and there were some precincts that had never seen one Republican vote ever cast that were turning out in big numbers. That's when I knew we might be in trouble."[7] And it proved to be the difference. The June 3 primary saw 318,000 votes cast, but on June 24, more than 382,000 were tabulated in the runoff, an increase of nearly 65,000. Cochran gained 194,932 total votes, McDaniel 187,265. In the end, McDaniel had fallen by just 6,500 votes in the initial count.

One major eye opener was Boss Perry's Hinds County. Cochran had won it handily on June 3. The fact that Cochran won such a liberal, and heavily black, county was not unexpected. What caught everyone's attention was the increase in voter turnout and the difference in Cochran's margin of victory in both votes. On June 3, there were 16,640 ballots cast in Hinds County, and Cochran won by a margin of 5,300 votes. On June 24, there were over 25,000 ballots cast and Cochran won by almost 11,000 votes. "In a race that Cochran won by 6,000 votes," said NBC, "that's pretty much your ballgame there."[8] But something was definitely fishy when Hinds County became the Republican stronghold in a primary election. It has never happened before and will likely never happen again without a similar "street money" operation. This was proven in the March 2016 Republican presidential primary, which saw 18,400 ballots cast in Hinds County, roughly 7,000 votes less than the 2014 runoff. As NBC said, that was the whole ballgame.

Other counties had similar question marks. *Business Insider's* Brett Logiurato explained how "Cochran won 22 of 25 Mississippi counties that had an African-American population of above 50%. And voter turnout in those 25 counties increased by almost 40%, up from about a 17% turnout increase overall."[9] For example, Jefferson County has a large black voting population that saw turnout soar 92 percent. That is unheard of. There were other surges in the Mississippi Delta counties of Quitman, Sharkey, Humphrey, and Coahoma. Overall the Delta region saw a 40 percent increase in turnout. "It's clear that Cochran's vote increases were correlated to the percentage of African-Americans who live in each county," wrote Harry Enten of the FiveThirtyEight blog. "The 10 counties where the incumbent senator improved most were those where blacks make up 69 percent or more of the population."[10]

In the end, as many as forty-thousand Democrats, voters that were casting both legal and illegal ballots, crossed over to pull the lever against Chris. Cochran increased his vote total by 38,000, most of them Democrats, while McDaniel, in true party-building fashion, increased his by 30,000, and you can bet that no more than a handful were of the Democratic persuasion. Had Cochran not had a surge of black voters, Enten wrote, he would have lost "by a little less than 8 points, or about 25,000 votes,"[11] which is the exact margin Chris led by in pre-vote polls. Chris McDaniel didn't just beat Cochran; he beat him badly. He beat a forty-one-year incumbent who has dozens of buildings named after him. Somewhere in the conscience of the Cochran team, they've got to understand that their way betrayed everything they had ever fought for, or at least pretended to fight for. They had to lie, cheat, and steal to win the election. Chris didn't. He ran on the issues. He never had anything to hide.

During the evening of June 24, I tried staying positive, but the truth is I was getting madder and madder, as were a great many other strong conservatives I talked with. Matt Kibbe of FreedomWorks, who has always said we must beat the Republicans before we beat the Democrats, encouraged me to stay positive and reminded me that if we lost we would fight again another day. But I knew the incredible amount of work Chris had put into a phenomenal campaign against insurmountable odds, as well as what this meant for the conservative movement as a whole. It was a shame to lose it in this fashion. I hoped this would have disastrous consequences for the Establishment in the future.

Awaiting the final results at his hotel near the convention center, Chris was deep in thought about what to do. Should he simply concede the election and move on, or should he fight what was obviously a very shady deal? The entire staff was unanimous in its desire to not concede.

When Chris finally emerged to speak to a throng of supporters tightly jammed in the convention center, I was a bit on edge about what he would say and how he would address the crowd. And when he began his speech, I was thrilled. It was sharp, defiant, and in some ways even Churchillian in its vows of resistance. Though he never mentioned a legal challenge, it was clear he was not conceding and would fight on somehow, someway. They could not be allowed to get away with this scot-free.

As Senator Michael Watson walked onstage, to shouts of "Write Chris In," he introduced Chris, saying to the crowd, "Ladies and Gentlemen, don't be deceived tonight. Amongst conservative Mississippians, Chris McDaniel won tonight! I firmly believe that and it's not over!" He then announced Chris McDaniel as *the Republican nominee for United States Senate.*"

When Chris took the stage to address his assembled supporters, I was excited at the prospect of fighting the Establishment. "We fought, we had a dream, and the dream is still with us," he opened. As to the unique happenings all around the state that night, he said, "There is something a bit strange, there is something a bit unusual about a Republican primary that's decided by liberal Democrats. So much for bold colors! So much for principle! I guess they can take some consolation in the fact that they did something tonight by once again compromising, by once again reaching across the aisle, by once again abandoning the conservative movement! I would like to know," he said passionately, "which part of that strategy today our Republican friends endorse. I would like to know which part of that strategy today our statewide officials endorse. This is not the party of Reagan! But we're not done fighting and when we are done it will be!"[12]

On this day, he said, "the conservative movement took a backseat to liberal Democrats in the state of Mississippi," to which a supporter shouted out, "It will backfire on them!" And indeed it would in the not too distant future. If this outrage could happen in one of the most conservative states in the nation, McDaniel continued, "it can happen anywhere and that's why we will never stop fighting!" This race had to happen, "for the very reasons you saw tonight," he said. "We are going to stand for those early principles. We are going to stand for our Founders. We are going to stand for the lessons of Reagan, even when sometimes it's difficult, even sometimes when those within our party shun us, or ostracize us, or ridicule us. We were right tonight!"[13]

He had always characterized himself as a fighter, such traits as coming as he often said from his Scottish and Irish heritage. When it's time to fight, he would often say in referencing politics, "you walk into a room and punch the biggest guy in there!" That's why he never feared facing off against Cochran, who was, politically speaking, the biggest guy in the room in Mississippi politics. And as he said in his announcement speech the previous October, "We shall go on to the end. We shall fight in academia. We'll fight in the classrooms and in the newspapers. We'll fight with growing confidence in the natural rights of mankind. We will fight in the marbled halls of Congress. We'll fight in the state capitols. We'll fight in the cities. We'll fight in the streets. We'll fight in the countryside. And, if for a moment, which I do not believe, this country and its liberty were somehow subjugated, I will expect a new generation of Americans to stand, with the Constitution as their guide, and reclaim what's rightfully theirs. This is our fight, if necessary for years, if necessary alone." How could he now walk away? He wouldn't.

In his non-concession speech, his intention was to make it clear that this was not a typical Republican primary. There was more at play. "I wasn't angry," he told me, "but I knew it was the right thing to do. And there were those who said it ruined my chance at future election, but I didn't care. I live every day to expose that type of madness, that type of betrayal, that type of abandonment of platform, so it will never happen again to someone else. It doesn't have to be me, but the conservative philosophy has to prevail. There's nothing radical about that mind-set; it's just if they think I'm going to walk away and quit, they are picking on the wrong person because there's nothing they can give me and there's nothing I want from them. The loss did not affect me. It was watching these so-called conservatives disavow and betray *everything* we believe in as a party simply for Thad Cochran and Haley Barbour to keep making money."[14]

For Cochran and his supporters, the victory was not fraudulent or politically unethical, but simply a great party-building effort, expanding the GOP's base of support to include Democrats, just as Austin Barbour told the press, the campaign "spent a lot of time bringing a conservative message to black voters." For Brother Henry, "it was one for the record books—and a model for how to grow the party." For Scott Reed, the campaign manager for Bob Dole's failed 1996 bid and the political strategist for the US Chamber of Crony Capitalism, the strategy "was to grow the electorate: base GOPers, independents, and Reagan Democrats."[15]

It was this last phrase, though, which was on the lips of a number of Cochran minions that gave many conservatives a good case of heartburn because this had been nothing like Reagan at all. "Reagan Democrats were conservatives, they were simply members of the Democrat party," said Dr. Milton Wolf, a conservative Senate candidate in Kansas. Thad Cochran "reached out to liberal Democrats to interfere with a Republican primary. It's a very different thing. Ronald Reagan knew to stand boldly for conservative principles of limited government and individual freedom, not what the current batch of Republicans stand for." Adam Brandon of FreedomWorks put it more succinctly, "This wasn't outreach. Outreach is promoting our values in other communities." This was "just spreading cash around."[16]

In the days after the vote, we waited for the assessments to come in from across the conservative nation. How would conservatives, particularly Tea Partiers, react to this? With anger, I hoped. But not everyone saw it that way. For "conservative" columnist George Will, it was about Mississippi voting "it's appetite" in keeping Cochran in office. "This bright-red state has the nation's lowest per capita income, the highest federal funding as a percent of revenue, and a surplus of cognitive dissonance between its professed conservatism and its actual enjoyment of the benefits Cochran can now continue to shovel its way." The Tea Party, wrote Will, came "face to face with a melancholy fact: Americans' devotion to frugal government is frequently avowed but rarely inhibiting."[17]

The problem with this line of thinking was that Chris, in a Republican primary, had won roughly 60 percent of the Republican vote. Republicans, then, did not vote for increased spending and more government. Liberal Republicans and thousands of liberal Democrats did. As John Hayward's piece in *Human Events* headlined, "Dems choose Thad Cochran as GOP Senate candidate."[18] This was not about an appetite for federal dollars; this was a major-league effort by the Republican Establishment, the Cochran campaign, and the Barbours to destroy Chris McDaniel's reputation by painting him as a racist. And all in the name of winning an election for selfish reasons. It was despicable and stomach turning, and every self-respecting Republican knew it. And many were downright mad about it.

But anger aside, were we just supposed to shut up and take it? Not all of us would. George Will proved the exception, not the rule. Strong conservatives were outraged, anger that was prevalent across the right-wing nation. As Mississippi Republican operative Gregg Phillips, now of VoteStand, said, "We watched them steal this election."[19] Now it was time to do something about it.

CHAPTER 13

THE CHALLENGE

While the Establishment Republicans were out to defend Cochran's tactics as a great example of expanding the party base, true conservatives were livid. They saw through the rhetoric and sought to expose the shenanigans and outright corrupt tactics of the party leaders in Mississippi. Senator Ted Cruz, speaking on the *Mark Levin Show*, called for an investigation. "What happened in Mississippi was appalling. Primaries are always rough and tumble. But the conduct of the Washington, DC machine in the Mississippi runoff was incredibly disappointing." That machine "spent hundreds of thousands of dollars urging some 30,000 to 40,000 partisan Democrats to vote in the runoff, which changed the outcome." This was not a party growing effort, Cruz said, but a recruitment of Democrats "to decide who the Republican nominee was," which "is unprincipled and wrong." And "the serious allegations of vote fraud" in the runoff "needs to be vigorously investigated and anyone involved in criminal conduct should be prosecuted." It would be the "only responsible thing to do."[1] Those calls for prosecution, coming from officeholders, were few and far between, and of course went unheeded.

Many conservative writers looked at the possible ramifications of this unbelievable racially polarizing effort. C. Edmund Wright headlined the race as "Despicable Haley Barbour and the Mississippi Mafia: They've no idea what they've done…" What Barbour and "his minions did the past three weeks in Mississippi has now set a new low standard for odious campaign tactics practiced by the Republican Establishment. The corrupt, unethical and immoral political cross-dressing . . . Haley and his team implemented over the past 21 days is simply breathtaking." There "was never even any pretense that Cochran understands, let alone concurs with, conservative base principles," he wrote. "He ran about as shamelessly liberal a campaign as any Mississippi Democrat would run. He didn't even pretend to be conservative. Did I mention that this was a Republican Primary?"[2]

John Hawkins of the website *Right Wing News* congratulated Cochran and the Republican Establishment on a "Pyrrhic Victory," a win that came with heavy losses and one that very well could shatter the GOP to pieces. It "wasn't an honorable victory," wrote Hawkins, as the "senile" Cochran touted his support for food stamps, paid "walking around money" to buy votes, and smeared Tea Partiers as racists.[3] Mollie Hemingway, a senior editor at *The Federalist*, made much the same point, arguing that longtime GOP voters could leave the party, and some seemed to be doing just that.[4]

Daniel Horowitz, writing for *Breitbart*, called it not a victory but "treachery," asking, much like Hawkins, how much longer the party could survive "when its leadership is inexorably against the ethos of its base." It cannot "be at war with its base forever and succeed." To campaign on liberal issues in contrast to the party platform is one thing, he wrote, but to accuse your own party "of being racist is downright despicable." The strategy only served to beat conservative voters "in order to reelect an ineffective incumbent who is barely lucid and will very possibly never serve out his term." But it's no different than what the Establishment does in Washington, as Republicans repeatedly use "Democrat votes to undermine and disenfranchise the GOP majority" and denounce conservatives for their positions. The Establishment condemns conservative challengers in Republican primaries but the "reality is that we are challenging these people precisely because they work in tandem with Democrats and empower them in growing government."[5] The Cochran strategy proved this without question.

Independent conservative journalist Charles C. Johnson, who helped to blow the lid off the whole race-baiting, vote-stealing effort, wrote that the "national GOP and Mississippi GOP establishments conspired to steal an election so that their government-funded gravy train could continue." Johnson pointed to "Karl Rove, Haley Barbour and his nephews, Romney consultant Stuart Stevens, and the National Republican Senatorial Committee" as being "engaged in a disgusting race baiting campaign to scare black voters into voting against McDaniel lest the Klan return."[6]

Niger Innis, a prominent black conservative, Tea Party activist, and national spokesman for the Congress of Racial Equality, writing in the *Daily Caller*, said the moderate Cochran had "disgraced his office and has come to illustrate exactly what is wrong with the establishment GOP. So concerned with winning reelection, Cochran's campaign affirmed what conservatives have long contended: the line between the Democrat and Republican establishment has been fully eroded." By engaging in such tactics to win reelection for Cochran, "the establishment GOP is willing to stoop to the lows we have seen from such Democrat cowards like Alan Grayson and Charlie Rangel," he wrote. "Is this what we can now expect from the establishment GOP, to simply shout 'racist!' and campaign based on race-baiting and fear instead of leadership and good ideas? These are dark days not only for the Republican Party, but for the American republic."[7]

John Fund in *National Review* flipped the argument around. What if, he wrote, "a tea-party candidate in some state had openly appealed to registered Libertarians to help him win a close primary runoff. There would have been howls of outrage that people who didn't agree with Republican values on social issues and foreign policy were being invited to decide a GOP race."[8] To me it was an interesting contrast but not a complete one. At least libertarians and conservatives have some things in common, like limited government, as Reagan once said the heart of conservatism is libertarianism. But this appeal by Cochran was as foreign to each other as capitalism is to communism.

As *Washington Times* editor Wesley Pruden wrote, Cochran's lobbyist friends "used race and resentment to aid his escape from oblivion."[9] Wrote one contributor at *Red State*, "The GOPe declared all out war . . . using the dirtiest of tactics, on the conservative base in Mississippi. This war was supported by all the national interests of the GOP establishment."[10] Steven Brodie Tucker of Virginia called it "the most disgusting and nefarious race baiting campaign ever devised by a republican reprobate and directed at conservative constitutionalist candidate" and vowed to "never forget" the "muck in Mississippi."[11] Leon H. Wolf at *Red State* said it was "rotten" down to the core.[12] Louis Woodhill of *Forbes* called it "egregious and disgusting."[13] Eliana Johnson of *National Review* referred to it a "two-faced victory,"[14] while Deneen Borelli, a prominent black conservative, wrote, "It's absolutely disgusting that the GOP establishment would stoop as low as left-wing radicals to maintain power."[15]

Matt Kibbe of FreedomWorks, who worked hard for Chris, called it "disgraceful," especially since the party seemed to acquiesce in it. "If the only way the K Street wing of the GOP establishment can win is by courting Democrats to vote in GOP primaries, then we've already won. Tonight is proof that the K Street establishment is intellectually bankrupt, and we are going to have to clean it up," he said on the night of June 24.[16]

Tea Party Express executive director Taylor Budowich said, "Unfortunately in Mississippi, nefarious campaign tactics seem to have won the day over ideas and a bold conservative vision." For Brent Bozell, nephew of conservative icon William F. Buckley, "Thad Cochran was able to squeak by against a previously little-known state senator thanks to the largesse of the Mississippi and Washington establishments." Dr. Milton Wolf, a Tea Party conservative challenging incumbent Kansas Senator Pat Roberts, said: "Tonight's election in Mississippi is yet another sign that the Washington Republican establishment has joined league with Democrats to declare all-out war on conservatives and our country is at stake. Even worse, NRSC chairman Jerry Moran spent hundreds of thousands of dollars of 'Republican' independent expenditure money turning out Democrats to manipulate a Republican primary in a safe Republican seat, showing just how low the party bosses are willing to go to protect fellow insiders."[17]

Conservative talk radio, which the Establishment hates anyway, was incredulous at the tactics used to knock down McDaniel. Glenn Beck, on his radio show, asked, "I have a question for every black Democrat in Mississippi. What the hell has this 90-year-old fart—a white Republican, the same white Republican that for years the Democrats have been telling you are nothing but old racists—you tell me exactly what Thad Cochran did for you?"[18] Aside from the fifteen dollars in their pocket on Election Day, Cochran has not done much in the way of real help.

On her show Laura Ingraham said, "When you have to win as a Republican by playing the race-baiting game that the left routinely plays, I would say that the taste of victory today should be quite bitter in the mouths of the Barbour family and Sen. Cochran himself. Do we really think that is the future of the Republican Party? Candidates who brag about how much bacon they'll bring home and who engage in those types of smear tactics with the help of the entrenched left, meaning people on the left who spend their morning, noon, and night smearing good people?"[19]

Perhaps Sean Hannity was the most bitter. "I am so angry at this Thad Cochran-Chris McDaniel race, I can't even begin to tell you," he said on his radio show the day after the runoff. "You know, between the flyer that was distributed in black neighborhoods and the robocall . . . why would these calls be made in a GOP primary? We all know the reason, because according to Mississippi law Democrats not voting in either party primary—remember, this was a runoff—were eligible to vote in the Cochran-McDaniel runoff. And Thad Cochran, seeing his power slipping away after many decades as a senator in Washington, you know, knew that his career was on the line here. And rather than run with dignity and honor and integrity and honor and decency, what did he do? He did just the opposite. And he was appealing to Democratic voters." So in order to win, Cochran "perpetrated the worst libel, the worst smear against conservatives, against the tea party, which is this false narrative that you hear every election cycle from Democrats: that conservatives are racist, that conservatives are mistreating the president because he's black. None of which is true."[20]

Talk radio king Rush Limbaugh also jumped on the appalling treatment of McDaniel and the use of blacks to decide a Republican race. "I wonder what the campaign slogan was in Mississippi the past couple days. 'Uncle Toms for Thad?' 'Cause I thought that the worst thing you could do as an African-American was vote for a Republican. Absolutely worst thing you could do. . . . Insider Republicans in the Senate bought 9 percentage points, 8 or 9 percentage points, from the black Uncle Tom voters in Mississippi. Well, you know what they call Clarence Thomas, Condoleezza Rice. Black Republicans, they call 'em Uncle Toms," he said on June 25, a comment that caused outrage in the left-wing media.[21]

The Republican Establishment, said Rush, "was a party to something to me that is reprehensible." Comparing it to a reverse of his "Operation Chaos" campaign in 2008, where he hoped to keep the heated Democratic presidential primary between Hillary and Obama going as long as possible, Rush told his listeners that the "Republican establishment was part of this Operation Chaos in Mississippi. This election, it has now been statistically proven, turned on Democrat voters from African-American counties," except the Republican Party backed and funded this effort. Reading aloud the content of one of the racist flyers, which, "combined with other efforts, secured a turnout of black Democrat voters in a Republican primary that gave Thad Cochran, in my view, a corrupt and undeserved victory." And the outcome was that the "most electable Republican candidate was thwarted by the Republican establishment," which was "part of this Operation Chaos in Mississippi."[22] And without it, he said, Cochran would have lost by at least 8 percent. Rush had it exactly right.

Chris also received support from the state chairman of the Missouri Republican Party, Ed Martin. His state had seen similar uses of race baiting against conservatives and he wanted it to stop. So he moved to bring a censure motion against Henry Barbour at the August 2014 meeting of the RNC in Chicago. He wrote in an op-ed:

> The question for we Republicans is simple: are we a party of principle that believes racial divisiveness is wrong whenever it occurs? Or are we a party of convenience that allows racial rhetoric as long as it's done by someone with enough political connections? I don't know the answer. I can only hope that when placed before the RNC, we don't close ranks and pretend that this is only a state matter. I don't believe that Republicans should risk losing the Senate in 2014 to protect Henry Barbour's actions in Mississippi.[23]

But at the meeting something strange happened. Rather than condemn Henry Barbour, the RNC gave him a standing ovation. It was sickening but it would come back to bite them when they least expected it.

Despite the treacherous RNC, Chris had vast conservative strength at his back, as well as overwhelming evidence of wrongdoing to prove his case, so he decided to do something about it. Rather than lie down and quit, like most Cochran supporters earnestly wanted him to do, he decided to take a stand and fight back by challenging the election results. As he said in his non-concession speech on the night of the runoff, there were "dozens of irregularities reported all across this state, and you know why. You've read the stories, you're familiar with the problems that we have," he said to shouts of "corrupt state" from across the room. "Now it's our job to make sure that the sanctity of the vote is upheld. Before this race ends we have to be absolutely certain that the *Republican* primary was won by *Republican* voters."

Receiving advice and encouragement from friends, family, lawyers, and supporters, everyone was behind his efforts to challenge the election results. He laid it out to me in an interview:

We had to get to the bottom of the truth. And I always told people I would fight for them, no matter the consequences. Had I stopped then, had I quit then, I would have been no different than those politicians in Washington. Because that would have been me attempting to salvage my political career as opposed to what I had always told the people, and that was that I would fight for them. So I wasn't about to become a sell-out politician. I was going to prove to everyone that I was exactly who I said I was when I was running. And of course when I did challenge the results my unfavorable numbers went up but I don't care about that. I know what we did was right. And I know what they did was wrong and I knew that every day we kept it in the press there was a chance for us to eventually clean this party up and make sure this doesn't ever happen again. So we did our best to keep it alive as best we could.[24]

The official challenge would come down to two basic problems. The first was legal crossover votes. There were some conservatives, like John Hayward of *Human Events*, who said that Chris should not base his challenge on legal crossover votes because such voters were definitely in line with the law. The main point of challenge on this issue was a larger one, that the simple appeal to those liberal voters was destructive to the party's platform and a detriment to its future and it also violated party rules—not to mention the fact that it was quite likely many of those voters were paid to crossover. Second, there was a great possibility that thousands of Democrats who had already voted in the Democratic primary on June 3 had illegally cast their ballots in the Republican runoff. There was no question that that was against the law.[25]

Chris was not the first to challenge an election but if successful he would be the first to win a challenge to a statewide race. There were a number of possible outcomes from a legal challenge: He could win the right to a new election and we would have to do this all over again for the third time or he could simply be named the Republican nominee. There was precedent for a new election, and that was seen as the most likely outcome.

Despite many conservatives calling out the unscrupulous manner in which Cochran won and Chris's willingness to fight for his principles, some Republican pundits criticized McDaniel's team's challenge of the results. One in particular was Ann Coulter, who believed Chris was "being led down a primrose path to political oblivion" by his supporters, who she derided as "clowns and nuts," as well as the "sore loser brigade," treating the race as if it were "a prom queen election," which would only kill Chris's career. Pointing to Richard Nixon in 1960, Bob Dornan in 1996, and John Thune in 2002, all who had races stolen from them by Democrats, Coulter emphasized that Nixon and Thune did not contest the results but won in future elections—Thune in 2004, Nixon in 1968. Dornan initiated a challenge and his career was finished.[26]

Our position was that the reason Democrat bullies, now Republican ones, continue to steal elections was because they knew we would not fight back. And we were certainly not alone in our defiance. "If the GOP is allowed to get away with how they won in Mississippi," wrote

Erick Erickson, "they will never really practice what they preach when it comes to limited government. There must be some consequence. I am just not sure what it should be. But I'm pretty damn sure it shouldn't be that the base is treated as the battered wife of the Establishment. Right now that seems to be the case."[27]

After all the races that had been outright stolen by the Democrats in the previous decades, many that Coulter had mentioned, someone had to finally stand up and fight back against this new Establishment, now to include both parties it seemed. And Chris McDaniel was that man.

Challenging Thad Cochran in an election was like taking on Mount Everest anew. For the difficult task ahead, the McDaniel legal team recruited squads of volunteers to find and gather the evidence needed for the challenge. These teams of investigators, almost all of them volunteers, would have to travel to most of the state's eighty-two counties and gather the evidence that illegalities and irregularities had occurred in sufficient quantities to change the outcome of the race. We all knew what had happened, but now it was time to prove it.

Gathering the evidence proved to be quite a challenge as the teams were thwarted at every turn. Our volunteers were not allowed to look at documents, which are public record. Others were told to come back on other days. A good many of the circuit clerks around the state are Democrats and a lot of them had good relations with Senator Cochran, and they didn't like the idea of being investigated. But the way our system works, every clerk does it differently, and there were thousands of irregularities. It was a daunting task to be sure.

One outside group that came to Mississippi to help was True the Vote, a voter integrity organization that fights for "free and fair elections for every American." True the Vote witnessed the roadblocks but also alleged that there were instances of willful destruction of evidence. The group filed a lawsuit in federal court calling for a restraining order against the state Republican Party. "Defendant county commissioners have continued to violate federal law by preventing access to election records," said organization founder Catherine Engelbrecht. "Now, we think we know why. If the affidavits we now have regarding the destruction of election documents and other similar stunning findings are true, then no Mississippian, no American, can trust the results of this election. Based on what we have seen—and all we have not been allowed to see—we now believe that unless the court steps in, illegal voting will go unchallenged, voters' rights will be diluted, voters' trust will be violated—and an unlawful and inaccurate election may be certified by the State of Mississippi." True the Vote claimed to possess evidence of "election subversion," "destruction of voters' absentee ballot applications and mandatory envelopes," and "illegal alterations of poll books." It certainly needed to be examined and reviewed by a court of law.[28]

For state party chair Joe Nosef, who one might think would want to ensure that his own party primary was on the level, said in a statement to *Breitbart* that he thought the True the Vote lawsuit story was a joke. "My initial reaction is I thought it was a headline from *The Onion*. Now I see how this group has earned their awful reputation."[29] So here was the party chairman, who prided himself at every turn as being a complete neutral in this contest, characterizing an organization that seeks free and fair elections for everyone as "awful." In the end, the Nosef side of the argument prevailed, as a federal judge threw out the suit. One wonders if this had been a Democratic lawsuit alleging Republican malfeasance against African-American voters, would the judge have tossed it so quickly. I think not.

In his challenge, Chris and his legal team first had to file an election challenge with the Mississippi Republican Party Executive Committee, headed by none other than Joe Nosef. Such a hearing seemed like a lost cause to many since it was quite obvious that the party was behind Cochran from the start, but unfortunately that is the correct procedure because a primary is a party function. As such, the party refused to hear the merits of the case, much less rule on it. In a letter to Chris's lead attorney, Mitch Tyner, Chairman Nosef placed blame on the refusal on the issue of time. "It is neither prudent nor possible in a single day for any political committee to process and review the significant amount of complex evidence necessary to make such a decision, and attempting to do so would be prejudicial to both candidates," he wrote. So Nosef moved to officially certify the results of the primary runoff, rather than look at any evidence. Chalk up another example of party one-sidedness.

But to Tyner, it was a bit of a setback. "The party was the perfect venue in which to hear the challenge since it was responsible for the election, but we will move forward with a judicial review as provided for under the Mississippi code."[30]

After losing out with the party, the next available option was to file with a court of law and Chris could file a suit in any county in the state where there were election irregularities, and they were all over the place. As this new process unfolded, Chris and his legal team, to the surprise of many, did not seek an election do-over but his recognition as the rightful nominee of the Republican Party. "We are not asking for a new election," Tyner said. "We're asking the Republican Party to simply recognize who actually won the election."[31]

It may have seemed a strange request to members of the media and the general public, but Tyner had Republican Party rules on his side. Although the Republican Establishment kept pointing to state law to support its position, the laws, at least in this case of an inter-party squabble, didn't apply to the nomination process according to a rule of the Republican National Committee, the same RNC that Henry Barbour belonged to. Specifically Rule 11, Section B states:

> No state Republican Party rule or *state law* shall be observed that allows *persons who have participated or are participating in the selection of any nominee of a party other than the Republican Party*, including, but not limited to, through the use of a multi-party primary or similar type ballot, to participate in the selection of a nominee of the Republican Party for that general election. *No person nominated in violation of this rule shall be recognized* by the Republican National Committee as the *nominee* of the Republican Party from that state."[32]

So under the RNC's own rules, the party could not recognize Thad Cochran as the nominee for the US Senate seat in Mississippi because of the participation of Democrats in a Republican Party process. It's as simple as that. But as this race, and the subsequent court challenge, showed for all to see, there's one set of rules for the elites and another for everyone else.

While the process moved slowly forward, the Republican Party Establishment, led by RNC Chairman Reince Priebus, remained completely silent, even though it was their rule in question and despite the fact that there were repeated calls for him to personally intervene in Mississippi. Iowa radio talk show host Steve Deace, a steadfast supporter of Chris, penned an open letter to Priebus, accusing him of "leading from behind" while the Establishment GOP used "Obama/Alinsky race-baiting tactics against their own base," a "betrayal that appears to have been at least partially master-minded by Henry Barbour, a member of your very own RNC." Republicans, he wrote, that have questioned this strategy are labeled "kooks" and "spoiled sports," a group that would have to include Rush Limbaugh, Mark Levin, *Breitbart*, and *National Review*. What happened to the concept of a "big tent?" he inquired.[33]

Famed conservative stalwart Richard Viguerie, who heavily backed Chris, also wanted to know why Priebus remained silent while this election was "hijacked" by the Establishment. Rather than ask conservatives to bolt the party, Viguerie demanded a full investigation of the allegations, for if it were allowed to go unchallenged, it would only continue in the future so long as the Establishment held the levers of power. If not, there would be grave consequences for the party and the movement.[34]

Despite all the roadblocks and obstruction, and the complete lack of support from the party, enough evidence was soon found that would have changed the outcome of the election in a big way. In a press conference, McDaniel and his team of attorneys provided initial evidence of at least 3,500 illegal crossover votes, 9,500 irregular votes, and more than 2,200 improperly cast absentee ballots. Those numbers would swell with additional investigations. In the official certified results, Cochran's margin of victory was a bit more than 7,600 votes, so McDaniel had ample proof, with the evidence he was allowed to gather, to verify that Cochran was not the legitimate Republican nominee. Had all those roadblocks not existed, and the team of volunteers been allowed to review public records in every county, many more improper ballots would have been found.[35]

So now the challenge and the evidence would have to be filed in a court of law. The main obstacle, however, was a state law that seemed to establish a twenty-day deadline to file an election challenge, a day that had long since past. And Cochran's legal team, consisting of attorneys from the Butler Snow firm, pointed to a specific law on the books, MS Code 23-15-921, which provides for a twenty-day deadline but the statute did not refer to a statewide race.[36]

By the time the legal challenge was filed in August, any twenty-day deadline had long since passed. But even if it did apply, why would the state have such a law in the first place? How could anyone challenging a statewide race possibly gather evidence in twenty days? It was if they were simply holding on to the ball until the clock ran out to prevent any preying eyes from seeing their handiwork, or shoddy work, whichever the case may be. However, McDaniel's team contended that the law did not apply. McDaniel's legal team pointed out a newer statute, MS Code 23-15-923, which did include statewide races, yet made no mention of a twenty-day deadline because the older statute had been partially repealed in 1986.[37]

Tyner also pointed out that when Speaker of the House Philip Gunn filed his own legal challenge back in 2003, in which he successfully challenged a Barbour, it was more than thirty days after the election, and he used the same statute that McDaniel was using and the issue of a deadline did not come up in the Gunn case. According to some media reports, the secretary of state's office, the state agency that is in charge of elections in Mississippi, admitted there was no twenty-day deadline to file a challenge.[38]

One Mississippi election law expert wrote about these two competing statutes. "The bottom line is this: the election code, as it stands today, contains no deadline for filing a contest in a state-wide primary," said John Pittman Hey, a man I've personally known for more than fifteen years. "Nobody who reads the two parallel sections would infer that there is a deadline in this case. There are no annotated cases showing that such a deadline exists or has been grafted into the statute by the courts. The secretary of state, our chief elections officer, stated that there is no such deadline."[39]

But this election was about so much more than mere questions of law. A little, seemingly insignificant legislative election in a Jackson suburb or a small thing like state law or party rules had no real ramifications for the state political machine, but unseating Thad Cochran would be the political equivalent of Hiroshima. In the end, the judge assigned to the case by the state supreme court, Hollis McGehee, sided with Cochran and dismissed McDaniel's challenge on a legal technicality. "Senator McDaniel's failure to file within 20 days precludes the court from going further and means that the motion to dismiss must be granted without prejudice," he ruled. The judge also agreed with Cochran's legal argument that a 1959 Mississippi Supreme Court ruling, *Kellum v. Johnson*, established the twenty-day deadline.[40]

Was this ruling really good law or just good enough to knock down Chris McDaniel? As John Pittman Hey wrote, "the notorious Kellum case (which engrafted a twenty-day deadline into the previous incarnation of the current law) was dropped from the statutory commentary by both major publishers of the Mississippi Election Code, whose editors apparently thought it was no longer relevant to the modern version of the statute."[41] But it was enough to suit the Establishment. They found a small sliver of space with which to squeeze through and block Chris's legal challenge. There was no way they wanted the merits of this case brought before a court and laid out before the people.

Chris was not quite finished, though. He still had one more option. After contemplating the issue for a few days, he decided to appeal the ruling to the state supreme court. He asked my opinion on the matter and I was frank and honest. If you don't file an appeal, I told him, you will spend the rest of your life wondering what would have happened. But I, like many others, including Chris himself, was very skeptical that the court would overrule the local judge. And there was certainly good reason since the state's highest court had already ruled against us some weeks before.

Back in July, when the whole episode over access to election records came to the forefront and True the Vote filed its lawsuit, Chris sought the court's intervention, with a *writ of mandamus*, that would have ordered every county in the state to give him access to the poll books containing all the information about the voters who had cast ballots on June 24. In other words, Chris wanted the un-redacted poll books, containing personal information about each voter, which is, by the way, public record, so that it could be determined if those voters were actually legal or not. The court denied the request. It was a concern but was no reason not to see what the court might say about the twenty-day deadline issue.[42]

In October 2014, in a 4 to 2 decision with three justices recusing themselves, the state high court upheld Judge McGehee's decision that the challenge could not proceed because of the missed deadline. "The case was not dismissed on substantive grounds. The case was dismissed on a procedural technicality," Chris told me. And it was clear to many that the court system simply did not want to hear the merits of the case. "To hear a case like that would have exposed massive wrongdoing, whether negligent or intentional, all over the state of Mississippi."[43]

It was an election that was simply unfair, unlawful, and downright wrong, all the way around. We discussed it one afternoon over pizza at Pasquale's.

There's no such thing as a fair election in Mississippi, and I thought I'd never say that. Now there are some counties that are incredibly fair, with men and women of integrity, but the state as a whole, with so much corruption and fraud going on, particularly in the Delta counties and Hinds County, there hasn't been a fair election in this state in a long, long time. And it really shook my faith in the entire system. I knew it was corrupt. But I thought the justice system was at least that last refuge of some degree of integrity. Any prosecutor worth his salt, state or federal, could have spent ten minutes and broken this whole thing up in no time. It would have been over. And they did nothing. . . . They want the system dirty because they know how they can profit from it and abuse it. They know that as long as they have the ability to utilize people like Crudup and others who will take their dirty money, they know that they will forever have an advantage over those who play the game honestly and with integrity.[44]

With the end of the legal challenge, the long, hard fought campaign was over, nearly a full year since it began in October 2013. There were no more speeches to give, no more arguments to be made, no more voters to convince, no more battles to fight. Now was the time to sit back, reflect, and see what the real outcome would be, for Chris, for those involved on his side, and for the party and the conservative movement. But just as Erick Erickson had written, there would be a consequence of what Daniel Horowitz had rightfully called treachery. As 2015 dawned, and the beginning of the presidential campaign, we would soon learn exactly what that consequence would be.

CHAPTER 14

REMEMBER MISSISSIPPI

eception. Deceit. Fraud. Theft. Trickery. There simply aren't enough words in the English language to describe the Establishment's conduct in the US Senate primary in Mississippi in 2014. But defeat conservatives they did only to nominate the quintessential RINO, Thad Cochran, rather than staunch conservative Chris McDaniel, who was clearly the choice of Republicans, to face a hapless Travis Childers in November in what was widely seen as an electoral foregone conclusion: Cochran's election to a seventh term in the United States Senate.

For Chris McDaniel, his campaign against Thad Cochran is having and will continue to have a lasting impact on American politics. "With this race I knew defeat was probable but I also knew that we would finally, once and for all, demonstrate the divide in the party. What I seek is not a perfect party but a party that is at least honest to its convictions, and we haven't had that in a long time in the Republican Party. I think it's something people will talk about for years to come."[1]

McDaniel policy advisor Keith Plunkett agreed. "What we did was to completely turn Mississippi politics on its ear," he told me. "Mississippi Democrat Chairman Rickey Cole said that years from now people will still be defining themselves by whether they were a McDaniel voter or a Cochran voter, and I agree with that. These power broker political operatives showed the people very clearly who they are and what they are really about. If Chris's run for Senate did nothing else but that then it was well worth it."[2]

There is no question that the race exposed the cast of character we conservatives are dealing with in the Establishment. "Cochran's campaign was built on lies," Melanie Sojourner told me. "Lies about Cochran's record. Lies about Chris's record. Lies about Chris's character. To the establishment nothing mattered but winning, and they had to do it by lying and cheating. It's a horrible legacy they left for what was a once great Mississippi GOP."[3]

"It showed how desperate they could become and how their desperation leads them to do things we never imagined," McDaniel said. "That's the legacy of Mississippi in 2014, a legacy of betrayal of one of their own, it was a legacy of brutality of one of their own, a legacy of slander and libel and illegal activity. It was a legacy that exposed the Establishment for what many of us assumed they could be and that was a group of individuals who only come around every four years to beg for our votes and then they disappear and hope we won't watch them lie and deceive and cheat and steal from the people of this country."[4]

These politicians, he continued, "come home, issue a couple of good press releases, tell us how conservative they are, then they govern based on their own selfish needs and those of the donor class. I'm hoping it's always a reminder of how far they will go to hold onto their moneymaking schemes. And I hope it's a wakeup call for people all over the country that they can use to advance a conservative agenda, one based in liberty and not collectivism, one based in the dignity of all people and not just the dignity of the wealthy. There's no question that it has exposed who our adversaries are."[5] And although he couldn't have foreseen it in the fall of 2014, his race would have far-reaching consequences, even emerging in the 2016 presidential campaign.

But in the fall canvass of 2014, across the nation the victorious Republican nominees embarked on the general election campaign with a common theme. No matter what state, what district, or what GOP candidate was on the ballot the issue was the same. The Republican Party, fresh off putting down conservative challengers across the country, ramped up their oft-used autumn rhetoric: *We need a Republican Senate, in addition to the House, so we can stop Obama, repeal his agenda, and push for conservative reforms.* That tactic worked once again, as a GOP surge won an astounding number of Senate seats, including the re-election of Thad Cochran in Mississippi, which had as much to do with dislike of the president and an extraordinary weak Democratic challenger than anything coming out of the mouths of Cochran or any of the Republican candidates nationwide.

But in his victory, Cochran gained the smallest vote total in his career, with slightly less than 60 percent of the vote. In his previous six Senate races, he had never gotten less than 61 percent, while most were landslides, including 100 percent in 1990 when no one bothered to challenge him and 71 percent in 1996. Though it may not seem like a big drop, the numbers show that potentially tens of thousands of conservatives, McDaniel supporters all, did not vote in the fall 2014 Senate election.

Then came the usual disappointment. Despite the soaring rhetoric and lofty conservative promises, Republicans once again embraced big government when the new Congress convened in January 2015, placating to the needs of their big donors. They cut deals with Obama, essentially giving him everything he wanted, and did not put forward anything that remotely resembled a conservative reform agenda.

Thad Cochran did his part for Establishment support for his seventh term by casting a vote for the Ryan-Obama omnibus spending bill, for Loretta Lynch as attorney general, for Common Core proponent John King for secretary of education, and was one of only a few Republicans to agree to sit down and meet with Obama's pick for the Supreme Court, Merrick Garland, who was to replace stalwart conservative Antonin Scalia. These latest Republican betrayals proved to be the last straw for conservatives.

Those of us professing the Christian faith are familiar with a very important teaching that our Lord Jesus Christ gave us: "A tree is known by its fruit." A good tree will only produce good fruit, He told us, while a bad one will produce bad fruit. Used in a political fashion, I contend that a conservative tree will produce conservative fruit, while a liberal tree will produce only liberal fruit. And we often see a lot of liberal fruit from Republicans in Washington, DC, causing conservatives to realize that it's time to break out the chainsaws.

And the chainsaws came out in force, first in 2015, as the very unpopular House Speaker John Boehner was replaced with Paul Ryan.

But things did not change. Speaker Ryan, immediately upon assuming office, handed Obama all of his requests in a new omnibus spending bill. Republicans then gave the president the keys to a disastrous Trans Pacific Partnership trade deal. When anger rose, Ryan self-righteously tried to kiss up to conservatives by reminding us, "Put down your arms. I'm one of you."[6] But he's shown himself not to be.

In 2016, the conservative insurgent rage continued to swell across the political landscape, as anti-Establishment presidential candidates immediately surged to the top of the heap in the presidential race, shocking Establishment pundits. The presidential race shaped up quickly to be a contest between grassroots outsiders versus the Establishment insiders, the same campaign dynamic that transpired in Mississippi. This is not a conflict between Democrats and Republicans, but a fight between the Establishment Machine and the People. The day after the Mississippi primary runoff, speaking about the Establishment race baiting of McDaniel, Rush Limbaugh said, "Now, it would be one thing if the Democrats did that. They do it every election cycle anyway. But for them to be joined, even if from a distance, by the Republican establishment here, simply confirms what we have long said on this program about establishment Washington. It is ruling class vs. country class. It's elites vs. the plebes. You and me are the plebes, and they are the elites, and they are aligning together."[7]

Cochran and the Barbour Machine knew this all too well, as did the entire Establishment Republican Party. If Chris McDaniel had prevailed in his campaign against the very symbol of the Establishment, a man who has been a major party figure for more than forty years, as well as its "greatest appropriator," then all bets were off. Chris could not be allowed to win. If he did, every old bull in Congress would suddenly become vulnerable and the Establishment would have a multitude of fires to put out every election cycle from now until the end of time. It would be open season on the Establishment Machine nationwide, and it may very well come apart at the seams. So if Republicans had to align with Democrats and completely trash and destroy the reputation of a good and decent man to keep control of the party, and ward off any would-be challengers in the future, then so be it.

And you couldn't find a better man than Chris McDaniel. He's always worked hard and never had any bad business dealings. He's always paid his taxes and never been to jail. The son of two devout teetotalers, he didn't even have his first beer until age thirty-eight. If Establishment forces can come into a small town like Ellisville, Mississippi and take the son of a deacon and make him sound like the Antichrist, then none of us have much of a chance. And it centers on how much money conservatives must raise to be successful in order to offset the Establishment narrative because their cohorts in the media control the storyline, and that's why conservatives are always at a disadvantage. So it is imperative that we all stand together.

No real conservative would have ever supported Loretta Lynch or the federal judges Cochran supported, or the trade pacts he voted for. We know that no real conservative would have ever voted to fund Obamacare the way he did, even though Ted Cruz and other conservatives fought hard to repeal it. And it is reasons like these that explain the rise of the anti-Establishment movement after Mississippi 2014.

Robert Reich, a former Clinton cabinet officer, wrote of this swell of anti-Establishment fervor happening in both parties. With the surge of Donald Trump on the right and Bernie Sanders on the left, one a "74-year-old Jew from Vermont who describes himself as a democratic socialist," the other a "69-year-old billionaire who has never held elective office," traditional candidates we are accustomed to are being decisively beaten. "Something very big has happened," he wrote, "and it's not due to Bernie Sanders' magnetism or Donald Trump's likeability. It's a rebellion against the establishment."[8]

Former Jimmy Carter pollster Pat Caddell, on *Breitbart* radio, opined that the 2016 presidential election "is not about ideology and it's not about issues. It's about insurgency. The system is on the verge of coming apart" and the politicians in Washington aren't going to be able "to put the genie back in the bottle." The Establishment political class, whose consultants are running most of the presidential campaigns, said Caddell, "have less feel for the electorate than the man in the moon."[9] And indeed that is true. As Reich wrote, "The establishment doesn't see what's happening because it has cut itself off from the lives of most Americans. It also doesn't wish to understand, because that would mean acknowledging its role in bringing all this on."[10]

With Establishment candidates going down right and left in the presidential campaign, being taken apart by insurgents, as Caddell and Reich pointed out, the insiders have no idea what's driving it. It's the exact point McDaniel made to me two months before the start of the presidential contests. "Many of these people live in a bubble," he said. "Their bubble consists of Starbucks, big expensive malls, nice wine, nice cars, the country club lifestyle, and they will only speak to each other. They have nothing in common with the average person. Nothing whatsoever. But the elites in Mississippi believed, and they make each other believe, that I wouldn't get over 20 percent of the vote, that I'd never win Madison County. Although I absolutely adore Madison County, it was not our primary focus. We were more focused on rural and blue-collar counties because those are the Mississippians that are hit hardest by Senator Cochran's abuse of his authority and power, whereas some of the Hinds and Madison people are associated with government in some fashion."[11]

But what was really behind this insurgent mood among conservatives? What greatly angered Republican voters across the nation? Many analysts could reasonably conclude that a likely culprit to this insurgency was the new Republican Congress failing to live up to promises they made in 2014, or that it was anger at Barack Obama. But we've seen this same song and dance before. How could anyone reasonably conclude that Establishment Republicans, with their visceral hatred of conservatives, would mount any kind of challenge to Obama? Could we honestly expect them to all of a sudden change their stripes? They didn't with George W. Bush and a Republican Congress, and they didn't this time either.

A Republican Senate, though, with the addition of Chris McDaniel, Dr. Milton Wolf, Matt Bevin, Joe Carr, and Greg Brannon, to go along with a successful conservative candidate in Nebraska, Ben Sasse, and the absence of Cochran, McConnell, and Lamar Alexander, as well as the other old bulls who retired, would have gone a long way toward pushing the leadership, if not replacing it, and putting the brakes on

Obama's socialism. Senators Cruz, Lee, and Paul would have had some powerful allies and reinforcements.

But the Establishment did not want that. Their congressional members returned to do what established members do—toss their oft-used campaign conservatism aside and govern as the liberals they really are, more in tune with the wealthy elites and not at all concerned about the needs of common, everyday Americans, the forgotten Americans that Trump reached out to. In this way, conservatives are treated, as Erick Erickson put it, "like a battered wife."

As conservatives, we've gotten used to being used, and it's certainly not the first time the Establishment has openly deceived us. This attitude is reflected in public opinion polls, the most shocking of which emerged in the fall of 2015 when a Fox News survey revealed that 62 percent of Republicans felt betrayed by their own party.[12] And even though many conservatives consider this latest backstabbing to be the final straw, something else is driving this insurgency. In his book *What America Needs: The Case for Trump*, Jeffrey Lord, a contributing editor of the *American Spectator*, writes that Donald Trump's appeal "has boosted the stature of other anti-Establishment Republicans. In the 2015 Kentucky governor's race, for instance, Republican Matt Bevin, written off by the pundits as a sure loser, won in a landslide, and a chastened Democrat operative ascribed the victory to 'Trump-mania.'"[13] This certainly has a ring of truth to it but before there was Trump-mania, there was McDanielmentum, a phrase coined after Chris surged to the lead over Cochran in the spring of 2014.

As Chris himself said on the campaign trail in Hattiesburg, stumping with Ron Paul, "I think we are the precise state at the precise time to lead a conservative revolution in Washington, D.C."[14] Though he was unsuccessful in his bid to lead the emerging movement from the US Senate, the revolution is happening now and the birth of it, the real turning point for it came with Cochran's "victory" over McDaniel and the way in which the Establishment portrayed conservatives in that race. The candidate himself was certainly treated like pond scum, but by extension every conservative in Mississippi and across America was likewise treated. No conservative contender, nor his supporters, has ever been treated as shabbily by the powers that be than Chris

McDaniel. No candidate has ever had as much negative money thrown at him. No candidate has ever been race-baited as extensively or as horribly as McDaniel. Ever.

No other conservative challenger in 2014 was so publicly—and very openly I might add—slandered by his own party as a friend of the Ku Klux Klan and other white supremacist groups or accused of wanting to throw a whole race of people out in the street to fend for themselves, and do so simply because of their race. Nor was there in any other race the widespread evidence of vote theft and shady, underhanded tactics. But all of that and much more happened to Chris McDaniel, and this treatment of a God-fearing, rock-solid conservative reformer who passionately wanted to change his state and the nation has caused the anger that changed the whole race for the White House and, quite possibly, the entire American political landscape.

The Establishment had no clue as to the angry beast they were unleashing by smashing a good man like Chris McDaniel in the manner in which they did and, by extension, all conservatives in the country. The anger was popping up around the nation soon after McDaniel's "loss" on June 24, as ABC headlined less than a week later: "Tea Party Anger Over Mississippi Ripples Across the States." Campaigning in Tennessee, Joe Carr, then challenging Lamar Alexander, heard from one of his voters about the McDaniel race, "We have gotten over the grief and we are mad as hell and our heads have exploded." Carr himself was "shocked that the establishment would go to such lengths to incorporate the message of liberal Democrats . . . soliciting their vote for the sole reason to stay in power. They are more interested in holding on to power than advancing the principles that embody the [Republican] platform. I think you are seeing a level of energy in Tennessee I have never seen before. They have done this at their own peril."[15] How right Joe Carr was.

Dr. Milton Wolf, campaigning in Kansas, told ABC News that voters there were "livid" about Cochran's victory. Conservatives, he said, "are infuriated by what the GOP establishment did in Mississippi. It's an absolute betrayal of what our party stands for. If the Republican establishment are using our resources and contributions to turn out Democratic voters, then what's the point of being Republican anymore?"[16]

Mollie Hemingway at *The Federalist* noted that several party voters were already vowing to bail out and it was all because of the McDaniel race. One said Cochran's tactics were, for him at least, "the last straw." The "GOP's strategy in this primary demonstrates to me is that the disdain, if not hatred, by the owners and operators of the Republican Party for the ordinary voter (me) is equal to or only marginally less than that of the owners and operators of the Democrat party," the voter wrote. "Openly encouraging Democrats to vote for Thad Cochran is like giving away tickets to fill seats that the public apparently doesn't think are worth paying for," wrote another GOP voter. "Any businessman would see this as the beginning of downward spiral that will result in bankruptcy for the circus."[17]

Adding insult to injury, the RNC sent out a very poorly worded fall campaign fund-raising e-mail that only rubbed salt in a very open wound. Written under the name of Chairman Reince Priebus, the e-mail, seeking campaign contributions, asked of those donors who had yet to submit a gift: "Did you abandon the Republican Party?" Anger boiled over on social media, with many conservatives vowing to leave the party and never contribute again. Dean Chambers of the *Examiner*, writing from his Virginia home, took the RNC to task, specifically mentioning the McDaniel-Cochran race. "This is no way to demonstrate support for the 'conservative principles' you claim to believe in and on the basis of this bad behavior and poor choice expect me to give them money so they can undermine conservative principle and good Republican candidates, over bad ones, even more," Chambers said. "If the GOP wants us to support them again, and donate money when they solicit it, they need to consistently stand up for conservative principles and support real Republicans when they run against charlatans like Thad Cochran and then show your clear non-support for a good candidate like Ken Cuccinelli. If they want our support, they need to get back to actually being Republicans again rather than trying to be Democrat Lite."[18]

Former Virginia attorney general and 2013 gubernatorial nominee Ken Cuccinelli, who was also sandbagged by the party powers, warned that the Establishment is "in danger of breaking this party in half. It isn't the conservatives that are going to do that. We're right where the Republican Party is supposed to be: smaller government, less power, more freedom, and they're running from that. They're the ones who are breaking this party apart. So if that happens . . . it's on the establishment folks who are doing it."[19] Even McDaniel himself said just days after the runoff that conservatives "don't feel welcome in the Republican Party anymore."[20]

By the fall of 2015, with the presidential campaign in full swing, the fury was roiling across the country. The people's wrath was aimed directly at the Establishment, and it galvanized insurgent Republicans and conservatives at the grass roots across the nation. There is little question about that. Public opinion polls began showing Republican voters moving into the camp of anti-Establishment candidates like Donald Trump, Ted Cruz, Rand Paul, and Ben Carson, and in many cases giving upwards of two-thirds of the vote to these outsiders. Establishment toadies never got out of the basement. Lindsey Graham, aka "John McCain Junior," hovered around one percent and never made it onto the major debate stage, dropping out in utter humiliation even before the first contest in Iowa, while many of the so-called experts were caught unaware with no explanation of what force was driving this bus.

The Iowa caucuses, held on February 1, 2016, proved that the polls were no fluke, as Cruz came out on top with 28 percent of the vote, Trump second with 24, and Carson fourth with 9 percent. Throw in Rand Paul's 5 percent and, just as the polls indicated, two-thirds of Republican voters chose anti-Establishment candidates. The face of the Establishment, Jeb Bush, got 3 percent. John Kasich received all of 2 percent, as did Chris Christie. In New Hampshire eight days later, Trump won huge with more than twice the vote of John Kasich, who threw millions of dollars into the race only to come in a distant second. Trump did it again in South Carolina on February 20, with Cruz nabbing 22 percent. Added to Trump's 33, and Carson's 7, that's 62 percent of voters turning from the Establishment. Same thing in Nevada, where Trump, Cruz, and Carson gained 72 percent of the vote, while on Super Tuesday, on March 1, Trump and Cruz won every contest except the Minnesota caucuses, which went to Marco Rubio.

And the treatment of McDaniel is a prime reason why this happened and why many conservative activists and evangelicals rallied around Ted Cruz and Donald Trump. Keith Plunkett, who co-chaired Ted Cruz's campaign in Mississippi, spoke to the presidential candidate specifically about the 2014 Senate race and its role in the 2016 upheaval. "Senator Cruz told us back in August 2015 that it was having an affect on the presidential race. Without the Mississippi Senate race, and all that happened, we wouldn't be seeing what we are seeing nationally, not at this level of anger."

As Erick Erickson wrote in September 2015, "McDaniel's name comes up repeatedly in conversations with conservative activists who have gone to Trump. They have concluded the GOP does not give a damn about them, so they do not give a damn about the GOP." So the "chickens are coming home to roost for the GOP now. They played for keeps. They won the battle. But it is looking more and more like they are losing the war. The funniest thing about it though is that they do not realize it and do not want to realize it."[21] Even Haley Barbour has conceded the point on Trump. "A lot of people wanna send Washington the bird," he told Katie Couric, "and they think [Trump's] the most perfect, giant middle finger they could imagine."[22] Yet Uncle Haley doesn't seem to realize that the bird is for him and the entire Republican Establishment.

In fact, the campaigns of two major GOP candidates, Rick Perry and Scott Walker, blew up on the launch pad because of a tie-in to the Barbour-Cochran race-baiting of McDaniel. Perry thought he had a legitimate shot, and perhaps he did until he hired Henry Barbour, and his campaign quickly imploded. Walker was seen as perhaps the eventual nominee, given his stand against the unions in Wisconsin, but then he hired Brad Dayspring, who, as a member of the NRSC, lobbed race-baiting bombs at McDaniel, and Walker found himself out of the race well before liftoff, to the shock of pundits everywhere.

But the Mississippi primary on March 8, with four candidates still in the race, proved to be the most stunning anti-Establishment contest yet, as an unprecedented 85 percent of voters cast their ballots for Donald Trump and Ted Cruz, while both Establishment candidates finished in single digits. No other state gave anti-Establishment candidates that much support, at least with that number of horses still in the race. As well it should be, for it was in Mississippi that the Establishment committed the worst atrocity of this war. "Mississippi was a turning point, absolutely a turning point, no doubt about it because it wasn't a battle for the heart and soul of the libertarian conservative Republican voter," said Adam Brandon, now president and CEO of FreedomWorks. "We won that, we won it, our arguments carried the day with that voting bloc. It's the desperation to turn to liberals to bail themselves out, bail their lobbyists out. . . . That's where they've been exposed."[23]

And that is the most lasting legacy of the Mississippi Senate election in 2014 and what it was really all about. True conservatives across the country rallied to the call of "Remember Mississippi." For Mississippi 2014 was the Alamo for the conservative movement. It was a clarion call for every true conservative in America, as Pat Buchanan used to say, "to ride to the sound of the guns." And to the horror of the Establishment, the people remembered Mississippi for it's the Magnolia State, often the butt of national jokes, that started this new political revolution, an insurgency that awarded the 2016 GOP presidential nomination and the White House, in an unprecedented fashion, to Donald J. Trump.

But the Establishment in Mississippi had to retaliate and mount a trophy on their wall. Melanie Sojourner, Chris's campaign manager, fell victim to the machine in her bid for a second term in the Mississippi Senate, all because she had the audacity to manage the McDaniel campaign. She lost her seat in 2015 by just sixty-seven votes to an eighty-year-old liberal Democrat, Bob Dearing, the same Bob Dearing she had beaten four years before with the backing of the state party. Not this time around, though.

After the votes were cast, Dearing led by a handful of votes with the usual stories of vote fraud. Yet this time several poll workers were arrested for breaking voting laws in Franklin County, which, by state law, should have disqualified the entire box and Sojourner had several very qualified and trained poll watchers who documented many instances of fraud and wrongdoing. The media, which has used gallons of ink to smear Sojourner and McDaniel for the "fake news" nursing home incident, spent almost no effort on actual arrests for voter fraud.

In the ensuing election challenge, Butler Snow, the law firm of Barbour and Cochran, sent two lawyers to represent Dearing the Democrat. And since Dearing couldn't even raise enough money to run his own campaign, there's no way he could have afforded two high-priced lawyers from Butler Snow. We can only speculate who was paying the freight on this one and what promise Dearing had to make to get the backing.

In the end, the issue went before the full Mississippi Senate. Chris was sure that they would simply call for a new election, rather than throw out the fraudulent boxes, which, had they done so, would have given the election outright to Sojourner. But in a shocking move, the Republican-controlled Senate overwhelmingly voted to seat Bob Dearing over Melanie Sojourner. The tax-and-spend liberal Democrat, who the GOP had trashed as a tax-and-spend liberal Democrat just four years before, won out over the archconservative senator who dared to speak out against the Establishment and manage Chris's campaign. Another woman trashed by the Republican Establishment. Make no mistake, the statewide Republican Party despises strong women like Melanie Sojourner. They need people to fall into place. They don't want leaders, they want dominoes, and she is not a domino.

But the Establishment in Mississippi was dealt a setback in the summer of 2017. The family of Mark Mayfield, who tragically took his own life just days after the 2014 runoff, filed a wrongful death lawsuit against those they believed were responsible. After conducting an independent investigation, the family came to their own conclusion: the fault lay with Cochran and his political machine. The suit named as defendants the mayor of Madison, Mary Hawkins Butler, several members of the Madison police force, the Butler Snow law firm, and attorney Donald Clark, who represented Cochran during the ordeal. The complaint cast blame exactly where it should have and completely exonerated the McDaniel campaign of any culpability.[24]

As for Chris McDaniel, he is very much involved in the fight against the Establishment, with no plans to ever give up. In 2016, the American Conservative Union, founded by William F. Buckley in 1964, named McDaniel the nation's top conservative for 2015 in recognition of his fight for conservative values. But the most often asked question is will he run again? Will he go through another grueling, grinding campaign? "Given all that was thrown at us we still beat them!" he said of his campaign against Cochran and the Establishment. "And, to tell you the honest truth, we'll beat them again next time!"

There's no quit in Chris McDaniel. For him the future of our country is too important to sit idly by and watch its demise. To fight against the Establishment is in his Scotch-Irish blood. If his name has to be dragged through the mud and his reputation trashed and tarnished in order to return the country to the constitutional republic our Founder's desired, then he will pay the price. The American Republic is more than worth the effort.

END NOTES

INTRODUCTION

1. Geoff Pender, "Voters Set To End Historically Bizarre Race, *Clarion Ledger*, June 21, 2014, http://www.clarionledger.com/story/news/2014/06/21/voters-set-end-historically-bizarre-race/11227879/.

2. Katherine Miller, "Did this happen in the Mississippi Senate primary, Scooby Doo, or a good John Grisham book? *Buzzfeed*, June 24, 2014, https://www.buzzfeed.com/katherinemiller/did-this-happen-in-the-mississippi-senate-primary-scooby-doo?utm_term=.weNlOZ5Kx6#.iadEkpNWdw.

3. Sean Sullivan, "The nastiest primary in the country is in Mississippi. And it's only getting uglier," *Washington Post*, May 21, 2014, https://www.washingtonpost.com/news/the-fix/wp/2014/05/21/the-nastiest-primary-in-the-country-is-in-mississippi-and-its-only-getting-uglier/?utm_term=.f87153ce8691.

4. Frank Corder, "Mississippi Republican Watchlist," July 17, 2012, http://yallpolitics.com/index.php/yp/post/32745/; Sam R. Hall, "Ranking GOP Rising Stars," *Clarion Ledger Blog*, July 24, 2012, http://blogs.clarionledger.com/samrhall/2012/07/24/ranking-gop-rising-stars/.

5. "Thad Cochran: The Quiet Persuader," Time, April 14, 2006, http://content.time.com/time/nation/article/0,8599,1183976,00.html.

6. Patrick Howley, "Bill Kristol is trying to get Tom Coburn or Rick Perry to run Third Party," *Breitbart*, March 19, 2016, http://www.breitbart.com/big-government/2016/03/19/bill-kristol-is-trying-to-get-tom-coburn-or-rick-perry-to-run-third-party/.

PROLOGUE

1. Breitbart News, "AP: McDaniel Runs to 'Save the Republic,'" June 15, 2014, http://www.breitbart.com/big-journalism/2014/06/15/ap-mcdaniel-runs-to-save-the-republic/.

2. Tiffany Parrish in an interview with the author on March 20, 2016.

3. Jack Fairchilds in an interview with the author on March 14, 2016.

4. Chris McDaniel, "Announcement Speech," Ellisville, MS, October 17, 2013, https://www.youtube.com/watch?v=Hb3B4gGcQ1E.

CHAPTER 1 CHRIS MCDANIEL: A SON OF MISSISSIPPI

1. Chris McDaniel in an interview with the author on June 20, 2016.

2. Malcolm Gladwell, David and Goliath: Underdogs, Misfits, and the Art of Battling Giants (New York: Back Bay Books, 2015), 140–143.

3. Walters, et al. v. Holder, et al., http://cases.justia.com/federal/district-courts/mississippi/mssdce/2:2010cv00076/71766/101/0.pdf?ts=1417658469.

CHAPTER 2: THAD COCHRAN: A LIBERAL WOLF IN CONSERVATIVE SHEEPSKIN

1. For more on the 1976 race, see Craig Shirley, *Reagan's Revolution: The Untold Story of the Campaign that Started It All* (Nashville: Thomas Nelson, 2005) and for more of Mississippi's role, see Jere Nash and Andy Taggart, *Mississippi Politics: The Struggle for Power, 1976-2006* (Jackson: University Press of Mississippi, 2006), 59.

2. Nash and Taggart, 62.

3. Ibid., 68.

4. Ibid., 67–68.

5. *Capitol Reporter,* September 14, 1978.

6. *Jackson Daily News,* May 22, 1978.

7. *Jackson Daily News,* August 19, 1978.

8. *Clarion Ledger,* October 31, 1978.

9. *Clarion Ledger,* January 16, 1979.

10. *Clarion Ledger,* January 28, 1979.

11. All material for Cochran's extensive voting record was gained from the American Conservative Union's Ratings: http://acuratings.conservative.org, FreedomWorks Scorecards: http://congress.freedomworks.org, and *Conservative Review*'s Scorecard: https://www.conservativereview.com/scorecard.

12. Douglas Brinkley, *The Reagan Diaries* (New York: Harper Perennial, 2009), 487; Chicago Tribune, April 4, 1987.

13. Brinkley, Diaries, 487.

14. On the Issues, "Thad Cochran on Abortion," http://www.ontheissues.org/Social/Thad_Cochran_Abortion.htm.

15. Thomas Jefferson to James Madison, December 20, 1787, in Papers of Thomas Jefferson, vol. 12, 442.

16. Richard L. Stroup and Bradley Townsend, "EPA's New Superfund Rule," Cato Institute's Review of Business and Government, 1993, page 71, https://object.cato.org/sites/cato.org/files/serials/files/regulation/1993/7/v16n3-8.pdf.

CHAPTER 3: THE SAGA OF UNCLE HALEY

1. For more information on the history of this machine, see Curtis Wilkie, *The Fall of the House of Zeus: The Rise and Ruin of America's Most Powerful Trial Lawyer* (New York: Broadway Paperbacks, 2011), 8–9, 35–38.

2. Bradford Plumer and Noam Scheiber, "Barbourism: The K Street Evil Genius Who Took Over Mississippi," *New Republic,* September 23, 2007, https://newrepublic.com/article/64947/barbourism.

3. Jere Nash and Andy Taggart, *Mississippi Politics: The Struggle for Power, 1976–2006* (Jackson: University Press of Mississippi, 2006).

4. Lucy Madison, "Haley Barbour will return to lobbying when governorship ends," CBS News, December 22, 2011, http://www.cbsnews.com/news/haley-barbour-will-return-to-lobbying-after-governorship-ends/.

5. Bradford Plumer and Noam Scheiber, "Barbourism: The K Street Evil Genius Who Took Over Mississippi," *New Republic,* September 23, 2007, https://newrepublic.com/article/64947/barbourism.

6. Ibid.; Donna Ladd, "The Truth About Barbour's 'Blind Trust,'" *Jackson Free Press*, August 29, 2007, http://www.jacksonfreepress.com/news/2007/aug/29/the-truth-about-barbours-blind-trust/.

7. Bradford Plumer and Noam Scheiber, "Barbourism: The K Street Evil Genius Who Took Over Mississippi," *New Republic*, September 23, 2007, https://newrepublic.com/article/64947/barbourism.

8. Bradford Plumer and Noam Scheiber, "Barbourism: The K Street Evil Genius Who Took Over Mississippi," *New Republic*, September 23, 2007, https://newrepublic.com/article/64947/barbourism.

9. Anna Schecter, "Former Tobacco Lobbyist Turned Governor Kills Statewide Anti-Smoking Program," ABC News, December 8, 2006, http://blogs.abcnews.com/theblotter/2006/12/former_tobacco_.html.

10. Bradford Plumer and Noam Scheiber, "Barbourism: The K Street Evil Genius Who Took Over Mississippi," *New Republic*, September 23, 2007, https://newrepublic.com/article/64947/barbourism.

11. Steve Wilson, "Ten Reasons the Kemper Project is bad for consumers," *Jackson Press*, June 3, 2015, http://thejacksonpress.org/?p=34451.

12. "Haley Barbour's Dirty Money: Lobbying for the Kemper County Coal Plant," A Report from the Sierra Club, https://content.sierraclub.org/creative-archive/sites/content.sierraclub.org.creative-archive/files/pdfs/100_248_HaleyBarbour_FactSht_03_low.pdf.

13. "Growth and Opportunity Project," Republican National Committee, http://goproject.gop.com/rnc_growth_opportunity_book_2013.pdf.

14. Steven Hsieh, "6 Conservative Who Support Raising the Minimum Wage," *Nation*, January 22, 2014, http://www.thenation.com/article/6-conservatives-who-support-raising-minimum-wage/.

15. Julian E. Zelizer, *The American Congress: The Building of Democracy* (New York: Houghton Mifflin, 2004), 704.

16. Chris Matthews, "America's Most Corrupt State Defends Itself," *Fortune*.com, July 28, 2014, http://fortune.com/2014/07/28/most-corrupt-us-state-mississippi/.

17. Jonathan Kaminsky, "Former Mississippi prisons chief pleads guilty in bribery case," Reuters, February 15, 2015, http://news.yahoo.com/former-mississippi-prisons-chief-pleads-guilty-bribery-charges-171944362.html;_ylt=A0LEVxz5H3NVaJcA0zhXNyoA;_ylu=X3oDMTEydTZqdTNtBGNvbG8DYmYxBHBvcwM0BHZ0aWQDQjAwWQDQjAwMjlfMQRzZWMDc3I.

18. Ross Adams, "Prison bribery case now up to $800M, prosecutors say," WAPT.com, April 12, 2016, http://www.wapt.com/article/prison-bribery-case-now-up-to-800-million-prosecutors-say/38965084.

19. WLOX News, "Walker gets max sentence: 60 months in prison," WLOX.com, June 16, 2014, http://www.wlox.com/story/25788108/walker-gets-max-sentence-60-months-in-prison.

20. Paul Hampton, "Judge holds Pickering in contempt in DMR records case," *Clarion Ledger*, May 27, 2014, http://www.clarionledger.com/story/news/2014/05/27/judge-holds-pickering-contempt-dmr-records-case/9653337/.

21. Anna Wolfe, "Mississippi gets D- grade in 2015 State Integrity Investigation," Center for Public Integrity, November 9, 2015, https://www.publicintegrity.org/2015/11/09/18437/mississippi-gets-d-grade-2015-state-integrity-investigation.

22. Deanne S. Nuwer, "Gambling in Mississippi: Its Early History," *Mississippi History Now*, http://mshistorynow.mdah.state.ms.us/articles/80/gambling-in-mississippi-its-early-history.

23. Timothy P. Carney, *The Big Ripoff: How Big Business and Big Government Steal Your Money* (Hoboken, NJ: John Wiley & Sons, Inc., 2006), 134–136.

24. Ibid.

25. Wilkie, *House of Zeus*, 15.

26. Wilkie, *House of Zeus*, 15, 39.

27. Ibid., 55.

28. Carney, *Big Ripoff*, 139.

29. Jake McGraw, "How did Mississippi smoke up billions from the tobacco settlement?" Rethink Mississippi, October 14, 2013, http://www.rethinkms.org/2013/10/14/mississippi-smoke-billions-tobacco-settlement-medicaid-inflation-short-term-thinking-anti-tax-dogma/.

30. NBC News, "Mississippi at a glance," from an original report from National Journal, July 16, 2008, http://www.nbcnews.com/id/25645168/ns/politics-decision_08/t/mississippi-glance/#.WOuLohiZPos.

31. Wilkie, *House of Zeus*, 55.

32. Ibid.; Karl Rove, *Courage and Consequence: My Life as a Conservative in the Fight* (New York: Threshold Editions, 2010), 34.

33. See http://www.butlersnow.com.

34. Keith Plunkett in an interview with the author on February 19, 2016.

35. "This Government Brought to You by Butler Snow," Cottonmouth Blog, December 17, 2013, http://cottonmouthblog.blogspot.com/2013/12/this-government-brought-to-you-by.html.

36. Ibid.

37. Ibid.

38. Chris McDaniel in an interview with the author on June 20, 2016; Butler Snow Press Release, March 2, 2015, https://www.butlersnow.com/2015/03/butler-snow-launches-economic-development-firm/; VisionFirst Advisors, http://www.visionfirstadvisors.com.

39. Max Blumenthal, "The Secret GOP Sex Diary," *Daily Beast*, July 23, 2009, http://www.thedailybeast.com/articles/2009/07/23/the-secret-gop-sex-diary.html.

40. See Elizabeth Creekmore Byrd website, http://elizabethcreekmorebyrd.com; John Bresnahan, "Pickering's wife sues alleged mistress," *Politico*, July 16, 2009, http://www.politico.com/story/2009/07/pickerings-wife-sues-alleged-mistress-025067.

41. Max Blumenthal, "The Secret GOP Sex Diary," *Daily Beast*, July 23, 2009, http://www.thedailybeast.com/articles/2009/07/23/the-secret-gop-sex-diary.html.

42. Alexander Burns, "Barbour Gang to Cochran's Rescue," *Politico*, March 19, 2014, http://www.politico.com/story/2014/03/haley-barbour-thad-cochran-republicans-104791.

43. Emily Wagster Pettus, "Emboldened after Cantor, tea party crows," AP, June 12, 2014, http://bigstory.ap.org/article/emboldened-after-cantor-tea-party-crows.

44. Thomas Jefferson to Horatio G. Spafford, March 17, 1814, in Albert Ellery Bergh, ed., *The Writings of Thomas Jefferson, Volume 14* (Washington, D.C.: Thomas Jefferson Memorial Association, 1905), 118.

45. Charles C. Johnson, "Haley Barbour's Dictators: Lobbyist Uses Third World Tactics in Mississippi Run off," Gotnews.com, July 15, 2014, http://gotnews.com/haley-barbours-dictators-lobbyist-uses-third-world-tactics-in-mississippi-run-off/.

46. Matthew Campbell and Dawn Kopecki, "Trent Lott's Firm Made a Fortune Lobbying for the Kremlin," *Bloomberg Politics*, May 14, 2015, https://www.bloomberg.com/politics/articles/2015-05-15/washington-insiders-reap-windfall-peddling-influence-for-kremlin.

47. Jaywon Choe, "Mississippi Governor Haley Barbour's Lobbying Group Tied To Iranian Nuclear Program," *Business Insider*, March 29, 2012, http://www.businessinsider.com/mississippi-governor-haley-barbours-lobbying-group-tied-to-iranian-nuclear-program-2012-3.

48. Melanie Mason and Maeve Reston, "Records contradict Mississippi Governor on lobbying work for Mexico," *Los Angeles Times*, March 23, 2011, http://articles.latimes.com/2011/mar/23/nation/la-na-barbour-mexico-20110324.

CHAPTER 4: THE STRANGLEHOLD

1. Matthew Boyle, "Mississippi Bloodbath: Open Warfare Breaks Out In Tea Party vs. Barbour Cochran," *Breitbart*, March 19, 2014, http://www.breitbart.com/big-government/2014/03/19/mississippi-bloodbath/; BGR Group, OpenSecrets.org, http://www.opensecrets.org/lobby/firmsum.php?id=D000021679&year=2014.

2. Ibid.

3. Keith Plunkett, "Cochran Enables Barbour to Skim Federal Money for Family and Clients," *Mississippi Pep*, March 30, 2014, https://mississippipep.wordpress.com/2014/03/30/plunkett-cochran-enables-barbour-to-skim-federal-money-for-family-and-clients/.

4. Timothy J. Burger, "Barbour contacts gain from recovery," *Bloomberg News*, August 19, 2007, as seen on the site Boston.com, http://archive.boston.com/news/nation/articles/2007/08/19/barbour_contacts_gain_from_recovery/.

5. Ibid.

6. Timothy P. Carney, "Thad Cochran's porking helps K Street but not Mississippi," *Washington Examiner*, June 21, 2014, http://www.washingtonexaminer.com/thad-cochrans-porking-helps-k-street-but-not-mississippi/article/2550029?custom_click=rss.

7. R. Jeffrey Smith, "Defense Bill, Lauded by White House, Contains Billions in Earmarks," *Washington Post*, September 29, 2009, http://www.washingtonpost.com/wp-dyn/content/article/2009/09/28/AR2009092803862.html.

8. Ibid.

9. Taxpayers for Common Sense, "Inouye, Cochran Benefit from Earmark Recipients," September 29, 2009, http://www.taxpayer.net/library/article/inouye-cochran-benefit-from-earmark-recipients.

10. R. Jeffrey Smith, "Defense Bill, Lauded by White House, Contains Billions in Earmarks," *Washington Post*, September 29, 2009, http://www.washingtonpost.com/wp-dyn/content/article/2009/09/28/AR2009092803862.html.

11. EaglePAC email in possession of the author.

12. Robbie Ward, "MSU may have violated political policy, ethics questioned," *Journal Politics*, March 5, 2014, http://journalpolitics.com/2014/03/05/mississippi-state-promotion-candidates-cochran-may-violated-political-activities-policy/.

13. Timothy P. Carney, "Thad Cochran's porking helps K Street but not Mississippi," *Washington Examiner*, June 21, 2014, http://www.washingtonexaminer.com/thad-cochrans-porking-helps-k-street-but-not-mississippi/article/2550029?custom_click=rss.

14. Matthew Boyle, "Monument Man: Thad Cochran's Unbelievable Skill For Having Federally Funded Buildings Named After Him," *Breitbart*, February 19, 2014, http://www.breitbart.com/big-government/2014/02/19/monument-man-thad-cochran-s-unbelievable-skill-in-having-federally-funded-buildings-named-after-him/.

15. Sam Hall, "Henry Barbour blasts state Sen. Chris McDaniel for possible challenge to Cochran," September 27, 2013, http://blogs.clarionledger.com/samrhall/2013/09/27/henry-barbour-blasts-state-sen-chris-mcdaniel-over-possible-challenge-to-cochran/.

CHAPTER 5: MUDSLINGING MAGNOLIA STATE STYLE

1. Patrick O'Connor, "Miss. Senate Hopeful Chris McDaniel Riffed on 'Mamacita,' Reparations," *Wall Street Journal*, April 10, 2014, http://blogs.wsj.com/washwire/2014/04/10/miss-senate-hopeful-chris-mcdaniel-riffed-on-mamacita-reparations/.

2. "Shocker: Senator McDaniel Agrees with Obama on a Major Issue," *Mississippi Conservative Daily*, April 11, 2014, https://mississippiconservativedaily.com/2014/04/11/shocker-senator-mcdaniel-agrees-with-obama-on-a-major-issue/.

3. "Slavery Reparations?", FactCheck.org, April 15, 2009, http://www.factcheck.org/2009/04/slavery-reparations/.

4. David Weigel, "An Unfair Hit on the "Next Todd Akin," *Slate*, May 19, 2014, http://www.slate.com/blogs/weigel/2014/05/19/an_unfair_hit_on_the_next_todd_akin.html; James Joyner, "Loretta Nall Campaigns for Alabama Governor on Cleavage," Outsidethebeltway.com, October 23, 2006, http://www.outsidethebeltway.com/alabama_gubernatorial_candidate_campaigns_on_cleavage/.

5. Jack Fairchilds in an interview with the author on March 14, 2016.

6. Tim Mak, "Barbour's 10 most barbed quotes," *Politico*, September 4, 2012, http://www.politico.com/story/2012/09/barbours-10-most-barbed-quotes-080668.

7. Ryan S. Walters, "Senator Chris McDaniel Supports Public Education, Just Not Mandated From Washington," *Mississippi Conservative Daily*, June 8, 2014, https://mississippiconservativedaily.com/2014/06/08/senator-chris-mcdaniel-supports-public-education-just-not-mandated-from-washington/.

8. Philip Elliott and Bill Barrow, "Barbour: McDaniel vulnerable on education stance," CNSNews.com, June 6, 2014, http://www.cnsnews.com/news/article/barbour-mcdaniel-vulnerable-education-stance.

9. Haley Barbour, *Agenda for America: A Republican Direction for the Future* (Washington, D.C.: Regnery Publishing, 1996), 128.

10. "Haley Barbour: GOP Platform Should Include Education Department Abolishment," Human Events, June 24, 2012, http://humanevents.com/2012/06/24/haley-barbour-gop-platform-include-education-dept-abolishment/.

11. Thad for Mississippi, "Chris McDaniel's Horrible Voting Record," http://thadformississippi.com/chris-mcdaniels-horrible-voting-record/; Ryan Walters, "Cochran Camp Distorts Chris McDaniel's Voting Records," *Mississippi Conservative Daily*, April 18, 2014, https://mississippiconservativedaily.com/2014/04/18/cochran-camp-distorts-chris-mcdaniels-voting-records/.

12. Patrick O'Connor, "Time Spent Outside Mississippi Dogs Sen. Cochran's Campaign," *Wall Street Journal*, May 22, 2014, http://blogs.wsj.com/washwire/2014/05/22/time-spent-outside-mississippi-dogs-sen-cochrans-campaign/.

13. Cochran told an interviewer that the first time he voted for a Republican for President was in 1968 when he supported Nixon over Humphrey. So in 1964, at the age of twenty-three (voting age was still twenty-one), Cochran would have cast his first vote for President for LBJ. See Perry Hicks, "Thad Cochran: An Unlikely Revolutionary," Gulf Coast News, December 17, 2006, http://www.gulfcoastnews.com/GCNfeatureThadCochranPt2.htm; also see Curtis Wilkie, Fall of the House of Zeus, 36.

14. These quotes came from a story in the *Clarion Ledger* by Geoff Pender, which is, for some strange reason, no longer available on-line. You can read it on the "Thad for Mississippi" website: http://thadformississippi.com/clarion-ledger-mcdaniel-voted-in-democrat-primary/. Or see *Mississippi Business Journal*, "Hoseman, McDaniel Begin War of Words," November 13, 2013, http://msbusiness.com/2013/11/hosemann-mcdaniel-begin-war-words/.

15. Ibid.

16. Ryan S. Walters, "A Tale of Two Ads: Chris vs. Thad," Mississippi Conservative Daily, April 24, 2014, https://mississippiconservativedaily.com/2014/04/24/a-tale-of-two-ads-chris-vs-thad/.

17. Radley Balko, "Meth isn't an argument for drug prohibition. It demonstrates prohibition's failure," *Washington Post*, October 15, 2015, https://www.washingtonpost.com/news/the-watch/wp/2015/10/12/meth-isnt-an-argument-for-drug-prohibition-it-demonstrates-prohibitions-failure/?utm_term=.02a7394217cc.

18. Rick Bella, "New Drug Report: Meth still Oregon's No. 1 problem, run mostly by Mexican drug traffickers," *OregonLive*.com, June 21, 2015, http://www.oregonlive.com/pacific-northwest-news/index.ssf/2015/06/new_drug_report_paints_a_less-.html.

19. Associated Press, "Mexican drug cartels shipping crystal meth from super labs to Mississippi," NOLA.com, March 2, 2014, http://www.nola.com/crime/index.ssf/2014/03/mexican_drug_cartels_shipping.html. Also see Ryan Walters, "Thad's Meth Ad: More Distortions from the Cochran Camp, MCD, April 28, 2014: https://mississippiconservativedaily.com/2014/04/28/thads-meth-ad-more-distortions-from-the-cochran-camp/.

20. Sam Hall, "Pro-Cochran PAC brings back disingenuous 'trial lawyer' label against McDaniel," *Clarion Ledger Blog*, February 24, 2014, http://blogs.clarionledger.com/samrhall/2014/02/24/pro-cochran-pac-brings-back-disingenuous-trial-lawyer-label-against-mcdaniel/.

21. Alexander Burns, "McDaniel accuses critics of 'slander,'" *Politico*, February 21, 2014, http://www.politico.com/story/2014/02/chris-mcdaniel-thad-cochran-mississippi-103771.

22. Ibid.

23. Ryan S. Walters, "A Dose of Reality in the Katrina Debate," *MCD*, February 26, 2014, http://mississippipep.com/2014/02/27/ms-conservative-daily-a-dose-of-reality-in-the-katrina-disaster-relief-debate/

24. Ibid.

25. Ibid.

26. Ibid.

27. Fox News, "Hurricane Pork," as reported on the site Taxpayers for Common Sense, August 31, 2009, http://www.taxpayer.net/media-center/article/hurricane-pork-fox-news.

28. Ryan S. Walters, "A Dose of Reality in the Katrina Debate," *Mississippi PEP*, February 26, 2014, http://mississippipep.com/2014/02/27/ms-conservative-daily-a-dose-of-reality-in-the-katrina-disaster-relief-debate/.

29. Maria Recio, "Haley Barbour relative defrauded FEMA after Katrina, judge rules," McClatchy, sited in the Modesto Bee, August 31, 2011, http://www.modbee.com/latest-news/article3136388.html.

30. Lisa Mascaro, "Does GOP's Mississippi showdown give Democrats a shot at Senate seat?" *Los Angeles Times*, June 4, 2014, http://www.latimes.com/nation/politics/politicsnow/la-pn-mississippi-senate-democrats-20140604-story.html.

31. Geoff Pender, "McDaniel, Cochran aide spar on state Capitol steps," *Clarion Ledger*, May 15, 2014, http://www.clarionledger.com/story/news/2014/05/15/mcdaniel-cochran-campaigns-accuse-distortion/9126819/.

32. These statistics can be found on the website OpenSecrets.org.

33. Jackie Bodnar, "Awkward: The Podesta Group Hosted a Breakfast Fundraiser for Thad Cochran, FreedomWorks. org, March 4, 2014, http://www.freedomworks.org/content/awkward-podesta-group-hosted-breakfast-fundraiser-thad-cochran.

34. Jeffrey Lord, "Donor Controversies Hit 'Mississippi Conservatives,'" *American Spectator*, July 8, 2014, http://spectator.org/articles/59885/donor-controversies-hit-mississippi-conservatives.

35. Alexander Burns, "Billionaires give to Cochran PAC," *Politico*, June 13, 2014, http://www.politico.com/story/2014/06/thad-cochran-pac-contributions-michael-bloomberg-sean-parker-107823; Shushannah Walshe, "Haley Barbour Not Backing Down in 'Nasty' Mississippi Race," ABC News, June 4, 2014, http://abcnews.go.com/blogs/politics/2014/06/haley-barbour-not-backing-down-in-nasty-mississippi-race/.

36. Tim Murphy, "GOP Senate Candidate Addressed Conference Hosted by Neo-Confederate Group That Promotes Secessionism," *Mother Jones*, October 23, 2014, http://www.motherjones.com/politics/2013/10/gop-senate-candidate-spoke-neo-confederate-conference-august.

37. Alan Lange, "Chris McDaniel headlining gun rally with 'white pride' vendor at event," *Y'all Politics*, April 2, 2014, http://yallpolitics.com/index.php/yp/post/37440/.

38. Chuck Ross, "Aide to Sen. Thad Cochran Arrested in Sex-For-Drugs Scheme," Daily Caller, April 24, 2015, http://dailycaller.com/2015/04/24/longtime-aide-to-sen-thad-cochran-arrested-in-chinese-sex-for-drugs-scheme/.

CHAPTER 6: "NOW IS THE TIME"

1. David M. Drucker, "Q&A: Chris McDaniel pledges 'conservative resurgence' in his bid to unseat longtime Sen. Thad Cochran in Mississippi," *Washington Examiner*, May 16, 2014, http://www.washingtonexaminer.com/mcdaniel-pledges-conservative-resurgence-in-bid-to-unseat-cochran/article/2548547.

2. Jay Cost, "The Real Lesson from Mississippi," *Weekly Standard*, June 26, 2014, http://www.weeklystandard.com/the-real-lesson-from-mississippi/article/795729.

3. Jonathan Strong, "Chris McDaniel's Quest," *National Review*, January 20, 2014, http://www.nationalreview.com/article/368862/chris-mcdaniels-quest-jonathan-strong.

4. Stuart Stevens, "Chris McDaniel Confirms the Worst GOP Stereotypes," *Daily Beast*, July 8, 2014, http://www.thedailybeast.com/articles/2014/07/08/chris-mcdaniel-confirms-the-worst-gop-stereotypes.html.

5. Dan Balz, "Cochran promotes DC Influence to fend off tea party challenge," *Washington Post*, May 30, 2014, https://www.washingtonpost.com/politics/cochran-promotes-dc-influence-to-fend-off-tea-party-challenge/2014/05/29/59a8a824-e6f6-11e3-8f90-73e071f3d637_story.html?utm_term=.151087bbf528.

6. Clarion Ledger Editorial, "Cochran, Palazzo should debate challengers," *Clarion Ledger*, April 26, 2014, http://www.clarionledger.com/story/opinion/editorials/2014/04/26/cochran-palazzo-debate-challengers/8216867/.

7. Emily Wagster Pettus, "Cochran-McDaniel debate unlikely," *Clarion Ledger*, May 2, 2014, http://www.clarionledger.com/story/news/politics/2014/05/02/cochran-mcdaniel-debate-unlikely/8618149/.

8. Keith Plunkett in an interview with the author on June 20, 2016.

9. Ibid.

10. Dan Balz, "Cochran promotes DC Influence to fend off tea party challenge," *Washington Post*, May 30, 2014, https://www.washingtonpost.com/politics/cochran-promotes-dc-influence-to-fend-off-tea-party-challenge/2014/05/29/59a8a824-e6f6-11e3-8f90-73e071f3d637_story.html?utm_term=.151087bbf528.

11. Janet Hook, "Chris McDaniel Interview: In Mississippi, 'Seniority is not what it used to be,'" *Wall Street Journal*, May 28, 2014, http://blogs.wsj.com/w.ashwire/2014/05/28/chris-mcdaniel-interview-in-mississippi-seniority-is-not-what-it-used-to-be/.

12. Matthew Boyle, "'Thad Cochran: I Grew Up Doing 'All Kinds of Indecent Things with Animals," Breitbart, June 12, 2014, http://www.breitbart.com/big-government/2014/06/12/thad-cochran-i-grew-up-doing-all-kinds-of-indecent-things-with-animals/.

13. Robert Costa, "In Mississippi, Senate hopeful McDaniel embodies what GOP fears about Tea Party," Washington Post, June 9, 2014, https://www.washingtonpost.com/politics/in-mississippi-senate-hopeful-mcdaniel-embodies-what-gop-fears-about-tea-party/2014/06/09/548d22ba-efe4-11e3-914c-1fbd0614e2d4_story.html?utm_term=.000e6e3c5b9f.

14. Ibid.

15. Molly Ball, "Thad Cochran, the Last of the Naïve Republicans," Atlantic, June 3, 2014, https://www.theatlantic.com/politics/archive/2014/06/thad-cochran-the-last-of-the-naive-republicans/372084/.

16. R. L. Nave, "Sen. Chris McDaniel to Announce Beginning of End of Political Career," Jackson Free Press, October 13, 2013, http://www.jacksonfreepress.com/weblogs/politics-blog/2013/oct/15/sen-chris-mcdaniel-to-announce-beginning-of-end-of/.

17. Alexandra Jaffe, "Poll: McDaniel gaining on Cochran in Miss. Primary, *The Hill*, April 8, 2014, http://thehill.com/blogs/ballot-box/senate-races/202973-poll-mcdaniel-gaining-on-cochran-in-ms-gop-primary.

18. Alex Pappas, Haley Barbour Dismisses Palin and Santorum as Self-Interested "Outside Celebrities," *Daily Caller*, June 2, 2014, http://dailycaller.com/2014/06/02/haley-barbour-dismisses-palin-and-santorum-as-self-interested-outside-celebrities/.

19. Matthew Boyle, "'McDanielmentum': Haley Barbour's Brother Endorses McDaniel, MS GOP Softens Tone," *Breitbart*, May 28, 2014, http://www.breitbart.com/big-government/2014/05/28/mcdanielmentum-jeppie-endorses/.

20. David Yates, "Miss. U.S. Senate runoff: 42 percent of Cochran's donations coming from PACs," *Legal News Line*, June 19, 2014, http://legalnewsline.com/stories/510517749-miss-u-s-senate-runoff-42-percent-of-cochran-s-donations-coming-from-pacs.

21. Matthew Boyle, "Exclusive Mark Levin: Tom Donohue's 'Chamber of Horrors' Is Democrats' Secret Weapon To Keep Senate," *Breitbart*, October 24, 2014, http://www.breitbart.com/big-government/2014/10/24/exclusive-mark-levin-tom-donohue-s-chamber-of-horrors-is-democrats-secret-weapon-to-keep-senate/.

22. Michelle Malkin, "The U.S. Chamber of Commerce vs. America," MichelleMalkin.com, January 24, 2014, http://michellemalkin.com/2014/01/24/the-u-s-chamber-of-commerce-vs-america/; Daniel Horowitz, "The Chamber of Cowards," Red State, April 17, 2014, http://www.redstate.com/2014/04/17/chamber-cowards/.

23. The emails can be seen here: https://mississippiconservativedaily.com/2014/04/17/exclusive-emails-between-ms-gop-chair-joe-nosef-and-the-mississippi-tea-party/.

24. Chris McDaniel in an interview with the author on June 20, 2016.

25. Ibid.

26. Denver Nicks, "Mississippi Senate Runoff Turns Into Battle for the Soul of the GOP," *Time*, June 23, 2014, http://time.com/2913762/thad-cochran-chris-mcdaniel-mississippi-runoff/.

27. Lisa Mascaro, "Does GOP's Mississippi showdown give Democrats a shot at Senate seat?" *Los Angeles Times*, June 4, 2014, http://www.latimes.com/nation/politics/politicsnow/la-pn-mississippi-senate-democrats-20140604-story.html.

28. Robert Costa, "In Mississippi, Senate hopeful McDaniel embodies what GOP fears about tea party," *Washington Post*, June 9, 2014, https://www.washingtonpost.com/politics/in-mississippi-senate-hopeful-mcdaniel-embodies-what-gop-fears-about-tea-party/2014/06/09/548d22ba-efe4-11e3-914c-1fbd0614e2d4_story.html.

29. Jonathan Weisman, "Democrats See a Break in a Gain for the Tea Party in Mississippi," *New York Times*, June 4, 2014, https://www.nytimes.com/2014/06/05/us/politics/democrats-see-a-break-in-a-gain-for-the-tea-party-in-mississippi.html?hpw&rref=politics.

30. Rasmussen Reports, "Election 2014: Mississippi Senate," https://mississippiconservativedaily.com/2014/05/12/once-again-travis-childers-will-not-beat-chris-mcdaniel-in-november/.

31. Paul Hampton, "Cochran has far higher favorability than McDaniel in poll," *Crawdaddy Blog*, Sun Herald, April 1, 2014, http://www.sunherald.com/2014/04/01/5461238/cochran-has-far-higher-approval.html?sp=/99/184/208/.

32. Sid Salter, "Entry of Taylor, Childers into House, Senate campaigns raise stakes," *DeSoto Times-Tribune*, March 3, 2014, http://www.desototimes.com/opinion/editorials/entry-of-taylor-childers-into-house-senate-campaigns-raise-stakes/article_3d5dfcab-a31a-59f7-8978-85836ef958aa.html.

33. Alexandra Jaffe, "Will Mississippi mudslinging give Dems a chance in South?" *The Hill*, June 24, 2014, http://thehill.com/blogs/ballot-box/senate-races/210320-will-mississippi-mudslinging-give-dems-a-chance-in-south.

34. Chris McDaniel in a personal interview on June 2014.

35. George Will, "Mississippi Republicans vote their appetite," Washington Post, June 25, 2014, https://www.washingtonpost.com/opinions/george-will-mississippi-conservatives-lose-a-battle-but-the-war-against-spending-continues/2014/06/25/25fe028e-fc82-11e3-932c-0a55b81f48ce_story.html?utm_term=.735ac49743d3.

36. Chris McDaniel in an interview with the author on June 20, 2016.

37. John McCormack, "Miss. Senate Candidate Chris McDaniel Distances Himself from Comments on Reparations and 'Mamacita,'" *Weekly Standard*, April 11, 2014, http://www.weeklystandard.com/miss.-senate-candidate-chris-mcdaniel-distances-himself-from-comments-on-reparations-and-mamacita/article/786794.

38. Patrick O'Connor, "Miss. Senate Hopeful Chris McDaniel Riffed on 'Mamacita,' Reparations," *Wall Street Journal*, April 10, 2014, https://blogs.wsj.com/washwire/2014/04/10/miss-senate-hopeful-chris-mcdaniel-riffed-on-mamacita-reparations/.

39. Nate Cohn, "Mississippi Primary Fight Is One of Geography as Well as Ideology," *New York Times*, June 3, 2014, http://mobile.nytimes.com/2014/06/03/upshot/mississippi-primary-fight-is-one-of-geography-as-well-as-ideology.html?referrer=&_r=0.

40. Sean Trende, "Can Travis Childers Win in Mississippi?" *Real Clear Politics*, June 4, 2014, https://www.realclearpolitics.com/articles/2014/06/04/can_travis_childers_win_in_mississippi_122864.html.

41. Alexandra Jaffe, "Cochran opponent faces more scrutiny over past comments," *The Hill*, April 10, 2014, https://thehill.com/blogs/ballot-box/senate-races/203216-mcdaniel-faces-more-scrutiny-over-past-comments.

42. Alan Lange, "February 28 was a bad day for Mississippi Democrats," *Y'all Politics*, March 3, 2014, http://yallpolitics.com/index.php/yp/post/37162.

43. Josh Kraushaar, "The Republican War Over Earmarks," *Atlantic*, March 31, 2014, https://www.theatlantic.com/amp/article/448944/.

44. Bill Barrow, "Mississippi Senate candidate runs to 'save the republic,'" *Boston Globe*, June 15, 2014, https://www.bostonglobe.com/news/nation/2014/06/14/miss-senate-candidate-runs-save-republic/Y04jIIYyYpeNRXBYSAUcQJ/story.html.

CHAPTER 7: A GRAND POWER PLAY

1. Geoff Pender, "Kelly pleads guilty to conspiracy in Cochran photo case," *Clarion Ledger*, June 8, 2015, http://www. clarionledger.com/story/news/2015/06/08/clayton-kelly-case/28680263/.

2. Keith Plunkett in an interview with the author on February 19, 2016.

3. Melanie Sojourner, the campaign's manager, graciously provided me copies of her emails on this subject. Also see, Matthew Boyle, "Update: McDaniel Campaign Asked Arrested Blogger to Take Video Down in Late April," Breitbart, May 18, 2014, http://www.breitbart.com/big-government/2014/05/18/mcdaniel-campaign-asked-arrested-blogger-to-take-video-down-in-late-april/.

4. Geoff Pender, "Cochran, colleagues defend travel with aide," *Clarion Ledger*, May 13, 2014, http://www. clarionledger.com/story/news/politics/2014/05/13/cochran-colleagues-defend-travel-aide/9045793/.

5. See https://www.legistorm.com.

6. Matthew Boyle, "Documents: Cochran Listed Aide's DC House as Address," *Breitbart*, May 4, 2014, http://www. breitbart.com/big-government/2014/05/04/cochran-listed-address-in-dc/.

7. Erick Erickson, "'She Gets Everything She Wants,'" *Red State*, May 29, 2014, http://www.redstate.com/ erick/2014/05/29/she-gets-everything-she-wants/.

8. Joel Gehrkle, "Democratic fundraisers hosted at home where GOP senator rents apartment from top aide," *Washington Examiner*, May 28, 2014, http://www.washingtonexaminer.com/democratic-fundraisers-hosted-at-home-where-gop-senator-rents-apartment-from-top-aide/article/2548998.

9. Manu Raju, "GOP senators wonder: Am I next?" *Politico*, May 9, 2012, http://www.politico.com/news/stories/0512/76078_Page3.html.

10. Matthew Boyle, "Thad Cochran's Executive Assistant Accompanied Him To 42 Countries on 33 Taxpayer-Funded Trips," *Breitbart*, May 12, 2014, http://www.breitbart.com/big-government/2014/05/12/cochran-s-executive-assistant-accompanied-him-to-42-countries-on-33-taxpayer-funded-trips/.

11. Ibid.

12. Matthew Boyle, "Thad Cochran Campaign: 'Sexist' to Ask Why Assistant Accompanied Him on Taxpayer-Funded Trips," *Breitbart*, May 14, 2014, http://www.breitbart.com/big-government/2014/05/14/thad-cochran-it-s-sexist-to-ask-me-why-i-brought-executive-assistant-to-42-foreign-countries-on-taxpayer-funded-trips/.

13. Matthew Boyle, "Thad Cochran's Executive Assistant Accompanied Him To 42 Countries on 33 Taxpayer-Funded Trips," *Breitbart*, May 12, 2014, http://www.breitbart.com/big-government/2014/05/12/cochran-s-executive-assistant-accompanied-him-to-42-countries-on-33-taxpayer-funded-trips/.

14. Legistorm.com: https://www.legistorm.com/trip/list/by/traveler/id/6422/name/Kay_B_Webber.html.

15. Congress.gov, "H.R.2364 - A bill to prohibit travel at Government expense outside the United States by Members of Congress who have been defeated, who have resigned, or retired," https://www.congress.gov/bill/93rd-congress/house-bill/2364/cosponsors?q=%7B%22search%22%3A%5B%22Cochran%22%5D%7D.

16. Dan Balz, "Cochran promotes DC influence to fend off tea party challenge," *Washington Post*, May 30, 2014, http://www.washingtonpost.com/politics/cochran-promotes-dc-influence-to-fend-off-tea-party-challenge/2014/05/29/59a8a824-e6f6-11e3-8f90-73e071f3d637_story.html.

17. New Albany News, "Thad Cochran, Scenes at a New Albany jewelry store," NAnewsweb.com, May 26, 2015, http://nanewsweb.com/thad-cochran-scenes-at-a-new-albany-jewelry-store/.

18. Louis Nelson, "Thad Cochran marries longtime aide Kay Webber," *Politico*, May 25, 2015, http://www.politico.com/story/2015/05/thad-cochran-married-kay-weber-118267.

19. Keith Plunkett in an interview with the author on February 19, 2016.

20. Melanie Sojourner in an interview with the author on March 22, 2017.

21. Campbell Robertson, "Dirty Tricks, Tea Party Suicide and Rising Mississippi Anger," *New York Times*, July 13, 2014, http://www.nytimes.com/2014/07/14/us/politics/mark-mayfield-a-tea-party-founder-became-the-unlikely-focus-of-a-big-controversy.html?_r=0.

22. Alexandra Jaffe, "Cochran campaign knew of wife's taping for weeks," *The Hill*, May 19, 2014, http://thehill.com/blogs/ballot-box/senate-races/206493-cochran-campaign-knew-of-wifes-taping-for-weeks.

23. Campbell Robertson, "Dirty Tricks, Tea Party Suicide and Rising Mississippi Anger," *New York Times*, July 13, 2014, http://www.nytimes.com/2014/07/14/us/politics/mark-mayfield-a-tea-party-founder-became-the-unlikely-focus-of-a-big-controversy.html?_r=0; Brett LoGiurato, "Clayton Kelly Arrested For Allegedly Photographing Thad Cochran's Wife," *Business Insider*, May 17, 2014, http://mobile.businessinsider.com/clayton-kelly-arrested-for-allegedly-photographing-thad-cochrans-wife-2014-5.

24. Alexandra Jaffe, "Cochran campaign knew of wife's taping for weeks," *The Hill*, May 19, 2014, http://thehill.com/blogs/ballot-box/senate-races/206493-cochran-campaign-knew-of-wifes-taping-for-weeks; Jackson Jambalaya, "Madison Police arrest Clayton Kelly for sneaking into Rose Cochran's room," Kingfish Blog, May 16, 2014, http://kingfish1935.blogspot.com/2014/05/madison-police-arrest-clayton-kelly-for.html.

25. Brian Walsh Tweet: https://twitter.com/brianjameswalsh/status/467744352610291716.

26. Jackson Jambalaya, "Madison Police arrest Clayton Kelly for sneaking into Rose Cochran's room," *Kingfish Blog*, May 16, 2014, http://kingfish1935.blogspot.com/2014/05/madison-police-arrest-clayton-kelly-for.html.

27. Melanie Sojourner in an interview with the author on March 22, 2017.

28. Daniel Strauss, "Meet The Blogger Who Risked It All For A Mississippi Tea Party Candidate," *Talking Points Memo*, May 21, 2014, http://talkingpointsmemo.com/dc/constitutional-clayton-clayton-thomas-kelly-chris-mcdaniel-thad-cochran.

29. Richard Sager in an interview with the author on May 10, 2017.

CHAPTER 8: THE VICTORY

1. Matthew Boyle, "Palin Touts McDaniel As 'Reinforcement' For Cruz, Paul, Lee," *Breitbart*, May 30, 2014, http://www.breitbart.com/big-government/2014/05/30/palin-touts-mcdaniel-as-reinforcement-for-cruz-paul-lee/.

2. Ibid.

3. Bill Minor, "USDA boss Walters has checkered past," *DeSoto Times-Tribune*, October 16, 2008, http://www.desototimes.com/opinion/usda-boss-walters-has-checkered-past/article_936e4c13-6d42-59ba-9e7a-ebb705b1db76.html.

4. Ibid.

5. Jennifer Ortega, "Tea Party official calls for help after being locked inside courthouse," WAPTNews.com, June 4, 2014, http://www.wapt.com/article/tea-party-official-calls-for-help-after-being-locked-inside-courthouse/2088779.

6. Dylan Scott, "Why Was Miss. Tea Partier in Locked Courthouse With Ballots On Election Night?" *Talking Points Memo*, June 4, 2014, http://talkingpointsmemo.com/dc/mississippi-tea-party-courthouse-locked-in.

7. Ben Jacobs, "Mississippi Tea Party Goes Watergate," *Daily Beast*, June 6, 2014, http://www.thedailybeast.com/articles/2014/06/06/mississippi-tea-party-goes-watergate.html.

8. Daniel Strauss, "Cochran Campaign: McDaniel Campaign Is 'Full of Criminals,'" *Talking Points Memo*, June 5, 2014, http://talkingpointsmemo.com/livewire/cochran-campaign-mcdaniel-camp-full-of-criminals-does-not-respect-rule-of-law.

9. Tammy Estwick, "Employee led tea party members into courthouse on election night," WAPT News, June 17, 2014, http://www.wapt.com/news/employee-led-tea-party-members-into-courthouse-on-election-night-official-says/26523454.

10. Matthew Boyle, "Cochran Campaign Staffer Arrested for Stealing Campaign Signs," *Breitbart*, June 23, 2014, http://www.breitbart.com/big-government/2014/06/23/cochran-campaign-staffer-charged-with-unlawful-destruction-of-chris-mcdaniel-signs/.

11. Erick Erickson, "'She Gets Everything She Wants,'" *Red State*, May 29, 2014, http://www.redstate.com/erick/2014/05/29/she-gets-everything-she-wants/.

12. Ibid.

13. Spencer S. Hsu, "Ex-Senate aide is sentenced in Abramoff case," *Washington Post*, January 5, 2011, http://www.washingtonpost.com/wp-dyn/content/article/2011/01/05/AR2011010506354.html.

14. Lauren French, "Sen. Thad Cochran aide, Fred Pagan, busted for meth in drug raid," *Politico*, April 24, 2015, http://www.politico.com/story/2015/04/thad-cochran-fred-pagan-meth-bust-117327.html.

15. Paul Hampton, "Barbour's son charged with assault in DC," *Sun Herald*, May 5, 2015, http://www.sunherald.com/2015/05/05/6212115/barbours-son-charged-with-assault.html.

16. Douglas Handshoe, "Oxpatch tussle in the political class?" Slabbed.org, October 16, 2013, http://slabbed.org/2013/10/16/oxpatch-tussle-in-the-political-class/.

17. Monica Hernandez, "Pickering and Hester arrested on simple assault charges," WLOX News, http://www.wlox.com/story/11649165/pickering-and-hester-arrested-on-simple-assault-charges.

CHAPTER 9: THAD THE KEYNESIAN

1. Linda Feldman, "Why Democrats are cheering over Mississippi primary," *Christian Science Monitor*, June 4, 2014, http://www.csmonitor.com/USA/Elections/2014/0604/Why-Democrats-are-cheering-over-Mississippi-primary-video.

2. Matthew Boyle, "Poll: McDaniel Opens 12-Point Lead Over Cochran," *Breitbart*, June 16, 2014, http://www.breitbart.com/big-government/2014/06/16/poll-shows-mcdaniel-with-12-point-lead/.

3. Anna Palmer, "McConnell to headline Thad Cochran fundraiser," *Politico*, June 6, 2014, http://www.politico.com/story/2014/06/mitch-mcconnell-nrsc-supports-thad-cochran-107527.

4. Matthew Boyle, "GOP Senators Scurry from NRSC HQ After McConnell's 'All In' for Thad Cochran Fundraiser," *Breitbart*, June 11, 2014, http://www.breitbart.com/big-government/2014/06/11/gop-senators-scurry-from-nrsc-hq-after-mcconnell-s-all-in-for-thad-cochran-fundraiser/.

5. Ibid.

6. Associated Press, "Celebrities dip into Thad Cochran vs. Chris McDaniel Republican runoff battle for Senate," *Gulflive.com*, June 19, 2014, http://blog.gulflive.com/mississippi-press-news/2014/06/celebs_dip_into_thad_cochran_v.html.

7. Katherine Skiba, "McCain's Years of Public Service Have Earned Him Enemies," *US News and World Report*, March 31, 2008, http://www.usnews.com/news/campaign-2008/articles/2008/03/31/mccains-years-of-public-service-have-earned-him-enemies.

8. Alexander Burns, "For Cochran, a Brett Favre ad blitz," *Politico*, June 18, 2014, http://www.politico.com/story/2014/06/2014-mississippi-senate-race-brett-favre-thad-cochran-108032.

9. Mississippi Conservative Daily, "Let Us Not Forget Haley Barbour's Other 'Endorsements,'" March 27, 2014, https://mississippiconservativedaily.com/2014/03/27/let-us-not-forget-haley-barbours-other-endorsements/.

10. Matthew Boyle, "Is Brett Favre's Cochran Endorsement Political Payback to Haley Barbour For Brother's Pardon?" *Breitbart*, June 19, 2014, http://www.breitbart.com/big-government/2014/06/19/is-brett-farve-s-cochran-endorsement-political-payback-to-haley-barbour-for-brother-s-pardon/.

11. Ibid.

12. Dan Balz, "Cochran promotes DC influence to fend off tea party challenge," *Washington Post*, May 30, 2014, https://www.washingtonpost.com/politics/cochran-promotes-dc-influence-to-fend-off-tea-party-challenge/2014/05/29/59a8a824-e6f6-11e3-8f90-73e071f3d637_story.html.

13. E.J. Dionne, "The Mississippi Paradox," *The National Memo*, June 5, 2014, http://www.nationalmemo.com/mississippi-paradox/.

14. "Cochran has 'word of warning' for likely McDaniel supporters," WJTV, June 12, 2014, http://www.wjtv.com/story/25766085/cochran-steps-up-attacks-on-mcdaniel.

15. "Cochran Speaks on McDaniel, Tea Party Calls for Nosef's Resignation, Nosef Responds," NewsMS.com, April 15, 2014, http://www.newsms.fm/cochran-speaks-mcdaniel-tea-party-calls-nosef-resignation-nosef-responds/.

16. Matthew Boyle, "Cochran Attacks Tea Party's McDaniel: 'Extremist' Who'd Be 'Dangerous' If Elected," *Breitbart*, June 10, 2014, http://www.breitbart.com/big-government/2014/06/10/thad-cochran-attacks-tea-party-s-mcdaniel-an-extremist-who-d-be-dangerous-if-elected/.

17. Philip Elliot and Emily Wagster Pettus, "Barbour: McDaniel vulnerable on education stance," AP via Yahoo News, June 6, 2014, http://news.yahoo.com/barbour-mcdaniel-vulnerable-education-stance-222729199--election.html;_ylt=AwrBTza6zZdTVH8Ap.VXNyoA;_ylu=X3oDMTEzaTg0a2U4BHNlYwNzcgRwb3MDMgRjb2xvA2JmMQR2dGlkA1NNRTQyMV8x.

18. Dan Balz, "Cochran promotes DC influence to fend off tea party challenge," *Washington Post*, May 30, 2014, https://www.washingtonpost.com/politics/cochran-promotes-dc-influence-to-fend-off-tea-party-challenge/2014/05/29/59a8a824-e6f6-11e3-8f90-73e071f3d637_story.html.

19. Ibid.; Jonathan Weisman and Theodore Schleifer, "Mississippi Race Points to Appeal of Partisanship," *New York Times*, June 23, 2014, http://www.nytimes.com/2014/06/24/us/mississippi-race-points-to-appeal-of-partisanship.html?_r=0.

20. Cliff Sims, "Handshakes and middle fingers: Alabama and Kentucky House Speakers engage in war of words," *Yellowhammer News*, September 11, 2014, http://yellowhammernews.com/politics-2/handshakes-middle-fingers-alabama-kentucky-house-speakers-engage-war-words/.

21. "10 Poorest States in America," CNBC, http://www.cnbc.com/id/101068491/page/11; Thomas C. Frohlich, "America's Richest (and Poorest) States," *Yahoo Finance*, September 18, 2014, http://finance.yahoo.com/news/america-richest-poorest-states-142726946.html; "Why Mississippi is Poor: Part One," Southern Political Watch, August 17, 2014, https://southernpoliticalwatch.wordpress.com/2014/08/17/why-mississippi-is-poor-part-one/.

22. James Joyner, "Britain poorer than all US states except Mississippi," *Christian Science Monitor*, August 28, 2014, http://www.csmonitor.com/USA/Politics/Politics-Voices/2014/0828/Britain-poorer-than-all-US-states-except-Mississippi.

23. Steve Wilson, "Reforms always a step behind Mississippi corruption," Watchdog.org, February 17, 2015, http://watchdog.org/200107/mississippi-corruption-3/.

24. Dan Balz, "Cochran promotes DC influence to fend off tea party challenge," *Washington Post*, May 30, 2014, https://www.washingtonpost.com/politics/cochran-promotes-dc-influence-to-fend-off-tea-party-challenge/2014/05/29/59a8a824-e6f6-11e3-8f90-73e071f3d637_story.html.

25. Chris McDaniel in an interview with the author on June 20, 2016.

"Zero-Sum Earmarks," Wall Street Journal, May 27, 2010, http://www.wsj.com/articles/SB10001424052748704026204575266651344397616.

26. Chris McDaniel in an interview with the author on June 20, 2016.

27. Ibid.

28. Ibid.

29. Dan Balz, "Cochran promotes DC influence to fend off tea party challenge," *Washington Post*, May 30, 2014, https://www.washingtonpost.com/politics/cochran-promotes-dc-influence-to-fend-off-tea-party-challenge/2014/05/29/59a8a824-e6f6-11e3-8f90-73e071f3d637_story.html.

30. Molly Ball, "Thad Cochran, the Last of the Naïve Republicans," *The Atlantic*, June 3, 2014, http://www.theatlantic.com/politics/archive/2014/06/thad-cochran-the-last-of-the-naive-republicans/372084/.

31. E.J. Dionne, "The Mississippi Paradox," *The National Memo*, June 5, 2014, http://www.nationalmemo.com/mississippi-paradox/.

32. Daniel Lippman, "Thad Cochran vs. Chris McDaniel: A closer look at the ad wars," Politico, June 23, 2014, http://www.politico.com/story/2014/06/thad-cochran-chris-mcdaniel-ads-federal-spending-conservative-credentials-108180. Also see, John McCormick, "Cochran Cites Virtuous Spending in Runoff With Tea Party," *Bloomberg*, June 19, 2014.

33. Linda Feldmann, "Mississippi braces for political earthquake in Senate GOP runoff," *Christian Science Monitor*, June 24, 2014, http://www.csmonitor.com/USA/Politics/2014/0624/Mississippi-braces-for-political-earthquake-in-Senate-GOP-runoff.

34. Mississippi Election Code, Secretary of State of Mississippi, http://www.sos.ms.gov/links/elections/home/tab5/MSCODE.pdf.

CHAPTER 10: RACE-BAITING 2.0

1. For more on the JCJC-Compton game, see Erle Johnston, Jr., *Mississippi's Defiant Years, 1953-1973: An Interpretative Documentary with Personal Experiences* (Forest, Miss.: Lake Harbor, 1990).

2. Joseph Crespino, *In Search of Another Country: Mississippi and the Conservative Counterrevolution* (Princeton: Princeton University Press), 268.

3. Nash and Taggart, 147–150.

4. Crespino, 268.

5. Ben Smith, "The Watermelon Thing," *Politico*, December 20, 2010, http://www.politico.com/blogs/ben-smith/2010/12/the-watermelon-thing-031591.

6. Kasie Hunt, "Barbour's critics say it's black and white," *Politico*, January 30, 2011, http://www.politico.com/story/2011/01/barbours-critics-say-its-black-and-white-048449.

7. Andrew Ferguson, "The Boy from Yazoo City," *Weekly Standard*, December 27, 2010, http://www.weeklystandard. com/boy-yazoo-city/article/523551?page=3.

8. Eric Kleefeld, "Barbour Praises Civil Rights-Era White Supremacist Citizens Councils," *Talking Points Memo*, December 20, 2010, http://talkingpointsmemo.com/dc/barbour-praises-civil-rights-era-white-supremacist-citizens-councils.

9. Kasie Hunt, "Barbour in KKK plate uproar," *Politico*, February 15, 2011, http://www.politico.com/story/2011/02/barbour-in-kkk-plate-uproar-049599; Jessica Yellin and Kevin Bohn, "Haley Barbour and NAACP at odds over redistricting," CNNPolitics.com, March 18, 2011, http://politicalticker.blogs.cnn.com/2011/03/18/haley-barbour-and-naacp-at-odds-over-redistricting/.

10. James Hohman and Kenneth P. Vogel, "Barbour apologizes after calling Obama's policies 'tar babies," *Politico*, November 10, 2014, http://www.politico.com/story/2014/11/haley-barbour-apology-obama-policies-tar-babies-112726.

11. Thad Cochran, Senate Biography, http://www.cochran.senate.gov/public/index.cfm/biography.

12. Daily Kos, June 14, 2005, http://www.dailykos.com/story/2005/06/14/121736/-Senators-who-refused-to-sign-anti-lynching-resolution; Sean Wilentz, "Lott, GOP, and the neo-Confederacy No surprise in senator's remarks. It's just the latest in an old story,"

13. Philly.com, December 20, 2002, http://articles.philly.com/2002-12-20/news/25360680_1_confederate-flag-sons-of-confederate-veterans-dixiecrat;

14. Tim Young, "9 Racist Things that Big Democrats Have Said and the Media has Forgotten," *Clash Daily*, April 30, 2014, http://clashdaily.com/2014/04/9-racist-things-big-democrats-said-media-forgotten/; Sean Davis, "6 Horribly Racist Comments from Obama Administration Officials," Media Trackers, June 20, 2013, http://mediatrackers. org/national/2013/06/20/6-horribly-racist-comments-from-obama-admin-officials.

15. David M. Drucker, "Democratic activists were behind controversial Klan ads in Mississippi," *Washington Examiner*, August 4, 2014, http://www.washingtonexaminer.com/article/2551630/.

16. Ibid.

17. Aaron Gardner, "No, the Racist Mississippi Primary Ads Weren't Just a Cabal of Elderly Democrat Women," *Red State*, August 6, 2014, http://www.redstate.com/aarongardner/2014/08/06/racist-mississippi-primary-ads-werent-just-cabal-elderly-democrat-women/.

18. "The Senate Race and the Black Vote," *Jackson Jambalaya*, June 26, 2014, http://kingfish1935.blogspot. com/2014/06/the-senate-race-and-black-vote.html.

19. Eliana Johnson, Meet Mitzi Bickers, *National Review*, June 27, 2014, http://www.nationalreview.com/article/381365/meet-mitzi-bickers-eliana-johnson.

20. Chuck Ross, "Pro-Cochran PAC Paid Embattled Consultant for Phone Calls," *Daily Caller*, June 26, 2014, http://dailycaller.com/2014/06/26/pro-cochran-pac-paid-embattled-consultant-for-get-out-the-vote-calls/?utm_referrer=http%3A%2F%2Ft.co%2FsLFwOqVeAK.

21. Scott Greer, "Robocalls Recruiting Dem Votes for Cochran Bashes Tea Party," *Daily Caller*, June 22, 2014, http://dailycaller.com/2014/06/22/robocall-allegedly-recruiting-dem-votes-for-gop-sen-cochran-bashes-tea-party-alleges-racism/.

22. "FNC Report: Haley Barbour Tied to Race-Baiting, Anti-Tea Party Radio Ads in MS," *Breitbart*, July 1, 2014, http://www.breitbart.com/video/2014/07/01/fnc-report-haley-barbour-behind-race-baiting-anti-tea-party-radio-ads-in-ms/.

END NOTES

23. Anna Wolfe, "PAC Trouble on the 'Horizon'"? *Jackson Free Press*, July 16, 2014, http://www.jacksonfreepress.com/news/2014/jul/16/pac-trouble-horizon/; Ryan S. Walters, "Alan Lange: Political Entrepreneur," *Mississippi Conservative Daily*, February 6, 2017, http://mississippiconservativedaily.com/alan-lange-political-entrepreneur/.

24. Jimmie Gates, "Bishop Ronnie Crudup says his PAC did everything legal," *Clarion Ledger*, July 9, 2014, http://www.clarionledger.com/story/news/2014/07/09/bishop-ronnie-crudup-says-pac-everything-legal/12422597/.

25. Sam Hall, "FEC reports raise issues over preacher, pro-Cochran PAC," *Clarion Ledger*, July 16, 2014, http://www.clarionledger.com/story/dailyledes/2014/07/16/all-citizens-for-mississippi-fec-report/12718801/.

26. Charles C. Johnson, "NRSC Accused of Illicitly Funding Black Church Super PAC," *Gotnews*.com, July 10, 2014, http://gotnews.com/nrsc-accused-of-illicitly-funding-black-church-super-pac/.

27. Charles C. Johnson, "New Evidence Links Cochran Campaign to All Citizens Ads," *Gotnews*.com, July 23, 2014, http://gotnews.com/new-evidence-links-cochran-campaign-to-all-citizens-ads/.

28. Katie Glueck, "Barbours spent on black turnout," *Politico*, July 16, 2014, http://www.politico.com/story/2014/07/2014-mississippi-elections-barbours-thad-cochran-chris-mcdaniel-109021.

29. The Hayride Blog, "The NRSC-Mississippi Thing Smells Fishier and Fishier," July 8, 2014, http://thehayride.com/2014/07/the-nrsc-mississippi-thing-smells-fishier-and-fishier/.

30. Erick Erickson, "I Do Not Believe It," *Red State*, July 8, 2014, http://www.redstate.com/erick/2014/07/08/i-do-not-believe-it/.

31. Charles C. Johnson, "NRSC Accused of Illicitly Funding Black Church Super PAC," *Gotnews*.com, July 10, 2014; http://gotnews.com/nrsc-accused-of-illicitly-funding-black-church-super-pac/#more-44.

32. Charles C. Johnson, "NRSC Funds Another Preacher in Cochran Race Baiting Scheme," *Gotnews*.com, July 15, 2014, http://gotnews.com/nrsc-funds-another-preacher-in-cochran-race-baiting-scheme/.

33. W. James Antle III, "Race-baiting the Tea Party," *American Conservative*, June 30, 2014; http://www.theamericanconservative.com/articles/race-baiting-the-tea-party/.

34. Erick Erickson, "CONFIRMED: Senate Republican Leaders Paid for Attacks Against Conservatives," *Red State*, July 15, 2014, http://www.redstate.com/erick/2014/07/15/confirmed-senate-republican-leaders-paid-for-attacks-against-conservatives/.

35. Charles C. Johnson, "NRSC Funds Another Preacher in Cochran Race Baiting Scheme," *Gotnews*.com, July 15, 2014, http://gotnews.com/nrsc-funds-another-preacher-in-cochran-race-baiting-scheme/.

36. American Liberty PAC, "The Shady Seven: GOP senators paid for attack ads against conservative Chris McDaniel," July 17, 2014, http://americanlibertypac.com/2014/07/the-shady-seven-gop-senators-paid-for-attack-ads-against-conservative-chris-mcdaniel/.

37. Stephen Koff, "As Tea Party vs. Establishment Dispute Simmers, Rob Portman says he disapproves of 'racist ads' that his and others' donations may have funded," *Cleveland Plain Dealer*, July 17, 2014, http://www.cleveland.com/open/index.ssf/2014/07/as_tea_party_vs_establishment.html.

38. Alexander Burns, "How Cochran Bounced Back," *Politico*, June 25, 2014, http://www.politico.com/story/2014/06/how-thad-cochrans-campaign-pulled-it-off-108276.

39. Stephen Koff, "As Tea Party vs. Establishment Dispute Simmers, Rob Portman says he disapproves of 'racist ads' that his and others' donations may have funded," *Cleveland Plain Dealer*, July 17, 2014, http://www.cleveland.com/open/index.ssf/2014/07/as_tea_party_vs_establishment.html.

40. "Mississippi: A Case Study in Republican Race-Baiting," Tea Party Patriots Citizens Fund, located at: https://dbgzvifxo1i3b.cloudfront.net/tppcf/32/MS-Case-Study.pdf.

41. David Martosko, "'The worst race-baiting ads I've ever seen': Radio ads in Mississippi senate race accused tea party candidate of Ku Klux Klan links and drove black Democrats to vote against him in a REPUBLICAN primary," Daily Mail, June 27, 2014, http://www.dailymail.co.uk/news/article-2672565/The-worst-race-baiting-ads-Ive-seen-Radio-ads-Mississippi-senate-race-accused-tea-party-candidate-Ku-Klux-Klan-links-drove-black-Democrats-vote-against-REPUBLICAN-primary.html.

42. "Mississippi: A Case Study in Republican Race-Baiting," Tea Party Patriots Citizens Fund, located at: https://dbgzvifxo1i3b.cloudfront.net/tppcf/32/MS-Case-Study.pdf.

43. Eliana Johnson, "Two-Faced Victory," National Review, June 25, 2014, http://www.nationalreview.com/article/381249/two-faced-victory-eliana-johnson.

44. Glynn Branch in an interview with the author on July 7, 2017.

45. Talib Bey in an interview with the author on September 24, 2017.

46. Star Parker, "McDaniel blows it in Mississippi by ignoring blacks," Syndicated Nationally by Creators, June 30, 2014, http://www.urbancure.org/washington/article.asp?id=488&t=McDaniel-blows-it-in-Mississippi-by-ignoring-blacks.

47. Chris McDaniel in an interview with the author on June 27, 2016.

48. Ibid.

49. John Fund, "Democrats Put Cochran Over the Top," National Review, June 25, 2014, http://www.nationalreview.com/corner/381171/democrats-put-cochran-over-top-john-fund.

50. Emma Foehringer Merchant, "The Haters and Losers Who Now Support Trump," New Republic, May 10, 2016, https://newrepublic.com/article/133352/haters-losers-now-support-trump.

CHAPTER 11: STREET MONEY

1. Matthew Boyle, "Rick Santorum Endorses Chris McDaniel," Breitbart, May 29, 2014, http://www.breitbart.com/big-government/2014/05/29/rick-santorum-endorses-chris-mcdaniel/.

2. Alexander Burns, "Mississippi Carnival: Palin vs. Favre," Politico, June 20, 2014, http://www.politico.com/story/2014/06/mississippi-election-sarah-palin-brett-favre-108105.

3. Matthew Boyle, "Ron Paul Tells Mississippi: My Son Rand Needs Chris McDaniel in Senate," Breitbart, June 15, 2014, http://www.breitbart.com/big-government/2014/06/15/ron-paul-tells-mississippi-my-son-rand-needs-chris-mcdaniel-in-senate/.

4. Matt Lewis, "Thad Cochran's Plan B: Woo Democrats," Daily Caller, June 5, 2014, http://dailycaller.com/2014/06/05/thad-cochrans-plan-b-woo-democrats/.

5. Sean Sullivan, "The nastiest primary in the country is in Mississippi. And it's only getting uglier," Washington Post, May 21, 2014, https://www.washingtonpost.com/news/the-fix/wp/2014/05/21/the-nastiest-primary-in-the-country-is-in-mississippi-and-its-only-getting-uglier/?utm_term=.f87153ce8691.

6. Charles C. Johnson, "More Evidence of Illegal 'Cash for Vote' Operation by Cochran Campaign Piles Up," GotNews.com, July 10, 2014, http://gotnews.com/more-evidence-of-illegal-cash-for-vote-operation-by-cochran-campaign-piles-up-see-more-at-httpgotnews-comindex-phpoptioncom_contentviewarticleid154more-evidence-of-illegal-cash-for-v/.

END NOTES

7. Geoff Pender. "Cochran camp says it 'screwed up' cash accounting," *Clarion Ledger*, July 8, 2014, http://www.clarionledger.com/story/politicalledger/2014/07/08/cochran-vote-buying-election-politics-mcdaniel-fec/12363785/.

8. Caitlin Huey-Burns, "Mississippi Runoff: Thad Cochran's Last Hurrah," *Real Clear Politics*, June 24, 2014, http://www.realclearpolitics.com/articles/2014/06/24/mississippi_runoff_thad_cochrans_last_hurrah__123079.html.

9. Jackson Jambalaya, "The Senate and the black vote," *Jackson Jambalaya*, June 26, 2014, http://kingfish1935.blogspot.com/2014/06/the-senate-race-and-black-vote.html.

10. Matthew Boyle, "Threats, Bribes, and the KKK: The Most Insane Story of the MS Senate Race," *Breitbart*, June 20, 2014, http://www.breitbart.com/big-government/2014/06/20/threats-bribes-and-the-kkk-the-most-insane-story-of-the-ms-senate-race/.

11. Keith Plunkett in an interview with the author on February 19, 2016.

12. Tea Party Race-Baiting Report: The Hayride, "Thad Cochran Is Going to Get Blown Out Next Week, And He Richly Deserves It," Thehayride.com, June 18, 2014, http://thehayride.com/2014/06/thad-cochran-is-going-to-get-blown-out-next-week-and-he-richly-deserves-it/.

13. Geoff Pender. "Hinds GOP chair paid by Cochran PAC," *Clarion Ledger*, June 16, 2014, http://www.clarionledger.com/story/news/2014/06/16/hinds-gop-chair-paid-cochran-pac/10593963/.

14. Ibid.

15. Matthew Boyle, "Chris McDaniel Rushes to Review Ballots from Tuesday's Election," *Breitbart*, June 27, 2014, http://www.breitbart.com/big-government/2014/06/27/mcdaniel-rushes-to-review-ballots-from-tuesday-s-election/.

16. Matthew Boyle, "Rumors Of Impropriety Swirl About Cochran Allies' Entreaties To Democratic Voters," *Breitbart*, June 17, 2014, http://www.breitbart.com/big-government/2014/06/17/rumors-of-impropriety-swirl-about-cochran-allies-entreaties-to-democratic-voters/.

17. Sam R. Hall, "FEC reports raise issues over preacher, pro-Cochran PAC," *Clarion Ledger*, July 16, 2014, http://www.clarionledger.com/story/dailyledes/2014/07/16/all-citizens-for-mississippi-fec-report/12718801/.

18. Matthew Boyle, "Threats, Bribes, and the KKK: The Most Insane Story of the MS Senate Race," *Breitbart*, June 20, 2014, http://www.breitbart.com/big-government/2014/06/20/threats-bribes-and-the-kkk-the-most-insane-story-of-the-ms-senate-race/.

19. Matthew Boyle, "Former DOJ Attorney: Illegal for Democrats to Vote in MS GOP Primary Runoff," *Breitbart*, June 18, 2014, http://www.breitbart.com/big-government/2014/06/18/top-ex-doj-attorney-it-s-illegal-for-democrats-to-vote-in-mississippi-s-gop-primary-runoff/.

20. Matthew Boyle, "Rumors of Impropriety Swirl About Cochran Allies' Entreaties To Democratic Voters," *Breitbart*, June 17, 2014, http://www.breitbart.com/big-government/2014/06/17/rumors-of-impropriety-swirl-about-cochran-allies-entreaties-to-democratic-voters/.

21. Anna Wolfe and Donna Ladd, "It's a Mad, Mad, Mad GOP Race for US Senate," *Jackson Free Press*, July 9, 2014, http://www.jacksonfreepress.com/news/2014/jul/09/its-mad-mad-mad-mad-gop-race-us-senate/.

22. Charles C. Johnson, "Cochran Campaign Manager, Staffer Busted in Illegal Vote Buying Operation," *Gotnews.com*, June 30, 2014, http://gotnews.com/cochran-campaign-manager-staffer-busted-in-illegal-vote-buying-operation/; Scott Wong, "No charges after strip club incident," *Politico*, December 9, 2011, http://www.politico.com/story/2011/12/no-charges-after-strip-club-incident-070181.

23. Arit John, "Conservatives Won't Let the Mississippi Election Go," *The Atlantic*, July 1, 2014, https://www.theatlantic.com/politics/archive/2014/07/conservatives-wont-let-the-mississippi-election-go/373806/.

CHAPTER 12: THE "DEFEAT"

1. Mississippi NAACP, "NAACP Will Monitor Tea Party Poll Watchers," June 23, 2014, http://naacpms.org/naacp-will-monitor-tea-party-poll-watchers/.

2. Daniel Strauss, "Mississippi Officials Will Monitor Voting in GOP Senate Runoff," *Talking Points Memo*, June 23, 2014, http://talkingpointsmemo.com/livewire/mississippi-senate-runoff-election-attorney-general-secretary-of-state.

3. Alexandra Jaffe, "Poll watchers warned in Mississippi," *The Hill*, June 24, 2014, http://thehill.com/blogs/ballot-box/senate-races/210340-mississippi-officials-question-legitimacy-of-conservative-poll.

4. Allie Jones, "Tea Party Resorts to Poll Monitoring for Miss. Senate Election," *Gawker*.com, June 23, 2014, http://gawker.com/tea-party-deploying-poll-watchers-in-racially-charged-m-1594699456.

5. Lloyd Marcus, Shame on Jonathan Capehart, *American Thinker*, June 16, 2014, http://www.americanthinker.com/blog/2014/06/shame_on_jonathan_capehart.html.

6. Perry Bacon, Jr., "More Controversy as Cochran, McDaniel Race Ends," NBC News, June 24, 2014, http://www.nbcnews.com/politics/elections/more-controversy-cochran-mcdaniel-race-ends-n139266.

7. Keith Plunkett in an interview with the author on February 19, 2016.

8. Robert Schlesinger, "Mississippi Big Talk," *US News and World Report*, June 26, 2014, https://www.usnews.com/opinion/blogs/robert-schlesinger/2014/06/26/cochrans-democratic-win-brings-hollow-threats-from-mcdaniel-tea-party.

9. Brett LoGiurato, "How A GOP Senator Everyone Thought Would Lose Pulled Off One of the Biggest Political Comebacks In Modern History," *Business Insider*, June 26, 2014, http://www.businessinsider.com/how-thad-cochran-beat-chris-mcdaniel-mississippi-runoff-senate-results-2014-6.

10. Larry Enten, "It Looks Like African-Americans Really Did Help Thad Cochran Win," *FiveThirtyEight*, June 25, 2014, https://fivethirtyeight.com/datalab/it-looks-like-african-americans-really-did-help-thad-cochran-win/.

11. Harry Enten, "It Looks Like African-Americans Really Did Help Thad Cochran Win," *FiveThirtyEight*, June 25, 2014, https://fivethirtyeight.com/datalab/it-looks-like-african-americans-really-did-help-thad-cochran-win/.

12. Jaime Fuller, "The fiery Chris McDaniel speech you have to see," *Washington Post*, June 25, 2014, https://www.washingtonpost.com/news/the-fix/wp/2014/06/25/the-fiery-chris-mcdaniel-speech-you-have-to-see/?utm_term=.a6a278ff5ad4.

13. Ibid.

14. Chris McDaniel in an interview with the author on June 27, 2016.

15. John Fund, "Democrats Put Cochran Over the Top," *National Review*, June 25, 2014, http://www.nationalreview.com/corner/381171/democrats-put-cochran-over-top-john-fund; Eliana Johnson, "Two-Faced Victory," *National Review*, June 25, 2014, http://www.nationalreview.com/article/381249/two-faced-victory-eliana-johnson.

16. Shushannah Walshe, "Tea Party Anger Over Mississippi Loss Ripples Across the States," ABC News, June 30, 2014, http://abcnews.go.com/blogs/politics/2014/06/tea-party-anger-over-mississippi-loss-ripples-across-states/.

17. George Will, "Mississippi Republicans vote their appetite," *Washington Post*, June 25, 2014, https://www.washingtonpost.com/opinions/george-will-mississippi-conservatives-lose-a-battle-but-the-war-against-spending-continues/2014/06/25/fe028e-fc82-11e3-932c-0a55b81f48ce_story.html.

18. John Hayward, "Dems choose Thad Cochran as GOP Senate candidate," *Human Events*, June 25, 2014, http://humanevents.com/2014/06/25/democrats-choose-thad-cochran-to-be-republican-senate-candidate-from-mississippi/.

19. Matthew Boyle, "Chris McDaniel Rushes to Review Ballots from Tuesday's Election," Breitbart, June 27, 2014, http://www.breitbart.com/big-government/2014/06/27/mcdaniel-rushes-to-review-ballots-from-tuesday-s-election/.

CHAPTER 13: THE CHALLENGE

1. Sean Sullivan, "Ted Cruz slams 'D.C. machine' over Mississippi runoff, wants voter-fraud investigation," *Washington Post*, July 7, 2014, https://www.washingtonpost.com/news/post-politics/wp/2014/07/07/ted-cruz-slams-d-c-machine-over-mississippi-runoff-wants-voter-fraud-investigation/?utm_term=.09e5f70c52c5.

2. C. Edmund Wright, "Despicable Haley Barbour and the Mississippi Mafia: They've no idea what they've done ..." cedmundwright.com, June 25, 2014, http://cedmundwright.com/despicable-haley-barbour-and-the-mississippi-mafia-theyve-no-idea-what-theyve-done/.

3. John Hawkins, "Congratulations to the GOP Establishment on Their Pyrrhic Victory in Mississippi Yesterday," *Right Wing News*, June 25, 2014, http://rightwingnews.com/republicans/congratulations-to-the-gop-establishment-on-their-pyrrhic-victory-victory-in-mississippi-yesterday/.

4. Mollie Hemingway, "Was Thad Cochran's Victory the GOP Establishment's Most Pyrrhic Yet?" *The Federalist*, June 27, 2014, http://thefederalist.com/2014/06/27/was-thad-cochrans-victory-the-gop-establishments-most-pyrrhic-yet/.

5. Daniel Horowitz, "This Is Treachery," Breitbart, June 25, 2014, http://www.breitbart.com/big-government/2014/06/25/horowitz-this-is-treachery/.

6. Steve Deace, "An open letter (plea) for RNC Chairman Reince Priebus to do something about Mississippi," *Washington Times*, July 23, 2014, http://www.washingtontimes.com/news/2014/jul/23/deace-open-letter-plea-rnc-chairman-reince-priebus/.

7. Niger Innis, "The Tea Party Is the Future of the GOP," *Daily Caller*, July 14, 2014, http://dailycaller.com/2014/07/14/the-tea-party-is-still-the-future-of-the-gop/?utm_referrer=http%3A%2F%2Ft.co%2Fq2VjAFsqtx.

8. John Fund, "Democrats Put Cochran Over the Top," *National Review*, June 25, 2014, http://www.nationalreview.com/corner/381171/democrats-put-cochran-over-top-john-fund.

9. Wesley Pruden, "Shameless race-baiting and betrayal in Mississippi," *Washington Times*, June 26, 2014, http://m.washingtontimes.com/news/2014/jun/26/pruden-race-baiting-and-betrayal-in-mississippi/.

10. Gawken Diary, "So, would it really be THAT bad if we don't win the Senate in November," *Red State*, June 27, 2014, http://www.redstate.com/diary/gawken/2014/06/27/really-bad-dont-win-senate-november/.

11. Steven Brodie Tucker, "The Muck in Mississippi," Varight.com, June 25, 2014, http://www.varight.com/opinion/the-muck-in-mississippi/.

12. Leon H. Wolf, "Rotten at the Core," *Red State*, June 27, 2014, http://www.redstate.com/leon_h_wolf/2014/06/27/rotten-core/.

13. Louis Woodhill, "Chris McDaniel's Lesson: Clueless Conservatism Loses," *Forbes*, June 26, 2014, https://www.forbes.com/sites/louiswoodhill/2014/06/26/chris-mcdaniels-lesson-clueless-conservatism-loses/#391d8df56556.

14. Eliana Johnson, "Two-Faced Victory," *National Review*, June 25, 2014, http://www.nationalreview.com/article/381249/two-faced-victory-eliana-johnson.

15. Deneen Borelli, "GOP Establishment Deals Race Card in Mississippi Senate Primary Contest," *FreedomWorks*, June 24, 2014, http://www.freedomworks.org/content/gop-establishment-deals-race-card-mississippi-senate-primary-contest.

16. Jackie Bodnar, "FreedomWorks for America Responds to the Mississippi Senate Runoff Results," *FreedomWorks*, June 24, 2014, http://www.freedomworks.org/content/freedomworks-america-responds-gop-mississippi-senate-runoff-results.

17. Alex Pappas, "Conservative Groups Angry After Cochran Wins With Help From Democrats," *Daily Caller*, June 25, 2014, http://dailycaller.com/2014/06/25/conservative-groups-angry-after-thad-cochran-wins-with-help-from-democrats/.

18. Melissa Leon, "Right-Wing Radio Fury Over Thad Cochran Win in Mississippi," *Daily Beast*, June 25, 2014, http://www.thedailybeast.com/articles/2014/06/25/right-wing-radio-fury-over-thad-cochran-win-in-mississippi.html.

19. Ibid.

20. Ibid.

21. Rush Limbaugh, "I Wonder If Thad Cochran's Campaign Slogan Was 'Uncle Toms for Thad,'" *Daily Rushbo*, June 25, 2014, http://dailyrushbo.com/rush-i-wonder-if-thad-cochrans-campaign-slogan-was-uncle-toms-for-thad/.

22. Rush Limbaugh, "Republican Establishment Took Part in Reprehensible Reverse Operation Chaos in Mississippi," *The Rush Limbaugh Show*, June 25, 2014, http://www.rushlimbaugh.com/daily/2014/06/25/republican_establishment_took_part_in_reprehensible_reverse_operation_chaos_in_mississippi.

23. Ed Martin, "Why I'm Moving to Censure Henry Barbour in the RNC Over Race-Baiting Ads," *Daily Caller*, August 6, 2014, http://dailycaller.com/2014/08/06/why-im-moving-to-censure-henry-barbour-in-the-rnc-over-race-baiting-ads/.

24. Chris McDaniel in an interview with the author on June 27, 2016.

25. John Hayward, "A Mess in Mississippi," *Human Events*, July 2, 2014, http://humanevents.com/2014/07/02/a-mess-in-mississippi/.

26. Ann Coulter, "Tea Party: Learn from Al Gore," July 9, 2014, http://www.anncoulter.com/columns/2014-07-09.html.

27. Erick Erickson, "Will There Be a Consequence?" Red State, June 26, 2014, http://www.redstate.com/erick/2014/06/26/will-there-be-a-consequence/.

28. Matthew Boyle, "True the Vote Alleges Pro-Cochran Officials Destroying Mississippi Election Evidence, Files Restraining Order," Breitbart, July 9, 2014, http://www.breitbart.com/big-government/2014/07/09/true-the-vote-files-restraining-order-against-ms-gop-alleges-pro-cochran-officials-destroying-election-evidence/.

29. Ibid.

30. Catherine Thompson, "Mississippi GOP To McDaniel: Take Your Challenge tCourts," *Talking Points Memo*, August 7, 2014, http://talkingpointsmemo.com/livewire/mississippi-gop-wont-hear-chris-mcdaniel-challenge.

31. Alexis Levinson, "Chris McDaniel Files Challenge to Mississippi Runoff Results," *Roll Call*, August 4, 2014, http://www.rollcall.com/news/home/chris-mcdaniel-files-challenge-to-mississippi-runoff-results.

32. See Republican Party Rules and Resolutions: https://www.gop.com/rules-and-resolutions/ (emphasis added).

33. Steve Deace, "An open letter (plea) for RNC Chairman Reince Priebus to do something about Mississippi," *Washington Times*, July 23, 2014, http://www.washingtontimes.com/news/2014/jul/23/deace-open-letter-plea-rnc-chairman-reince-priebus/.

34. Richard Viguerie, "Reince Priebus: Why the Silence on Mississippi?" *ConservativeHQ*.com, July 1, 2014, http://www.conservativehq.com/article/17626-reince-priebus-why-silence-mississippi.

35. Jeremy Diamond, "Six weeks later, McDaniel challenges Mississippi runoff result," CNNPolitics.com, August 4, 2014, http://www.cnn.com/2014/08/04/politics/mcdaniel-state-gop-election-challenge/.

36. MS Code 23-15-921: http://codes.findlaw.com/ms/title-23-elections/ms-code-sect-23-15-921.html.

37. MS Code 23-15-923: http://codes.findlaw.com/ms/title-23-elections/ms-code-sect-23-15-923.html.

38. See a legal argument by John Pittman Hey's here: https://mississippiconservativedaily.com/2014/10/26/john-pittman-hey-how-partisan-prejudice-and-legal-trickery-bludgeoned-to-death-mcdaniels-effort-to-get-to-the-bottom-of-illegal-voting/.

39. Ibid.

40. "Judge dismisses McDaniel election challenge," WLOX.com, http://www.wlox.com/story/26405267/judge-dismisses-mcdaniel-election-challenge.

41. John Pittman Hey's legal argument: https://mississippiconservativedaily.com/2014/10/26/john-pittman-hey-how-partisan-prejudice-and-legal-trickery-bludgeoned-to-death-mcdaniels-effort-to-get-to-the-bottom-of-illegal-voting/.

42. Associated Press, "Mississippi Supreme Court denies Chris McDaniel request to revisit ruling on poll books access," gulflive.com, July 25, 2014, http://blog.gulflive.com/mississippi-press-news/2014/07/mississippi_supreme_court_deni_7.html.

43. Chris McDaniel in an interview with the author on June 27, 2016.

44. Ibid.

CHAPTER 14: REMEMBER MISSISSIPPI

1. Chris McDaniel in an interview with the author on June 27, 2016.

2. Keith Plunkett in an interview with the author on February 19, 2016.

3. Melanie Sojourner in an interview with the author on March 22, 2017.

4. Chris McDaniel in an interview with the author on June 27, 2016.

5. Ibid.

6. Amber Phillips, "Paul Ryan to conservatives: Put down your arms. I'm one of you," Washington Post, February 1, 2016, https://www.washingtonpost.com/news/the-fix/wp/2016/02/01/paul-ryan-to-conservatives-put-down-your-arms-im-one-of-you/?utm_term=.16a0829809b8.

7. Rush Limbaugh, "Republican Establishment Took Part in Reprehensible Reverse Operation Chaos in Mississippi," *The Rush Limbaugh Show*, June 25, 2014, http://www.rushlimbaugh.com/daily/2014/06/25/republican_establishment_took_part_in_reprehensible_reverse_operation_chaos_in_mississippi.

8. Robert B. Reich, "The end of the establishment?" *Chicago Tribune*, February 23, 2016, http://www.chicagotribune.com/news/columnists/sns-201602231330--tms--amvoicesctnav-b20160223-20160223-column.html.

9. Mike Flynn, "Pat Caddell: 2016 Election About Insurgency, Not Ideology," January 25, 2016, http://www.breitbart.com/big-government/2016/01/25/pat-caddell-election-about-insurgency-not-ideology/.

10. Robert B. Reich, "The end of the establishment?" *Chicago Tribune*, February 23, 2016, http://www.chicagotribune.com/news/columnists/sns-201602231330--tms--amvoicesctnav-b20160223-20160223-column.html.

11. Chris McDaniel in an interview with the author on June 27, 2016.

12. Dana Blanton, "Fox News Poll: Outsiders rule 2016 GOP field, support for Biden nearly doubles," Fox News, September 24, 2015, http://www.foxnews.com/politics/2015/09/24/fox-news-poll-outsiders-rule-2016-gop-field-support-for-biden-nearly-doubles.html.

13. Jeffrey Lord, What America Needs: The Case for Trump (Washington, DC: Regnery, 2016), 4.

14. Matthew Boyle, "Ron Paul Tells Mississippi: My Son Rand Needs Chris McDaniel in Senate," Breitbart, June 15, 2015, http://www.breitbart.com/big-government/2014/06/15/ron-paul-tells-mississippi-my-son-rand-needs-chris-mcdaniel-in-senate/.

15. Shushannah Walshe, "Tea Party Anger Over Mississippi Loss Ripples Across the States," ABC News, June 30, 2014, http://abcnews.go.com/blogs/politics/2014/06/tea-party-anger-over-mississippi-loss-ripples-across-states/.

16. Ibid.

17. Mollie Hemingway, "Was Thad Cochran's Victory the GOP Establishment's Most Pyrrhic Yet?" The Federalist, June 27, 2014, http://thefederalist.com/2014/06/27/was-thad-cochrans-victory-the-gop-establishments-most-pyrrhic-yet/.

18. "RNC angers many with fundraising email: 'Did you abandon the Republican Party?" July 27, 2014, http://yeahstub.com/rnc-angers-many-with-fundraising-email-did-you-abandon-the-republican-party/.

19. Shushannah Walshe, "Tea Party Anger Over Mississippi Loss Ripples Across the States," ABC News, June 30, 2014, http://abcnews.go.com/blogs/politics/2014/06/tea-party-anger-over-mississippi-loss-ripples-across-states/.

20 Alex Pappas, "McDaniel: 'Conservatives Don't Feel Welcome' In GOP, Daily Caller, June 26, 2014, http://dailycaller.com/2014/06/26/chris-mcdaniel-many-conservatives-dont-feel-welcome-in-the-republican-party/.

21. Erick Erickson, "The Chris McDaniel Legacy Haunts the Republican Party," Red State, September 8, 2015, http://www.redstate.com/erick/2015/09/08/the-chris-mcdaniel-legacy-haunts-the-republican-party/.

22. Haley Barbour's revealing assessment of Trump supporters," Yahoo News with Katie Couric, March 15, 2016, http://news.yahoo.com/video/haley-barbour-revealing-assessment-trump-022427421.html;_ylt=A0LEVx9eH.9W0zAAYHtXNyoA;_ylu=X3oDMTEyNXVlY2YxBGNvbG8DYmYxBHBvcwMxMxBHZ0aWQDQjE3MTVlMQRzZWMDc3I-.

23. Shushannah Walshe, "Tea Party Anger Over Mississippi Loss Ripples Across the States," ABC News, June 30, 2014, http://abcnews.go.com/blogs/politics/2014/06/tea-party-anger-over-mississippi-loss-ripples-across-states/.

24. Emily Wagster-Pettis, "Lawsuit: Mississippi political scandal pushed man to suicide," Clarion Ledger, June 29, 2017, http://www.clarionledger.com/story/news/politics/2017/06/29/lawsuit-mississippi-political-scandal-pushed-man-suicide/438893001/.

CPSIA information can be obtained
at www.ICGtesting.com
Printed in the USA
LVOW12s2306061217
558942LV00001B/26/P